RESEARCH METHODS

FOR

INEXPERIENCED RESEARCHERS

RESEARCH METHODS

FOR

INEXPERIENCED RESEARCHERS

Guidelines for Investigating the Social World

Coreen J. Leacock • S. Joel Warrican • Gerald St. C. Rose

IAN RANDLE PUBLISHERS
Kingston • Miami

Revised edition, 2015
First published in Jamaica, 2009 by
Ian Randle Publishers
11 Cunningham Avenue
Box 686
Kingston 6
www.ianrandlepublishers.com

© 2009, 2015 Coreen J. Leacock, S. Joel Warrican and Gerald St. C Rose

National Library of Jamaica Cataloguing in Publication Data

Leacock, Coreen J
    Research methods for inexperienced researchers : guidelines for investigating
the social world / Coreen J. Leacock, S. Joel Warrican, Gerald St. C. Rose

    p.   ; cm.

    Bibliography : p.

    ISBN 978-976-637-883-7 (pbk)

Cover design and book design by Ian Randle Publishers
Printed in United States of America

TABLE OF CONTENTS

LIST OF FIGURES

PREFACE

The idea of writing this book dawned after several years of lecturing in research methods in education at both the graduate and undergraduate levels. In these courses we often come across students who must produce a piece of research, and who are reading research methods books but are left in the dark about what is required of them. We often found ourselves having to produce handouts for these students, using language and examples that the students found useful. After much prompting, we finally decided to compile everything into a text that would provide guidance for those who must conduct research, but who lack experience and the background to do so with confidence.

The readers of this text will find a heavy bias towards research in education. This is because we are all in the field of education and initially the text was aimed exclusively for people in that field. However, after some reflection we decided to widen the focus to other fields in the Social Sciences. Despite this widening, many of the examples are still related to education. We feel though that despite the content, the methods of research are very relevant to other fields in the Social Sciences.

This text is not intended to be the only one that students will consult when they engage in research. We prepared it as a gentle introduction to powerful concepts that are relevant to the world of social research. It is expected that once students develop a basic understanding of these concepts, that they will expand their reading to other sources. Indeed, we have even recommended some works that they may find useful.

Based on our experience, we believe that this text will be useful to researchers in the following categories:

- Students studying at the sixth form, associate degree, undergraduate and graduate levels;

- Educators, community workers and others in the public and private sector needing to do research.

We trust that our style of delivery makes your journey into the world of social research a pleasant and productive one. We wish you every success.

Kindest regards

C.J. Leacock, S. J. Warrican and G. St. C. Rose.

1

INTRODUCTION TO SOCIAL RESEARCH

INTRODUCTION

Before embarking on a research project, it is good sense to have an understanding of some basic theories and issues associated with research. In this chapter, we will introduce you to some of these. We will briefly discuss ways of knowing, before focusing on research as a way of knowing. We will define research, examine types of research, and explore different perspectives on research. After studying this chapter, you will also have a sense of purposes for conducting research, who benefits from research and who should and/ or could conduct research. Finally, we discuss the role of social research in the context of the Caribbean, suggesting some ways in which research can and should be the basis for decisions across the region. You should be aware that this is not an exhaustive coverage of all of the theories and issues surrounding social research. However, it provides a sound foundation on which we sincerely hope that you will go on to build as you strive to hone your skills and knowledge in this area. So, take a deep breath, square your shoulders and forge on with the reading of the chapter.

SOCIAL RESEARCH IN THE CARIBBEAN

During the closing years of the twentieth century, territories in the Caribbean undertook many reforms as they sought to take their citizens into the twenty-first century. Many of the decisions made in connection with these reforms were and still are informed by research conducted in other regions. For example, it is not uncommon for systems in the region to be making decisions based on dated research. For some reason, research findings seem to take a long time to reach our shores. Additionally, much of this research is not even relevant or appropriate to our context. Often, officials fool themselves into believing that research conducted in large countries can be made applicable by taking their findings and scaling them down to match the smaller systems within the region. By now it should be clear to these officials that this view is erroneous and that the Caribbean is 'ripe' for systematic investigations into social phenomena that take the unique context of the region into consideration.

Unfortunately, in some areas of social endeavour, much of what is practised in the Caribbean is based on tradition and not on research. But having established earlier that research is the superior way of knowing, it seems vital that this should be the means of identifying what should be good practice. This is not to say that traditional practices are bad, but in recent times, many of these have been challenged by those who believe that they are failing to meet the needs of a generation that is growing up in a global village where failure to keep up with the advancement of technology could seriously affect their social, emotional and economic development. Conducting research is therefore a means of verifying if this is actually the case, and if it is so, what can be done to improve conditions for the next generation.

Another reason why more research should be conducted in the Caribbean is that the findings can add to the body of knowledge about social phenomena. Once widely disseminated, it could be very useful to individuals and organisations both within the region and those in other countries who interact with Caribbean people. For example, many organisations outside of the region (such as funding and other aid agencies) often appear not to understand the social systems within the region and therefore when engaging in transactions, tend to attach conditions that may not be within the best interest of the region. Exposure to Caribbean research could serve to enlighten these organisations and foster a better understanding of the needs of the people of the region.

Often when the need for research is acknowledged in the Caribbean, the thought is to bring in consultants from abroad to do it. This should not always be necessary, as there are people in all social fields who are capable of conducting rigorous research. However, a caveat must be given. As in any research situation anywhere in the world, both the researchers and the users of the research must be aware of the motives and/or agenda behind the research. It is possible that persons conducting this research may have a vested interest in the outcomes, and this may cloud their judgement. While this is not unique to Caribbean researchers, the possibility may be more acute because of the influence of relationship within small states. For this reason, Caribbean social researchers should develop an awareness of small state issues that can have an impact on their work and should take these into consideration when conducting research.

Having issued the above caveat, we must emphasise that there are genuine benefits that can be had from home-grown research. For example, the findings can be interpreted based on intimate knowledge of the Caribbean context, and hence the conclusions drawn would be more valid than when such interpretations are done without this knowledge. This would be of great benefit to the social institutions of the region as their decision-making would be guided by more relevant research findings. Again, this is not to discount the value of studies done by researchers from outside of the region. This is merely to say that research conducted by local researchers could provide an added dimension to the mosaic of knowledge that is generated about this unique region. It is the responsibility of Caribbean people to put their perspectives and lived experiences on the global radar.

WAYS OF KNOWING

Today the word *knowledge* is tossed about liberally. We hear of knowledge industries, knowledge markets, and access to knowledge. But where does this knowledge come from? How do we come to know? The answer is that there are several ways of knowing, some less credible than others in people's eyes. Some of the ways in which people come to know include:

Intuition – As humans, we come to know some things through intuition, that is, without conscious reasoning. For example, most primigravidae (first time mothers) intuitively know how to meet the needs of their newborn babies, even though they may protest that they do not know what to do.

Common sense – Knowledge based on sound judgement in practical matters. Knowledge is generated after a weighing of alternatives and coming to a decision about what is best or right. This knowledge often influences how an individual behaves in future situations.

Experience – Knowledge is based on the experience of individuals. For example, experience has left some teachers with the 'sure' knowledge that using a particular teaching approach will benefit all students, regardless of their individual characteristics.

Authority – Knowledge based on authority can be had from many sources. For example, some people look on the authority of religious books such as the Bible for knowledge. Authority may also be conferred on persons whose scholarly and professional achievements have caused others to respect and accept their views as credible knowledge. Often, knowledge based on authority is expounded in speeches, textbooks and other forms of writing.

Reasoning – there are different types of reasoning that lead to knowledge. First there is deductive reasoning. With this kind of reasoning, one starts with major premises or generalisations and through logical deduction, arrives at specific conclusions. An example of deductive reason is:

> All Kweól-speakers learn well if instructed in French.
> Annette is a Kweól-speaker.
> Therefore Annette will do well when instructed in French.

With *inductive reasoning*, one starts with a number of cases of a specific observation and formulates a generalisation based on these. For example:

> A number of Kweól-speakers are observed to be doing well when
> instructed in French.
> Therefore it is reasoned that all Kweól-speakers will do well if instructed
> in French.

Of course, you can also have reasoning that involves a combination of these two approaches.

Research – Knowledge is generated by means of systematic investigation of phenomena. It is knowledge produced in this way that should be most valued. Of all the ways that people use to arrive at knowledge, research has the advantage in that the knowledge is based on evidence derived through the scientific method.

While the other ways of knowing should not be discounted, they tend to be limited or sometimes even erroneous. They leave too much to chance and whimsy to be used to guide decision-making. For example, knowledge gained through intuition may be inadequate since intuition can be influenced by factors such as likes and dislikes, past experiences and preferences, which can cloud your reasoning. Likewise, knowledge gained by experience can be distorted. This is evidenced by the fact that two people can have the same experiences but go away with something different from it. Or it could be that what was experienced might not be representative of the particular phenomenon and thus does not paint a true picture of what normally exists. In a similar vein, sole reliance on reasoning could produce questionable knowledge. For instance, in the example given about deductive reasoning, the premise that all Kweól speakers learn well when instructed in French might be flawed and therefore the conclusion would also be flawed. (That's the thing about deductive reasoning. If the premise from which you start is flawed, then the conclusion is likely to be flawed.) Without systematically testing this premise through research, educational decisions may be made based on this 'knowledge' to the detriment of many Kweól speaking students.

Unlike the other ways of knowing, as mentioned before, research is based on solid evidence. This is why in the fields of social endeavour where decisions made can have a far-reaching impact on the society, knowledge gained through this way of knowing should be preferred.

CHARACTERISTICS OF RESEARCH

Research can take many forms, but regardless of what shape it takes, there are certain characteristics that it should possess. First, research is *systematic*. This means that it follows a formal procedure; it is not haphazard. No matter what form your research takes, it should follow the process of the scientific method. Broadly stated, this process involves five steps. You must begin by selecting and clearly defining a problem. Next you must make plans for conducting the research. After that, you must execute your plan. Then you must analyse the data collected and finally you must draw and state your conclusions.

A second characteristic of research is that it is *empirical*. This means it is based on evidence that is observable; therefore apprehendable through the senses. This evidence should take the form of some kind of information – for example test scores, field notes or responses to questionnaires – that you can organize, and use as a basis for formulating and testing hypotheses and/or answering questions. The final result is the generation of knowledge. This is what makes knowledge generated by research superior to that obtained by the other ways of knowing.

An extremely important characteristic of research is that it is *trustworthy*. This means that research should be both reliable and valid. Reliability refers to the consistency of the results obtained and replicability of the research. Validity is concerned with the accuracy with which the results can be interpreted. It is the trustworthiness of your research that gives credence to the knowledge it generated.

Finally, research is *versatile*. Versatility here means that research can be used for a variety of purposes such as exploration, description and explanation. Thus, you may engage in research to explore a phenomenon about which little is known. For example, in the Caribbean there is the common view that girls are out-performing boys in most areas in the curriculum. You may conduct a pilot study to explore this. For this purpose, you may use a small sample of students from say two schools. After drawing your conclusions, you may conduct a larger follow-up study to describe the phenomenon, finding out in what ways girls are out-performing boys, as well as the extent to which this is so. Finally, you might conduct a study to explain what factors seem to be contributing to any observed differences in performance. The purpose for which you are conducting the research would influence your decisions about research design, participants, and instrumentation and data analysis procedures. More will be said about this in later chapters.

We must point out that research can draw on all the other ways of knowing mentioned above. For example, as a researcher, you will find that deductive and inductive reasoning, along with the combined deductive-inductive approach, play an important part in the research process. The difference is that research calls for verification before something is accepted as knowledge.

Apart from exploratory, descriptive and explanatory, there are other ways of classifying research.

TYPES OF RESEARCH

Research is often classified according to broader categories than the three mentioned above. In fact, those three may be subsumed by the broader categories. For example, research can be classified according to its wider purpose or according to its methodology.

Basic versus Applied Research

When research is classified according to its purpose, it may be either basic or applied. *Basic research* is the term used for research that is concerned with the development or refining of theory. The researcher is not interested in the practical application of the theory, but merely in establishing it. For example, research into how children learn would be basic research, as would be research into developing a new method of teaching some concept. Once the theory or method is developed, it is left to those interested in practice to establish optimum conditions for its use. This can be done through applied research.

Applied research refers to research where the aim is to ascertain how theories can best serve the interest of different people. Here the researcher applies the theories in different settings, with different participants and under varying conditions and notes the outcomes. This then leads to decisions about practice. Thus, based on applied research, for example, a particular policy on treating people who are HIV positive may be adopted. Applied research is often itself divided into three smaller categories: evaluation, development and action research.

Evaluation research is carried out to make decisions about the worth of alternative entities. For example, researchers may conduct an evaluation study to decide whether to expand a training programme for unemployed youth based on a pilot project. The researcher would try to answer questions such as:

Is the programme cost effective?
Is the programme meeting the needs of the unemployed youth?

Development research, also called research and development (R&D), is conducted to develop effective products for use. For example, the Ministries of Health in the Eastern Caribbean may want a series of informative pamphlets on teenage drinking that reflects the cultures of the region. Researchers may be engaged to investigate what such a series should include and to develop an appropriate product.

Action research is carried out to solve practical problems in the social world. This type of research is especially relevant to practitioners who are often seeking ways of improving their practice. Because of the value of this research approach, it will be examined in greater detail in a later chapter.

Quantitative versus Qualitative Research

When research is classified by methodology, it often follows a quantitative or qualitative mode. Generally, whether research is described as quantitative or qualitative depends on the way in which the data are collected, the nature of the data and the methods of analysis. *Quantitative research* tends to involve the use of instruments such as questionnaires, rating scales and tests that yield numerical data, or data that can be quantified. Data analysis procedures tend to be statistical, with the aim being to test hypotheses.

Quantitative research tends to rely on deductive reasoning for hypothesis testing.

Qualitative research typically involves the collection of large quantities of narrative data, usually by interviews, field notes from observations or textual data from documents, photographs, diaries, journals and so on. Analysis tends to involve coding for themes, patterns, anomalies, key events and anything else that can shed light on the phenomenon being investigated. Qualitative research often relies on inductive reasoning to generate hypotheses and theories.

Many researchers try to force their research into a strictly quantitative or qualitative mould, but this is not always advisable or practical. In fact, it is more likely that a piece of research would involve a combination of the two approaches. Do not put limits on your skills by seeking to be a 'quantitative' or a 'qualitative' researcher. You should try to become skilled in both approaches, and then use whichever best suits the piece of research that you are conducting. The two approaches are not mutually exclusive, but can be used to complement each other in ways that enhance the research process.

The qualitative or quantitative nature of a study is often influenced by the researcher's philosophical orientation. Though there are many philosophical perspectives, generally they can be grouped into two broad categories: positivist and anti-positivist.

POSITIVIST VERSUS ANTI-POSITIVIST PERSPECTIVES

Philosophical notions of what is knowledge often influence research. Some people (positivists) hold the philosophical view that knowledge is objective, absolute and unchanging; others (anti-positivist) see it as subjective and relative. These viewpoints determine what these people are willing to accept as legitimate means of coming to know about something and, by extension, what approaches they deem appropriate for research.

Positivist researchers advocate research in which the researcher approaches the study in an impersonal way. The researchers must see themselves as objective observers, gathering information about a phenomenon without having any influence on it. They believe that their personal predisposition or those of their participants of the study do not affect their expert interpretation of the data. They tend to favour research approaches in which the researcher 'controls', manipulates or measures conditions. This approach to research usually involves the use of deductive reasoning, and instruments that yield numerical data that are analysed statistically.

Right now you may be noticing the similarities between the positivist paradigm and quantitative research. In fact, some inexperienced researchers erroneously believe that these two concepts are synonymous. This is not the case! Whereas positivists advocate quantitative methods, quantitative research is not exclusive to the positivist paradigm.

On the other hand, *anti-positivist* researchers do not believe in the notion of objective truth. Their approach to research often takes into account the personal characteristics of both the researcher and the participants, which they believe can influence the information gathered during the research. Because they believe in the existence of multiple truths, anti-positivists advocate approaches that seek to access the various views of the research participants, usually through individual or small group interviews. Anti-positivists are more receptive to qualitative research approaches, but they do not reject quantitative approaches. This of course rules out the notion held by some that anti-positivist approaches equal qualitative research.

THE WAY FORWARD

In this chapter, we have provided some insight into issues relating to social research. We hope that what we have presented will encourage discussion and also fire your zeal for learning more and acquiring the skills necessary for contributing to this field within the region.

The remainder of this book is designed to introduce you to the process of conducting social research. We start by giving some general information about different approaches to research, followed by a number of chapters, each dealing with an aspect of the research process. Although you may read the chapters in the order in which they are written, each one can stand on its own.

The act of conducting research is not a linear one as the arrangement of the chapters might suggest, and there is no need to read the chapters in the specific order in which they are written.

As we mentioned earlier, there is a dire need for trained social researchers throughout the region. We want to encourage you to continue to acquire as much knowledge as you can in the field and to hone your skills. We now wish to add a special word to classroom teachers, since our background is in education and we have a special affinity for educational research. So to you classroom teachers, there are many reforms in education that will affect you. Innovations or programmes will be introduced in the schools and you are in a prime position to lead the way in research in these settings. In fact, that is why we included a chapter on action research with a heavy emphasis on classroom activities! For those who are not classroom teachers, you too have vested interest in the field. We also encourage you to make your contribution since the systems can benefit greatly from the multiple perspectives that this would produce. For those who are not in the field of education, do not overlook this chapter! The principles of action research can be applied in any social setting in which you are in a position to effect change. Feel free to adopt and adapt the guidance and ideas presented on action research to your needs.

Our final admonitions before going into the research process: developing skills in research takes time and practice. But even after you have been at it for some time, never become complacent. Always seek to improve what you do. Learn from the experiences of others and maintain high integrity to ensure that whenever research from the region goes on the world scene, people will pay attention because they recognise its quality! It is for this reason that we felt compelled to tackle the issue of ethics right up front. From the start we want to emphasise good practice and integrity. This book is designed to gently introduce new and inexperienced researchers to concepts and issues in conducting trustworthy social research. We encourage you to read it as one of the core texts that you consult as you move into the field. But even if you already have some experience with research, the guidance and advice presented may still provide new insights and renew your zeal for engaging in this most enlightening and rewarding activity. So readers, press on and enjoy!

2

THE ETHICS OF SOCIAL RESEARCH

INTRODUCTION

Research is a means of generating knowledge. The quest for knowledge is such an important, basic and worthwhile human endeavour, that some may think that it should be pursued at any cost. However, in social research, the sources of information are often themselves human and as such, deserve to be treated with respect and dignity. As new or inexperienced researchers, you need to be aware of certain conventions that govern how to conduct research. You need to learn about conducting research with heart, compassion and sensitivity. You need to learn about research ethics. This chapter deals with ethics in social research. Its aim is to draw to your attention certain guidelines and principles on which you should draw when you conduct research. This chapter is placed right at the beginning of the book for a reason! We believe that whatever you do in research should be governed by certain basic ethical principles which we will raise here. As you read the other chapters and consider the various bits of advice on how to carry out certain activities and why, we want you to always bear in mind the ethical concerns that may be involved. So, let us get on with it!

ETHICS: ARE THEY NECESSARY?

In social research, as in several aspects of human endeavour, we interact with other people on a professional level and are dependent on their cooperation in order to make progress towards our goals. To guide this professional interaction, there are certain standards of behaviour, called ethical *principles*, which have been established. These rules and conventions distinguish professionally acceptable behaviour from that which is professionally unacceptable. In very brief and general terms, ethical principles ensure good professional practice. Over the years, various professional organisations have stipulated particular codes of practice to govern the behaviour of members of the organisations, those who work within the given profession, or in any given geographical location. The Australian Association for Research in Education, the British Educational Research Association, and the American Psychological Association all have codes of practice that guide their members and other researchers. These codes of practice do not only guide the researcher but also provide protection for both the researcher and the participants.

As researchers, it is customary to collect information from others. Sometimes we ask the participants about places, events, other people and things, but more often than not, we ask them about themselves, their work, their lives, their feelings about some matter that we are interested in, and so on. The conclusions of the research depend greatly on the information which the participants provide, so that if our research is to be meaningful, then the data we collect must be as true as possible to the real situation. In other words, we depend on our participants to tell it like it is! This means that we must engender in them a spirit of trust, so that they feel comfortable in providing the kind of information that will be helpful to our research without feeling that they will be disadvantaged or embarrassed in any way. Remember that, as long as we are dependent on their word, for example when we use interviews, questionnaires, or some form of self-report, they can tell us whatever they feel inclined to indicate, and we have to accept that as the data provided. So then, there must be a mutual acceptance of trustworthiness, on their part and on ours.

Researchers must be ethically concerned about the subject matter of their investigation, as well as about the methods, techniques and procedures intended to acquire relevant research data, the appropriate analysis of data, as well as the conclusions drawn and the reporting and publication of their findings. All of these areas are of great importance and they are all areas to which the pertinence of ethical principles needs to be addressed. Burns (2000) however tells that some researchers feel that ethical rules or guidelines that attempt to define limits may be too rigid, thus limiting the effectiveness of the research and denying research into aspects of human behaviour where knowledge would be valuable. He discusses ethical principles and codes of practice in relation to several research concerns; voluntary and involuntary participation, informed consent, deception, role-playing, debriefing, privacy and confidentiality, right to discontinue, experimenter obligations, publication of findings, stress, and intervention studies.

Fraenkel and Wallen (2000) refer to the list of ethical principles published by the Committee on Scientific and Professional Ethics of the American Psychological Association for the conduct of research with human participants. They state very clearly that these principles suggest three very important issues which every researcher should address, namely; the protection of participants from harm, the ensuring of confidentiality of the data collected, and a question pertaining to the deception of participants. Should participants know the truth, the whole truth, and nothing but the truth as far as the research is concerned?

These are all weighty matters to be considered. But, if you are going to produce solid research of which you can be proud, then you must pay attention to them. So then, let us consider each of these three issues as they relate to the kinds of social investigations that you are most likely to be carrying out early in your research career.

ISSUE 1: PROTECTION OF PARTICIPANTS FROM HARM

Harm, in a research context, may refer to emotional disturbance, psychological discomfort, physical danger or any kind of injury or risk that would be damaging to participants. It is your responsibility as the researcher to ensure that nothing you do subjects the participants of your study to any of these conditions, that is, that no harm is likely to result from carrying out the research procedures, whether intentionally or not. This means that you should not ask your participants to do anything that can endanger them, nor should you withhold anything from individuals that might protect them from harm or be beneficial to them. For example, you may decide to investigate the effects of tobacco smoking on teens. Now there is enough evidence that suggests that smoking can be harmful. It would therefore be unethical to try to deter a teen from quitting the practice because it would interfere with your data!

Participants may also be harmed by the way you report your findings. For example, some of the topics that you may explore in social research may involve contact with people who engage in activities that they may want to keep out of the limelight. They may consent to cooperate with you for your study on the grounds that you do not expose them or their activities. If you agree to this, then you must think about how you will act if you become aware of any of these illegal activities. Do you rush off to the police station? After all, this person is breaking the law! Even if you decide not to go to the law, you may then write up your research report in such a way that readers cannot help but know who your sources are and the nature of their activities. Again, you may be exposing that person to harm. In small states, such as are many of the Caribbean territories, it may be easy to identify these people. You should therefore be very careful what you report.

When you undertake a piece of research, one way of protecting your participants from potential psychological harm is to ensure that they consent to be involved in your study. It can be distressing for people to learn that they were being studied without their knowledge; meaning, information that they provided in the capacity of a friend or acquaintance was used for some other purpose. This can certainly cause emotional disturbance and psychological discomfort. It is therefore ethical to obtain consent before involving anyone in a research project. What you tell them about what you are doing will be discussed later. It is noteworthy that in acting ethically and obtaining consent, you would also be protecting yourself. It is therefore very much worth the effort to prepare a document of consent and have participants sign it.

ISSUE 2: CONFIDENTIALITY, ANONYMITY AND RESEARCH DATA

When you are about to collect research data, it is important that your participants are acquainted with the nature of the research and the type of information that will be required. Investigators conducting surveys recognise the importance of gaining accurate information and so will usually ask their sample to give frank answers under the conditions of confidentiality and anonymity. These conditions are usually interpreted by researchers as not allowing the reader to make linkages between the information provided and the person providing the information.

Let us firstly examine the issue of anonymity. If something is done anonymously, then it is not possible (or at least not easy) to identify the doer. One of the reasons some believe that self-completed questionnaires are great data collection tools is that they can be completed anonymously. It is felt that research participants are more likely to tell 'the truth, the whole truth and nothing but the truth' if they are confident that they cannot be identified. (Of course anonymity can also be the scourge of data collection. But more about this later). The question is then, is it ethical to place markings on questionnaires and distribute them in such a way as to be able to trace them to specific respondents? Not if anonymity has been promised to the respondents! Think of the mistrust that this would create for future researchers who may ask these respondents for assistance.

What can you do to keep your promise of anonymity? Here are a few suggestions.

- Do not ask any questions to which the response would clearly identify the respondent.
- Do not covertly place any markings on the data collection instruments that can be traced to the respondent.
- If the participants complete the instruments while you wait, avoid having to personally collect them. Provide a receptacle (e.g. an envelope or a taped-shut box with a slot) in a place where the participants can privately deposit the completed instrument.
- Sometimes you may want to collect data from the same people on more than one occasion and be able to match each participant's responses, but keeping the respondents anonymous to you. To do this, you may consider using a third party (an individual or organisation) as the collection agent. Let us say that the respondents are asked to write their names on a cover sheet that is attached to the instrument. When the instrument is returned to the third party, this cover sheet should be removed and a code unique to each individual participant affixed before it is passed on to you in your capacity as researcher. This way, the third party, who may have no interest in the research, keeps the identification list and you never get to see it. Hence, for all intents and purposes, the participants remain anonymous. It would be unethical on your part to seek out the identity of any of the participants.

In the small communities such as those found in the Caribbean, or anywhere else in the world for that matter, even anonymously administered data collection instruments may not ensure anonymity. This may occur in instances when there are so few with access to certain information that if that information appears in a report, the source can be identified. Other situations in which anonymity may not be possible are when interviewing and observation are involved. So, when anonymity cannot be guaranteed, how can you protect your participants? By offering confidentiality.

To offer confidentiality means that you would not reveal the identity of the sources of your data, either by naming them or by reporting in such a way that they can be identified. It also means that you would not include in your research report anything that the participant asks you not to report. Thus, you must be careful about making the information about or from your sources public. If you are trusted with information in confidence, it often means that the participant does not want that information to be given to anyone else unless the bond of confidence has been released, (that is, the participant gives permission) or the information is put in the public domain by someone else. Let's suppose that during a research project about some other topic, several participants give you information about drug use in a prestigious school, but under confidential cover, so to speak. Should you make any statements in your research about drug use at the particular school? Strictly speaking, the answer is 'No!' If the purpose of the research is to determine, among other things, the extent of drug use in the school, then that purpose should be made clear to the participants so that they understand that any information they give you about that activity is likely to be used in your report. The participants still have the right however, to request that you do not divulge certain information that they may give you, especially if doing so can put them in danger. No matter how much you believe this information might enhance your report, you should respect this confidence. It is the ethical thing to do. Further, though you may be aware of the sources of your data (you sat down with them to interview them), you may keep them anonymous to the public not only by paying attention to how you report your findings, but also by using pseudonyms rather than real names.

Researchers may unintentionally breach their obligation to provide confidentiality and anonymity by the way in which tabular data analyses are produced. The likelihood of this increases when small samples are being used and there are several categories being accounted for. It sometimes happens that the printout from statistical programmes may inadvertently make it possible for persons to be identified. The researcher needs to be aware of this and take the necessary action to prevent such disclosure. This means that you should pay attention to how you report your findings. For instance, in small states such as those in the Caribbean region, where there may be only one or two people holding certain positions, you may want to be careful about how much information you include in your study if you do not want these individuals to be identified even though you haven't provided their names. In large countries such as the USA, a researcher may report a controversial opinion offered by the Head of the Obstetrics department in a large city hospital and not expose the individual. If such a statement is attributed to someone in that position in Barbados or St Kitts or St Lucia, it is highly likely that anyone reading the report would identify the participant since in these small countries, there is often only one 'large' hospital.

Sometimes, you may be faced with what appears to be a clash between ethics and law. So, what about legal aspects related to data collected? In many places, it is illegal to use drugs or engage in certain forms of sexual activity. What should you do if you come across data that point to illegal activity? If you have given your word with respect to confidentiality and anonymity, you are honour bound to protect your data and sources. Essentially this boils down to a possible conflict between ethics and the law. There are sometimes complex issues relating to 'the public's right to know' which, particularly in the fields of journalism and politics, can become quite serious. The *New York Times* reporter Judith Miller, a Pulitzer Prize-winning journalist, spent 85 days in jail protecting her confidential source in the White House CIA leak case.[1] Spence (2005) in an article entitled, 'The Reporter's right not to tell supports the public's right to know',[2] declares that 'the problem with the disclosure or non-disclosure of confidential sources is that it seems to involve a troubling paradox. It presents two equally valid but unacceptable propositions: disclose and act unethically, or not disclose and break the law.' He goes on to state that, 'Because laws must be grounded in ethical principles for their justified legitimacy and not only on legal enforcement through fear of punishment, ethical principles must take precedence when the law conflicts with ethics.'

You should see, then, that when considering your research areas, and the kinds of data you want to obtain, and what you may need to do to obtain those data, you need to be prepared to go the whole way in respecting the declarations of confidentiality and anonymity that you proffer to your participants. So when you are planning your research, think about possible ethical issues that may arise and reflect on how you would deal with them. But remember, though there are some ethical stances with regard to anonymity and confidentiality that are non-negotiable, sometimes it may come down to your own conscience, convictions and values on which you must depend. It is therefore a good idea to anticipate any concerns, ask yourself how far you are willing to go to protect your data and sources and...be prepared!

ISSUE 3: DECEPTION ON YOUR MIND?

One question which social researchers often ask themselves is, 'will the participants in the study give a true picture of what normally happens or how they actually feel?' This may lead them to consider how best to get the 'right' information from these participants. Fearing that the precise nature of the research may cause the sample to behave out of the ordinary, some degree of deception may be contemplated, all for the cause of the 'greater good.' But is this unethical?

The issue of deception is troublesome because both proponents and detractors offer reasonable arguments for their positions. This leads some to conclude that there are instances where deception is clearly out of place and other instances where it is obviously necessary, since some studies could not be carried out unless some deception of participants is involved. The general policy we recommend is that deception should be avoided. Though we do not advocate deception, as mentioned before, proponents will argue that some studies cannot be successfully undertaken without some deception. But even when this is the case, there are guidelines to govern how the participants are to be treated. For example, Northern Illinois University, in a document[3] that offers guidelines for conducting research with human participants, advises that when applying to carry out a study that involves deception, the researcher should, among other things, clearly justify why deception is necessary and explain what they will say to the participants after the study is complete. It suggests that informing the participants after the study helps the researcher to discharge the obligation to address any negative consequences that the deception may have had.

As with other ethical issues, whether you use deception or not again depends on your own conscience, convictions and values. For instance, you may believe that withholding the truth about your research from participants with whom you have made personal contact is unethical, but have no qualms about positioning yourself in such a way as to eavesdrop on private conversations between people who are unaware of your presence or your intentions to use their words as data. Others may find this behaviour unethical! The point we are making here is that though we advocate avoidance of deception, we are aware that others believe that it is sometimes warranted. If you should take the latter stance for a research project, then you should be prepared to justify your actions, both to the participants when you reveal the true nature of your work and also in any written report of your study.

As you can see then, as a social researcher you have certain important responsibilities such as protecting your participants from harm, refraining from violating their trust by breaking the bonds of anonymity and confidentiality, and lastly avoiding garnering participation through deception. These all involve decisions that are influenced by ethics, ethics that are guided by not only the formal prescription of professional organisations and associations, but also by your own values. These decisions may also have legal ramifications. These are all good reasons for you as a social researcher to anticipate any ethical dilemmas you are likely to encounter while conducting your study and think about how you might resolve them. It might save you and your participants a whole lot of worry later on.

Having said all the above, we want to shift our attention to a special group of people with whom you may want to work – children.

RESEARCH WITH CHILDREN

There are several vulnerable groups that you may find yourself working with as a researcher, but perhaps the most vulnerable of these are children. In the Caribbean, as indeed in many other parts of the world, children are socialised to be mindful and respectful of their elders and others in authority. The position of power and control that adults usually enjoy over children is sometimes exploited by researchers who want to use them as sources of data. But there are ethical guidelines that should be taken into consideration if you are planning to do a study that involves children.

It is generally accepted that minors have to be protected. Not only are there laws designed to do so, but institutions with responsibility for seeing after the welfare of children are also governed by regulations for this same purpose. Often, when children are to be involved in studies, the researchers make contact through the institutions in which they spend a substantial amount of time: schools. Consequently, education authorities – Ministries and Departments of Education, school boards, management committees, parent-teacher associations, and so on – offer some protection as official channels through which researchers must go to obtain access to school children. Thus, ethics dictate that if you want to make contact with children in the school setting, then you should seek permission through the appropriate channels. It would therefore be unethical to ask a friend who is a teacher to administer a questionnaire to a class on your behalf without the knowledge or permission of the school's administrators. However, we believe that being granted this permission only relates to *access* to the children, not to their guaranteed participation. This means that you should still ask the students to participate in the research. To do this, you should explain as simply as possible the nature of the research and then give them the option to participate or abstain. You should also make it plain that there is no penalty attached to abstention. Why is this necessary? Because of the relationship between children and adults, children often feel pressured to participate in research activities. And sometimes, the pressure is not imagined! Teachers have been known to threaten students with punishment if they showed reluctance to complete a questionnaire or take a test for research purposes. While you might try to persuade the children to participate, if they are adamant that they do not wish to do so, then you should respect their decision. If you don't, you may find that the data you collect are as far from reality as day is from night!

If you are planning to collect data from children by visiting them at school, it would be a good idea to inform the school authorities about the nature of the research. This should include showing them your data collection instruments to have them vetted. This is because there are some research areas that are inappropriate for children and others that require parental permission for the involvement of their children. In other words, the school, acting in the place of a parent, can allow access for you to approach students to ask them to participate in your research for some topics, but not all topics. Research that touches sensitive areas requires parental permission for underage children. Unfortunately, it has been known for researchers, perhaps unaware of acceptable practices, to pay little heed to the ethical responsibilities which such situations demand, and to venture to collect data from students in classes, having secured by some means, the assistance of comrades who teach the particular groups in which the researcher is interested. These attempts are often brought to a speedy halt by angry parents and guardians who descend on the school or on education officials demanding reasons for the multitude of searching and possibly inappropriate questions put to their sons, daughters and wards. It is particularly to be borne in mind that there are certain topics that may not legally or morally be put to minors, and certain questions that cannot be asked even with the consent of relevant adults. This is true when you have to deal with sensitive areas such as students' awareness or involvement in activities related to drugs, sex, their parents' personal lives and so on. Researchers have been known to face the possibility of legal action for knowingly or unknowingly, ignoring these guidelines.

Working with children can truly test your values. Children, especially young ones, are notorious for divulging all kinds of personal information to adults that they trust. Ask any kindergarten teacher! So what if a child reveals something that you believe indicates that the child is in danger, what would you do? Further, if this information is given in confidence, then you are bound by the same standards that govern confidentiality with adult participants. You should think about these and other challenging situations if you are going to be working with children. The key concern is the protection of the children as sources of data. Children are often powerless in the world of adults, your task as an ethical researcher is to avoid doing anything to exploit this vulnerable group in society.

ETHICS, STATISTICS AND DATA ANALYSIS: 'LIES, DAMNED LIES, AND STATISTICS!'

There are many people who are uncomfortable with numerical data and even more who are unable to analyse them well. Often when statistics are quoted, some listen with awe and respect, others with disbelief and even mirth. As a researcher, you would at least want your research data and subsequent analysis to be treated with respect, if not awe but certainly not with disbelief or mirth. To achieve this, your data should be credible. This means that you should avoid doing anything that might appear underhanded and may call your findings into question. To ensure this, you should pay attention to the ethics related to data analysis. Ethical principles applied to your data and their analysis help to give credible results. Beginning researchers may, on occasion make a typographical error, unintentional errors of computation or misinterpretation, but there is no justification for delibrate falsification. As a researcher, you must know and use appropriate methods of data analysis, and state the results to which these analyses lead. The temptation to 'massage' the data to induce nonexistent trends and patterns must never be contemplated. Even if such unethical practice is not discovered at the time of the grading of your study, think of the embarrassment you will face when as an established respected professional, your misdeed is uncovered. Such dishonesty perpetrated in the past could call into question your integrity in all subsequent research or professional actions. Once a cheat, always a cheat!

Research students often feel that their aim in conducting a piece of research is to 'prove' something. If their data do not seem to be providing the kinds of results that they would like to have, they often explore a multitude of ways of finding that formula, or technique, or 'minor modification' that would help them to achieve 'success.' This often amounts to falsification and is unethical. It is likewise just as unethical if you are mathematically inclined and you deliberately use inappropriate techniques in the hope that the 'non-mathematical' reader would ignore them or become so confused that they just accept them. Sammons (1975) takes a careful look at the various concerns relating to ethical issues in statistical work and explains the International Statistical Institute (ISI) code which regulates the use of statistical data and procedures. Referring to the code, Sammons states that:

> While statisticians operate within the value systems of their societies, they should attempt to uphold their professional integrity without fear or favour. In particular they should not engage or collude in selecting methods designed to produce biased results, or in misrepresenting statistical methods by commission or omission... In particular statisticians are bound by a professional obligation to resist approaches to data collection, analyses interpretation, and publication that are likely (explicitly or implicitly) to misinform or to mislead rather than to advance knowledge (533).

What does this mean for you as a researcher? Well for one thing it is unethical to 'cook' your data so that they reflect your expectations. Remember, even if your expectations are not met, this does not mean your research is worthless. It also means that you should not attempt to dupe readers by resorting to shenanigans to conceal perceived inadequacies in your data. For example, using percentages to disguise a small sample size can be misleading and thus, unethical. 'Fifty percent of the participants' sounds more substantial than 'two out of four participants', but it can be misleading! Ethical behaviour dictates that you present whatever your data reveal. If it is not what you expected, then find legitimate ways of explaining the discrepancies. This often leads to a more meaningful study in the long run.

ETHICAL ISSUES IN WRITING

In the previous section we addressed the ethics involved in dealing with your data, and how you present your findings. But that is just one aspect of reporting your study. In this section we will pay attention to other considerations related to writing your report and we will start with a big one right up front, plagiarism. One of the most glaringly unethical practices in written reports of research is plagiarism. In essence, plagiarism is the stealing, yes, stealing of another person's ideas, written or unwritten, published or unpublished and putting them forward as your own. This is a problem for many students and beginning researchers as they usually do not have a clear or specific idea as to what exactly constitutes plagiarism. Educational institutions consider this such an important aspect of professional behaviour that they produce materials for all students and faculty advising them how to avoid the dangers and the likelihood of plagiarism. So then, what is plagiarism? It is using someone else's work, such as words and or ideas without giving the originator credit for them. Plagiarism is a serious offence. In today's information-driven world where much store is placed on intellectual property, if you are found guilty of plagiarism you may be suspended from your educational institution, criminally charged, or have a civil claim brought against you. You should pay attention to your institution's guidelines regarding citing other people's work. The excuse of ignorance is often not tolerated so it is in your interest to become aware of standards for acknowledging work that is not your own, and use them! Let us consider some areas where the potential for the unethical practice of plagiarism is great. Let us start with your literature review.

Though technical information on writing a literature review is provided in a later chapter, we cannot discuss ethics without making a few points about this. The new or inexperienced researcher often puts forward as their defence, when they are accused of plagiarising, the assertion that 'I put it in my own words.' You should however be aware that even if you use your 'own words,' if the ideas expressed in those words are not yours, then you need to acknowledge the source. Another area of potential unethical behaviour relating to reviewing literature stems from that ubiquitous source of information, the Internet. As you may know, you can get all sorts of information from the Internet, good, bad and ugly, as they say. Some inexperienced researchers have been known to download materials from this source and use it (sometimes with several paragraphs 'cut and pasted' into the review) without acknowledging the source. When taken to task, their defence is that there was no author; it was just on a website. If that is the case, then you should acknowledge the website. Otherwise your actions may be viewed as dishonest. There are several different styles of acknowledging sources of ideas and all of them offer guidelines for citing electronic sources.

FINAL WORDS

We started this chapter by pointing out that the purpose of social research is to generate knowledge about phenomena in the social world. If this knowledge is to be taken seriously and to contribute to the understanding of our social environment, then what we produce must be of a high standard. It must be viewed as credible. To achieve credibility for your research, you must follow the rules. Many of the rules are embodied in ethical principles. It is in your interest when planning your study to think about potential ethical issues that may arise and to reflect on how you might resolve them. Remember though that there are times when the ethics you apply will be governed by your own conscience, convictions and values. This means that you should also reflect on these when you are planning your research. Ask yourself what you are willing to do to get your research done and consider your potential behaviour in light of acceptable ethical standards. Above all, whatever your decisions, be prepared to justify them, both orally and in writing.

Now that we have created the appropriate mindset for a researcher, let us explore the research process. Are you as excited as we are? Then let's go!

NOTES

1. Details of this case and of the reasons given by the reporter for her stance may be obtained from http://www.cnn.com/2005/POLITICS/09/30/cia.leak/index.html.
2. Available online at http://www.smh.com.au/news/opinion/the-reporters-right-not-to-tell-supports-the-publics-right-toknow/2005/09/12/1126377253683.html.
3. Online at www.orc.niu/orc/human_research/deception.pdf. Retrieved December 4, 2007.

3

READY, SET, GO!
BEGINNING THE RESEARCH PROCESS

INTRODUCTION

Many inexperienced researchers have great anxiety when the prospect of producing a research paper looms before them. They agonise over questions such as what do I research? Where can I find a good problem? What is meant by 'problem' anyway? In this chapter, we will provide information that we hope will lessen such anxiety and make the research process one that you approach with much enthusiasm. We will help you to identify sources of researchable problems, to select a research area, and to focus your research into something manageable. After reading this chapter, you should be in a good position to write a clear problem statement, as well as concise research questions or hypotheses. You should also be in a good position to contextualise your research and offer a coherent rationale for conducting it.

FINDING A RESEARCH PROBLEM

The first thing that you need to do when embarking on a research exercise is to identify a general research area. This can sometimes be the hardest part of the research process because you must find an area about which you have some knowledge and interest. In some cases, your course of study may necessitate that you choose a topic from a specific area. For instance, if you are doing a course of study in sociology, then you may be expected to choose a topic that reflects sociological issues. But generally, you may have more flexibility in choosing an area to research. As you go about selecting your problem area, there are some guidelines that can help you to recognise a 'good' problem area. A good problem area has certain characteristics. Let us examine these now.

CHARACTERISTICS OF A GOOD RESEARCH PROBLEM

There are hundreds of research problems that can be investigated. You however must find the one that is right for you. A research problem that is good for you should meet the following criteria:

1. It should be of interest to you. Far too often, inexperienced researchers are lured into conducting a study in which they have little interest. It may be that it is something that is of interest to their supervisors or somebody else, but not to them. The fact is, you are the one who will be spending long hours with this research. You are the one who will be eating, sleeping and breathing with this research on your mind. You are the one who will have to engage in activities, sometimes tedious activities, related to this research. If it is not of interest to you, then it makes your task more difficult than it needs to be. Therefore, while you may seek advice on what area to research, the final decision should be yours, and you should find a problem that is of interest to you.

2. It should be within your expertise. A good problem is one that you have the skill and knowledge to investigate. This does not mean that you should be an expert in the area before you begin your research. What it means is that you should understand enough about it to know what would contribute to knowledge in that area. This might call for you to read extensively in the area before selecting a research problem if your knowledge base is weak.

3. It should be worthwhile or significant. A good problem is one that is of theoretical or practical value to your field. Investigation in the area should contribute something of worth and therefore trivial topics should be avoided. On the other hand, significant does not mean earthshaking. The fact is that there are very few areas in the social world that have not been researched already. Hence, there may not be many totally new, earthshaking revelations to be uncovered. However, your problem could be significant in that it offers a different perspective on the area. Thus, for example, you could apply some already researched theory to a novel context, with different types of participants. The Caribbean is an exciting place to be carrying out social research because of the diversity of social settings available. Much of the research comes out of larger countries with social systems that differ greatly from what exists in the region. You could ask what would be the findings if these studies were carried out in St Lucia or in Dominica or the British Virgin Islands. How would the findings differ? How would they be similar? This gives significance to the problem, especially if it is an area that is of concern within the region and that would contribute to improvement of the lives of the people in the region.

4. It should be 'do-able'. A good research problem is one that can be investigated. This means that, for example, you should have access to the data needed for the research. Therefore, it makes no sense planning to investigate how the use of computers in public libraries affects their operations if the public library system is not yet computerised. Nor is it a good idea to try to investigate philosophical or ethical issues for which answers may be a matter of conscience. Therefore, you might want to avoid problems such as 'Should all students take religious education in school?' What data would you collect? How would you analyse it? How meaningful would the findings be? Clearly, there are other issues associated with such a problem that would render this topic un-researchable, and hence one to be avoided.

5. It should be manageable. A good research topic is one that you can manage within whatever limitations you may have. For example, it must be something that can be done within the time available to you. If you have a school term in which to produce your thesis, then it would be unwise to select a problem area that requires a full academic year to collect the appropriate data. Nor would it be wise to select a research problem that would cause you to incur great expenses if you have limited funds. For example, you may want to avoid embarking on a piece of research that requires you to travel to many communities if the bus fares or cost of petrol would put a strain on your finances. It would be better for you to select a problem that can be investigated in settings to which you have reasonable access without straining your resources.

The characteristics mentioned above should help you when you are trying to select a problem for investigation. It should be clear that what might be a good problem for one person might not be appropriate for someone else. You should therefore try not to compare your problem with anybody else's. Remember you are the one who will spend hours with your research. Therefore, you should ensure that you select a problem that will hold your interest and attention even when you are tired and under stress. Your research and the challenges that it presents should constantly excite you.

SOURCES OF RESEARCH PROBLEMS

Now that you are aware of some features of a research problem, you must go out and find one. There are several sources of research problems for you to explore. An excellent source of research problems is theory. The notion of a theory is that it has not been established as fact and is therefore open to testing in different contexts. Testing of theories is a meaningful and worthwhile activity that helps to establish them as facts or relegate them to the realm of perpetual theory. So if there is some theory that you believe can be properly tested in your social setting, and it meets the other criteria mentioned above, you may want to do your research in that area. Admittedly however, research problems associated with theory may be a bit too challenging for most inexperienced researchers, so you may want to avoid such research problems until your research skills are more developed.

Research problems may also be found within your context. There are always issues of concern within any social system. Perhaps a new policy is being introduced in an organisation. You might want to conduct research into the effectiveness of this new policy. Or perhaps teachers are concerned about some behaviour that is emerging among the students that might be having an effect on their learning. Would it be worthwhile to investigate this phenomenon to ascertain the true extent of its effect? In the past decade, educational reforms have been introduced in almost all of the Caribbean territories, as in many other countries worldwide. In many of the OECS territories, there is the introduction of universal secondary education. What are some of the effects of this reform? What are the effects of technological reforms in the schools, in banking, in health institutions? Could you investigate the effects of such reforms? As was mentioned before, the start of the twenty-first century ushered in exciting times for researchers in the Caribbean. For example, there are issues related to the Caribbean Single Market and Economy (CSME); the privatisation of institutions such as hospitals; concern about the environment; and issues relating to health and family life. These are all areas that can provide topics of investigation that would be relevant to the sub-region.

Another good source of a problem is research literature. Students looking for a research problem have been known to spend hours in the journals section of the library at their institutions browsing journals in the hope of finding something of interest to them. Reading abstracts and summaries of previous research might ignite a spark in you that can set you on your way towards a productive research exercise. It is true that sometimes, inexperienced researchers find that reading research articles can be daunting. Do not be deterred; it gets easier with practice, and we offer some tips in the next chapter which deals with reviewing literature that should make that task less harrowing for you. Further, in these days of electronic media, you might also want to use the Internet to find out what educational issues are currently being discussed and explored on the international scene. You might find something there that could help you to identify a research problem that you would want to explore within the context of the Caribbean.

Sometimes new researchers despair that if this research was done before, then how will they find something novel to do. Take courage! As mentioned before, novel does not mean never ever done before. You can introduce novelty by perhaps refining some aspect of the reported research, or by replicating it in a different setting, or even developing the research beyond what was reported. As mentioned before, many of the reported studies are done in countries outside of the region. You have the unique privilege of exploring these ideas within the Caribbean region.

One other source of research problems that should not be overlooked or minimised is your own experience. People who are engaging in social research for the first time are members of several social systems. As such, there might be some phenomena that you observed, or that others brought to your attention that may be worth investigating. Remember, it must not be trivial or something that is of concern to no one but you. If you discuss your idea with others and they all ask 'so what? Who cares?', then the meaningfulness of your problem may be questionable. If you are a secondary school student, is it worthwhile to investigate your hunch that if the dustbin is placed at the back of the class instead of at the front there will be less paper for the cleaners to sweep up at the end of the day? On the other hand, a research topic that examines school students' preferences on music and its possible effects on their academic performance is more likely to meet the above criteria.

The advice given here should help you with the task of identifying a research problem. No doubt, your supervisor and others will also give you advice. Talk to your colleagues, to students, to parents and anyone who is interested in social matters. The staff at your institution can also be sources when you are looking for an area to research. Talk to your supervisor or anyone else there who you believe might be able to point you to a researchable problem. But, remember you are only looking for ideas. You should not allow yourself to be forced to undertake research simply because your supervisor says you should. The ultimate choice is yours.

FOCUSING YOUR RESEARCH PROBLEM

When you first identify a research problem, you may find that it is very general. For example, you may decide to investigate the use of computers in education. This is a wide area that can be approached from many different angles and in different contexts. In this form, the investigation might be too large for a single researcher working within a relatively short period. It would therefore be necessary for you to focus your research problem. This means that you must narrow the topic down to something more manageable. It can be tempting to try to do too much in one research project, but that will only result in superficial and/or unclear findings. It would be better to focus on a specific topic within a larger area. If you are truly motivated, you can gradually investigate other aspects of the problem area later.

Focusing your research, also referred to as delimiting the research, is a task in which you set the boundaries of your study. This is where you decide what or who is to be included in the research and what or who is to be excluded. Setting boundaries is important because it guides you in choosing your research design, and in selecting your participants, data collection methods and data analysis techniques. It also guides your choice of literature to review. There may be many pieces of literature in the general area of your research. You do not want to spend your limited time reading materials that are irrelevant to your study, nor do you want to write a review that is so unfocused that readers cannot see where you are going with the research. Setting careful and clear boundaries for your research reduces the possibility of this happening. A well-delimited study also helps readers of your work to understand the contexts and individuals to which any generalisations may be made.

We must mention here that delimitation of your research is not the same thing as limitations of the research. Delimitation is a deliberate act designed to control the research, making it focused and clear. A limitation however is a condition that weakens your research. It is a condition over which you have little control, but that can affect the findings of your research. For example, let us say that you were studying young people's attitudes towards people who are HIV-positive and you plan to collect your data from school children during the first term of the academic year, over a 13-week period. However, since this is usually during the hurricane season in the Caribbean, let's say school was disrupted by the passage of two major hurricanes during this time and your data collection period was reduced to eight weeks. As a result, you may not be able to gather the quantity of data you wanted, and therefore the conclusions you can draw can at best be only tentative. This is a limitation, since you have no control over the weather and you may not have time to redesign your research. Sometimes conditions that can have an effect on your research findings are known from the start, but are conditions over which you have no control. In reporting your research, you should acknowledge these limitations and discuss the possible impact on the research. Then when you present your findings and conclusions, you can remind the reader of the limitations.

Delimiting or focusing your research helps you to eliminate one flaw that many students tend to report as a limitation. It is not uncommon to read under the heading 'Limitations of the Study' the sentence 'There was not enough time to collect all the data needed.' On examination, there is nothing to indicate that this was the result of some unforeseen or some known but uncontrollable event. In many cases, it is simply the result of poor planning, or an attempt to undertake a project that was too large for the time available. This is a flaw, not a limitation. While limitations are unforeseen and/or events out of your control, flaws can be identified and eliminated before you begin your research.

WRITING YOUR PROBLEM STATEMENT

When you have decided on your research topic and what the focus will be, your next task is to formulate a problem statement. The problem statement identifies the intent or purpose of the research. Formulating one calls for much thought on your part because this statement guides what data you collect, from whom you collect it, how you analyse it and how you interpret the results of your analysis. A good problem statement tells the readers what the focus of your research is, and clues them to the types of questions that you are going to try to answer.

A basic rule for writing your problem statement is: Always state your research problem in a complete grammatical sentence in as few words as possible. Your research problem should be so clearly and concisely stated so that anyone reading it should be in no doubt about your intentions or about the purpose of the research. If your problem statement is not clear and precise, it might be an indication that even you are not clear on what you are setting out to do. This can have an impact later when you try to analyse whatever data you collect since you may not be sure what you are looking for, or what questions you are trying to answer. A good piece of research therefore begins with a good problem statement.

A well-written problem statement usually identifies the variables, in which you are interested, the specific relationship between those variables that you are examining, and where possible, the types of participants involved. Figure 3a below gives examples of problem statements. Remember, each statement must be a grammatically stated sentence that is clear and concise.

Figure 3a
Examples of Statements of Research Problems

1. This study investigates the factors that influence voters' choice of political parties.

2. The purpose of this study is to investigate primary school teachers' attitudes towards students with special education needs in mainstream classrooms.

3. This study investigates the impact of warning labels on cigarette cartons on people's attitudes to smoking.

4. This study investigates the impact of Hurricane Janet on the physical, social and economic infrastructure of Barbados.

5. This study investigates the effects of a constructivist approach to teaching mathematics on the mathematics achievement of students pursuing the Caribbean Advance Proficiency Examination (CAPE) in St Vincent and the Grenadines.

6. The purpose of this study is to investigate the relationship between physical attractiveness of individuals and the perception of members of the university community about their HIV/AIDS status.

A good problem statement defines all the relevant variables either directly or operationally. There are many concepts used in social research for which dictionary definitions do provide clarity. To avoid vagueness and ambiguity, operational definitions should be used. An operational definition explains a concept in terms of operations or processes. For instance in problem statement #5 in Figure 3a above, the variables to define are 'constructivist approach' and 'mathematics achievement.' The term 'constructivist' has different meanings for different people. It is therefore important that you tell the reader how you are using the term. Thus, you might define 'constructivist approach' as 'allowing the students to engage in various activities that are designed to lead them to an understanding of given concepts in mathematics'. Similarly, you might define 'mathematics achievement' as students' performance in the Caribbean Advanced Proficiency Examination (CAPE).

The statement of the research problem should be given in the introductory chapter or section of your report and should be accompanied by the presentation of the background of the problem. The background of the problem should include something on the context of the problem being investigated and justification or rationale for conducting the research. This is where you explain the significance of the research, why it is worthwhile and how it can contribute to knowledge in your field. Some people advocate that you should state your research problem before going into this presentation, since it sets the stage for the discussion that follows. However, you may also present your background and rationale for doing the study and lead into your problem statement. It is a matter of choice, guided by what is most suitable for your particular style. Figure 3b below gives an example of how you may report the background of your research and the justification or rationale for conducting the research, followed by the statement of the research problem. It is in this section of your report that you might also want to present your research hypotheses or questions.

Figure 3b
An Excerpt from the Background and Rationale for Conducting a Piece of Research, Followed by the Problem Statement

> It is often said that the contribution of the jury members to the work of the judiciary is extremely important. It therefore seems to be more than worthwhile to provide feedback on this most important phase of the criminal justice system, so that the relevant authorities might be aware of the impact which it has on those who are called to render valuable service and discharge their civic duties most faithfully... This study investigates the feelings of jurors about jury service. It seeks to capture the jurors' perceptions of their contributions to the system and what might be done to make this contribution more meaningful....
>
> Source: Rose, G. S. (2006). A Survey Investigating the Feelings and Attitudes of a set of persons summoned for Jury Service in one of the Supreme Courts of Barbados. Unpublished Paper.

FORMULATING AND STATING RESEARCH HYPOTHESES

After stating your research problem, you could formulate research hypotheses that you will test. The outcome of the testing of your hypotheses provides information about the problem that you are researching. It is therefore important that you formulate relevant hypotheses. The following sections should help you to make good decisions about this.

Purpose of the Hypothesis

A hypothesis is a statement about expected relationships or difference between variables based on a hunch. The use of the word 'hunch' should not be taken to mean that you are making a wild guess. On the contrary, your hunch should be based on theory, past experience, observations and/or information gathered from other sources. Thus, using the example of the constructivist approach mentioned earlier, you may have a hunch that this approach may be more effective in fostering understanding of mathematics concepts based on the theories of learning associated with it. You may therefore make a statement of expectation along these lines. Your hypothesis is stated in such a way then, that it can be tested.

As mentioned in chapter 2, one common misconception held by many inexperienced researchers is that their task is to 'prove' their hypothesis. This belief leads many of them to despair when their data do not prove or confirm their expectations. It also leads to some of them giving in to the urge to 'cook' the data so that it produces the expected results. Not only is this practice unethical, it is also unnecessary. It is not the researcher's task to prove anything. As a researcher, your task is to test your hypothesis. To do this, you collect data that will either support your hypothesis or not. Since you formulate your hypothesis based on some theory you read or some personal experience or information from others, if the data you collect do not support it, then it is your task to try to explain why. These considerations make your research exciting, since they could highlight factors that were not apparent to previous researchers and theorists. You could be making important contributions to knowledge in the area.

Stating the Hypothesis

As mentioned earlier, a hypothesis is a statement of expected (or suspected) relationship or difference between research variables. A research hypothesis is a definite statement predicting a particular research outcome. It provides a tentative explanation of the relationship or difference between two or more well defined or operationalised variables. Examples of research hypotheses are:

1. There is a relationship between the age of voters and their preference of political party.
2. Primary school teachers who received training in special education hold more positive attitudes towards special needs students in mainstream classroom than do those who received no training.
3. Students studying mathematics for CAPE who are taught using a constructivist approach achieve higher in the subject than do those who are taught by a traditional approach.

In each of the examples above, there is a predicted relationship between two variables. Figure 3c below shows the variables involved in each example.

Figure 3c
The Pairs of Variables Involved in the Hypotheses

Hypothesis	Variables	
1	(i)	Age of voters and
	(ii)	preferred political party
2	(i)	Status of teachers' training in special education and
	(ii)	teachers' attitudes to special needs students in mainstream classrooms
3	(i)	Teaching approach in mathematics and
	(ii)	students' achievement in mathematics

To some extent, your hypothesis may be seen as a highly specific version of your problem statement, and as with your problem statement, the variables in your hypothesis should be clearly defined or operationalised. Thus for Hypothesis 1 above, there might be two conditions that define the age of voters: either they are 25 years old or younger or they are older than 25 years. Further, party preference may be for a democratic party or a socialist one. The idea is that you should clearly define your variables.

Types of Hypotheses

Hypotheses can be categorised according to how they are derived or how they are stated. The classifications we will discuss are the directional, non-directional and null hypothesis. Hypotheses are inductive if they are derived from observations. Here, variables may appear to be related in a number of situations and a tentative hypothesis may be formulated. Thus, for example, you may notice that some students' essays are of very good quality. You may then find out that most of these students report that they are members of a dramatic society. You may then hypothesise that students who are involved in dramatic activities produce better quality essays than students who do not engage in such activities. This would just be a tentative explanation for the high standard of the essays produced. Thus, inductive hypotheses are formulated after data has been collected and analysed. These tend to be associated with qualitative approaches to research. On the other hand, deductive hypotheses are derived from theory. They provide evidence that support, expand or contradict a given theory, often suggesting studies that may be conducted in the future. These hypotheses are formulated before data is collected. In fact, data is collected in order to test deductive hypotheses. Deductive hypotheses are usually associated with quantitative research approaches.

Hypotheses may be stated in a manner that suggests that you expect to find a relationship or difference between two variables. Such hypotheses are called research or declarative hypotheses. Further, a research hypothesis may be non-directional or directional. A non-directional hypothesis merely indicates that you expect that a relationship or a difference exists. No guesses are made about the nature of the relationship or difference. Thus, a non-directional hypothesis might state:

> There is a significant relationship between age of voters and their
> preference of political party.
> Or
> There is a significant difference in attitudes towards children with
> special needs in mainstream classrooms between teachers who
> have training in special education and those who do not.

Notice that for the first hypothesis we did not attempt to guess at which age group is likely to have which preference. Likewise, for the second hypothesis, we did not attempt to predict which group of teachers might have a more positive or negative attitude. All we are saying is that we expect a significant relationship or a significant difference in attitude.

On the other hand, a directional hypothesis indicates the nature of the expected relationship or difference. Thus, such a hypothesis might state:

> Voters in the 25 years and under age group are more likely to
> have a preference for socialist political parties than do voters in
> the 25 years and over age group.
> Or
> Teachers who have training in special education have more
> positive attitudes towards children with special educational needs
> in mainstream classrooms than teachers with no training.

For directional hypotheses, not only do you state that you expect a relationship or a difference, but you also suggest what that relationship or difference might be. Directional hypotheses tend to be used only in situations when you are very confident about the nature of relationship or difference.

Whether you use non-directional or directional hypotheses it is important when you are carrying out statistical tests to ascertain the nature of any relationship or difference between the given variables. The nature of your hypotheses will influence how you use and interpret the statistical tests.

A hypothesis may be stated in a form other than as a research or declarative hypothesis. You could also state it as a null hypothesis. A null hypothesis is a statement indicating that no relationship or difference is expected between the two variables. Stated as null hypotheses, the two examples given above would read:

> There is no significant relationship between age of voters and
> their preference of political party.
> And
> There is no significant difference in attitudes towards children
> with special needs in mainstream classrooms between teachers
> who have training in special education and those who do not.

Null hypotheses are especially important if you are using statistical tests of significance since it is the null hypothesis that these tests evaluate. Tests of significance help you to make the decision either to reject the null hypothesis or fail to reject (retain) it. More will be said on this in chapter 11. Suffice to say that you should be able to write a sharp and concise null hypothesis, with the variables involved clear to the reader.

As with your problem statement, your hypotheses must be clearly and unambiguously stated. If you do not state them clearly and unambiguously, you may be deluding yourself that you know what you are doing and what you are looking for. As a result, you may collect insufficient or irrelevant data from unsuitable participants, and in the end, be unable to test your hunch adequately. For instance, if you are investigating the relationship between age of voters and preference of political party, you would need a sample that includes people who are eligible to vote who are in the required age ranges. It would not be wise to include people who are below the voting age, non-nationals who are ineligible to vote or even people who can vote but choose not to be registered to do so. In addition, you have to be clear what you mean by party. Do you mean from an ideological standpoint (Democratic versus Socialist) or whether you want to refer to specific parties (People's Power Movement versus Freedom Fighters Faction) regardless of their ideology? Being clear on this will guide what you ask the participants. The bottom line is, you must ensure that whatever data you collect and the people from whom you collect them are appropriate for testing your hypotheses. This could prove difficult if your hypotheses lack clarity.

Sometimes inexperienced researchers believe that they must always have hypotheses when they are embarking on research. This is not necessarily the case. There are some instances for example when you as a researcher will have no theory, past experience or other information from which to formulate hypotheses. In such cases, you may be on a 'fishing trip', that is you are trying to understand the status of some phenomenon. For such exploratory research it might be more prudent to use research questions.

FORMULATING RESEARCH QUESTIONS

Not all research paradigms embrace the scientific deductive approach, with its emphasis on hypothesis testing. Indeed not all research problems can be addressed in this manner. Sometimes hypotheses are inappropriate but that does not mean that the research problem is not worthwhile. There are instances in which not enough is known about the phenomenon for hypotheses to be formulated. Thus, exploratory research may be necessary. Here the researcher formulates questions that are likely to shed light on the phenomenon. This is often the type of research that produces inductive hypotheses that others go on to test.

As with hypotheses, research questions should be well thought out. They too should be clearly and unambiguously stated so that the variables of interest are evident. Suppose for example that you wanted to explore teachers' attitudes towards children with special educational needs in mainstream classrooms. But the concept of integrating students with special educational needs into mainstream classrooms may be somewhat new to the Eastern Caribbean region and little is known about how people feel about it. Rather than hypothesising about it, you may simply want to ask specific questions to which you will seek answers by collecting and analysing data. Thus, you may formulate research questions such as:

What are the current practices in relation to educating students with special educational needs?

How do teachers feel about having students with special educational needs in their mainstream classrooms?

What do teachers believe would be needed for successful integration of students with special educational needs in their mainstream classrooms?

Notice here that you would make no definite attempt to hypothesise about which teachers may be feeling what. That does not mean that you may not have some expectations. However, you are not willing to stick your neck out about them until you have done some exploratory work. Thus, you may select a sample of teachers from appropriate settings and carry out your investigation. Based on the findings, you (or some other researcher) may formulate hypotheses about teachers and their attitudes towards students with special educational needs in mainstream classrooms in your country and go on to test those hypotheses in different settings, perhaps at primary, secondary and tertiary levels. The thing to remember is that your research questions should be well stated with the variables of interest clear since these will influence who is involved in your study and what data you collect.

By now you would have noticed our repeated advice to ensure that your variables are clear and well defined. You might be wondering why. In the next section, we will be discussing variables and their role in the research process.

VARIABLES

The concept of variables, introduced earlier in this chapter is one with which you should become very familiar and comfortable. One of the dictionary definitions of the word 'variable' is 'able to be changed or adapted'. This suggests that variables can take on different appearances at times. In research terms, variables are conditions or characteristics that you, the researcher, manipulate, control or observe. As the dictionary definition implies, these conditions or characteristics may take on different values. Using the research problem about voters' party preference, the variable 'age of voter' will change depending on the particular participant. For example 'age of voter' may take on the value '25 years or under' or it may have the value 'over 25 years old,' depending on the age of the individual. Similarly, if we had a variable called 'number of cigarettes smoked in a day' for the study on smoking habits, this variable would take on the values of 0, 1, 2, 3, and so on, depending on how many cigarettes the participant smoked in a day.

In research, there are different labels given to variables. But two very common types of variables that you will need to understand are independent and dependent variables. You should be well aware of them and their relationship to your research from the start. Let us explore these two types of variables.

Types of Variables

The main types of variables that you need to be concerned with in your research are independent and dependent variables. However, these are not the only ones of which you must be aware. There are other types of variables that can have an impact on your research. For example, you may read of moderator variables, intervening variables or even organismic variables. These may sometimes be referred to as confounding variables since, if you do not take them into account, they can influence the conclusions that you are able to draw from you research findings. These concepts are especially significant if you are doing an experimental study. But since the notion of independent and dependent variables may be related to most types of research, we will discuss them here.

Independent Variables

In experimental research, independent variables are those conditions that you would try to manipulate in order to observe their effect on some other variable. In a study where you are interested in finding out the effects of two different approaches to instruction on the rate of teenage pregnancy, you may have several communities in which to collect data. You could manipulate the method of instruction by exposing young people in a number of communities to a programme that promotes abstinence. In other communities, the programme could be about protection and in a third group, a programme that involves both messages could be introduced. You would decide which programme each group gets. Then you would observe the effects of the programmes by monitoring the rate of pregnancy among the young girls in the various communities. Thus, the programme would be your independent variable. When the independent variable is one that can be manipulated by the researcher, it is called the experimental or treatment variable.

Sometimes, the independent variable may be a characteristic that you cannot manipulate. For instance, you may want to find out whether females and males feel differently about something. Here the independent variable would be the gender of the participants; however, you cannot assign a gender to any of them. Independent variables such as gender, age, race and other inherent attributes that cannot be manipulated but can be studied are called organismic variables. Using one of our research problems mentioned earlier, if you were examining whether there is a difference in the number of cigarettes smoked by smokers in different age groups, then the age of the smokers would be your independent variable. Just as how you would separate the communities into groups according to the programme that they received and then look at the pregnancy rate, for research, you would group the smokers according to their age and then look at how many cigarettes were smoked by the various groups.

Notice that in the first example, you the researcher had some control over which group got what treatment. In the second example, you have no control over people's age. They are as old as they are. In cases where the independent variable is not manipulated (a treatment assigned), it is also called the grouping variable. This is due to the separation of the research participants into groups of those with a pre-existing characteristic or attribute and those without it.

Dependent Variables

If you are carrying out an experimental study, then you are likely to be attempting to establish a cause-effect relationship, with the treatment variable being the cause. The effect or the outcome of manipulating the variable is called the dependent variable. Thus, in a case where you are looking at the effects of three different programmes on rate of teenage pregnancy, the dependent variable would be the rate of teenage pregnancies. The concept of dependent variables is also used in other types of research besides experiments. In a study of the perceptions about the HIV status of individuals, you may use a rating scale to assess the participants' perceptions about the individuals in question. Here, the dependent variable would be the ratings indicated by the participants. Or in a more qualitative study, the dependent variable could be views, opinions or beliefs. In general then, the dependent variable is the characteristic or condition that you expect to change or vary for different groups (independent variable). It is the characteristic or condition on which all the research participants are assessed and which you make no attempt to manipulate.

Identifying Independent and Dependent Variables

Whether you use hypotheses or research questions, it is always useful to identify your independent and dependent variables from the start. This helps you to clarify operational definitions and also helps you to decide on matters such as what would be the best research design to adopt, which participants would be appropriate to help you test your hypotheses or answer your research questions, and what data you would need to collect. One way of identifying your independent variable is to ask yourself: 'Which variable am I going to use to separate the participants into groups?' or 'Which variable am I going to manipulate?' To identify your dependent variable, you may ask: 'On which variable am I going to assess all the participants?' Let us see how that might work.

Let us say that you had the following hypothesis.

> There is a difference in the quality of essays produced by third form secondary students who used computers for essay writing and those who used only paper and pencil.

To identify the independent variable, ask what variable am I going to use to group the students? The answer is, according to how they learn to write essays, either with the computer or with paper and pencil only. Thus, the independent variable is the method that students use to write their essays. There are two conditions here: (1) with computers and (2) with paper and pencil only. To identify the dependent variable, ask on what variable am I going to assess all the students? The answer is, on the quality of their essays. Thus, quality of the essays is the dependent variable. You would then go on to say what you intend to look for to determine quality. Figure 3d summarises this.

Figure 3d
Identifying and Defining Independent and Dependent Variables in a Hypothesis

Hypothesis:	There is a difference in the quality of essays produced by third form secondary students who used computers for essay writing and those who used only paper and pencil.	
Independent Variable:	Method used to write essays	There will be two groups of students, one writing essays using computers and the other using paper and pencil only.
Dependent Variable:	Quality of the essays	Identified by assessing the content, coherence and use of language.

What about if you have research questions instead of hypotheses? Let us consider an example. Suppose your research question is:

What attitudes do bank employees have towards working on weekends?

Here you are not manipulating any of the variables. So you might decide to group the bank employees according to several different existing characteristics, for example age, gender, marital status, or any others that you believe would shed light on the presence of differing opinions (See Figure 3e). All of these can be independent variables. When the employees are grouped by age, you may want to use the different age groups; by gender – male and female; by marital status – single or married. The dependent variable would be the attitudes that the employees hold towards working on weekends. This you might assess by questionnaire or an attitude scale.

Figure 3e
Identifying and Defining Independent and Dependent Variables in a Research Question

Research Question:	What attitudes do bank employees have towards working on weekends?	
Independent Variable(s):	Existing Characteristics of the employees	
	(a) Gender	Employees grouped as male or female
	(b) Age	Employees grouped accord to age group (< 25 years, 25–34 years, 35–44 years, 45+ years)
	(c) Marital Status	Employees grouped according to whether they are married or not
Dependent Variable:	Attitudes towards working on weekends	Assessed by means of an attitude scale/questionnaire items

Identifying the independent and dependent variables tends to be a bit more complicated when research questions are being used, or where no variables are being manipulated, since a characteristic that is the independent variable for one question could be the dependent variable for another question. For example, in a study of bank employees' attitudes towards working on weekends, you may have two research questions: the ones mentioned above and this one:

Is there a difference in the rate of absenteeism among bank employees who have different attitudes towards working on weekends?

> For this question, the employees can be grouped according to their attitudes towards working on weekends as indicated by their responses on the questionnaire or attitude scale, so this would be your independent variable. You may end up with two groups of employees: one group that displays positive attitudes and another with negative attitudes. You could then assess the rate

of absenteeism of the employees in each group. That would be
your dependent variable. Thus, the employees' attitude towards
working on weekends was the dependent variable for the first
question but the independent variable for the second one.

The ability to identify the independent and dependent variables associated with research hypotheses and research questions is honed with time and experience. So use every opportunity to practise. Try to identify them in research articles that you read or in other people's research. In time this task could become painless and even automatic.

THE END OF THE BEGINNING

You might realise by now that although you are at the beginning stage of your research, by the time you have reached this far, you would have made some decisions about your research design, data collection and analysis. This is indeed how the process works. Doing research is not a linear process as it sometimes appears to be, where you start and finish one aspect before going on to another. What you do from the start affects what you do later and you must be aware of this. You must always try to assess how your chosen hypotheses or research questions can inform how you collect your data, how you analyse it and how you report your findings, even if only tentatively. You may find that as you get deeper into your research that you need to adjust certain aspects, for example, your research questions. This is all part of the process. But these beginning activities outlined in this chapter are very important.

Though it was not highlighted here, since it is dealt with in detail in the next chapter, we must emphasise that while engaging in these beginning activities, you should be reading extensively in your research area. A sound knowledge of the research area helps you to make sensible decisions about what is feasible and what might not be. It helps you to identify issues that are germane to your research area. It also helps you to identify any weaknesses in previous research in the area so that you can avoid them or rectify them in your own work or strengths that you can incorporate. Further, while reading journal articles and books in the area of research you may be directed to reliable instruments that can be used in your research. Reading in the problem area is vital at the early stages of your research and in the next chapter we give you some advice that can make that task fairly painless.

Thus then, by the end of these initial activities you should have a relatively clear understanding of the problem that you are researching. You should have clarified your problem statement, formulated appropriate hypotheses and/or research questions, and identified the variables of interest to you. If this is done well, you should also have a pretty good idea of what research design to use, what data you need to collect and from whom, as well as how you will analyse it. Indeed it is truly worth the turmoil that you may experience at the start of your research, for once these things are clear to you and you can express them with equal clarity in writing, then you are well on your way to an extremely exciting and enjoyable experience of producing a worthwhile piece of research.

4

REVIEWING LITERATURE

INTRODUCTION

The literature review is seen by many, especially young researchers, as an evil which they wish could be avoided. As a result, it is often poorly done. We do hope that after you have read this chapter, if you are one of those haters of literature reviews, your perspective will change and that you will come to the realisation of its immense importance. Hopefully, the information that we present to you in this chapter will help in the process of reviewing the literature. You should be in a better position to determine which literature is relevant to your study, how to source literature, indexing literature located and/or read, reading and critiquing the literature, annotating literature, compiling a list of references and importantly, writing a literature review. One word of advice, you must be prepared to make the library your friend. Remember that the library is where most of the materials you will review reside.

WHY DO A LITERATURE REVIEW?

In conducting a literature review, you must first recognise that, like all other phases of the research process, it should be undertaken in a systematic way. To do it well, you will need to identify and locate materials, evaluate their relevance to the problem you are researching, and analyse them to determine for example their strengths and limitations.

The review is important for several reasons. First, you do not want to disillusion yourself. It certainly would not help your mental state in anyway if you were to later find out that what you thought was ground breaking research was actually a highly researched problem. We are not suggesting that if a problem has been highly researched before that you should not tackle it also, but that it would be good if you are aware of any such previous studies. Examinations of similar studies to the one you are about to undertake may save you unnecessary headaches. Through these studies, you may gain methodological insights into how you can go about conducting your study. You are able to see what worked or did not work for other researchers. You in fact can add a new dimension to the study of a problem if you are aware of what was done previously. You may have discovered that all the studies ignored something that you believe could have affected the findings in some way. If for example, in studies of adolescents' home practices, you were to discover that only the adolescents were consulted in the data gathering process, you may consider this a major weakness. You may decide then to build on such studies by getting the perspectives, not only of the adolescents, but also of the parents or significant others in the home. You may also wish to study a problem that, though highly researched, has never been investigated in your setting. In areas such as the Caribbean this point has special significance since much of what guides practice in the region is often research conducted in foreign settings like the USA and UK.

The literature review is also important because you can learn from what was done before. You are able to see how other researchers controlled the scope of their problem. The topic you wish to investigate may be quite wide and as such, you would have to delimit your study. You must make choices as to how wide and how deep you want your investigation to go. An example of this could be an interest in studying male academic performance. With this interest, you may have to make the decision as to whether you study males at all levels of the education system or whether you confine it to just one level. Our advice is that for the small-scale research that you will be expected to do at the certificate, associate degree or undergraduate level, you would be better off delimiting the study to one level. The general rule of thumb is that it is better to go for depth than to conduct a study that is wide in scope but very superficial.

Importantly also, a review of the literature facilitates the interpretation of the results of your study. Having reviewed the literature, you would be able to comment on your findings in comparison to other studies. You would be able to provide answers to the questions that will aid your analysis. Based on your review, you will be able to say whether your findings are in agreement with or contradict other studies. Naturally, if your results contradict those in the studies that you reviewed, you would be expected to offer possible explanations for the discrepancies.

We are aware that doing the review can be challenging but it needs not be painstaking. One of the major challenges that young researchers face is to know how broad their review should be. The problem often is to determine what literature is relevant to the study. We of course are not in a position to assess the relevance of any material to your study. It is a rather subjective process that must be left to your judgement. Our advice is to avoid the urge of using every piece of material that you can put your hand on. The key is to determine what is directly relevant to your study and aim for a well-organised review. A sign of a good literature review is not necessarily in its width but how the materials that you determined to be relevant are utilised. In all you do, aim for a review that is well focused.

IDENTIFYING AND LOCATING LITERATURE

Identifying and locating literature are two important steps in doing the review. For most problems that you will investigate there will be many sources of literature. One of the major complaints by students embarking on the journey of reviewing literature is that they cannot identify materials relevant to their study. One needs only to know where to look and how to conduct the search.

The many sources of literature can be divided into two major categories: primary and secondary. A primary source is where a study is reported by the actual person who conducted it. A secondary source is where someone is reporting on a study conducted by someone else. That is to say it is not original; it is the interpretation of another person. As a researcher, you should always strive to obtain primary sources of literature since as the saying goes, it is better to get the information from the 'horse's mouth'. This does not mean though that secondary sources are not important. Often, it is the secondary sources that will point the way to the primary sources. For example, a book may give an account of a study done by another researcher. Having made this citation, the author would provide a full reference of the study. Thus, to read a more detailed account of the study, you may then need to use the reference to locate the original work.

In the event that there is truly very little written about your problem, there is still no need to worry. You can still produce a well-developed literature review. The key is to locate materials that though not focusing specifically on your topic, still has some bearing. In investigating issues related to volunteering in the Eastern Caribbean, you may discover that there is very little research in that area within the region. However, in doing your review, you can draw on literature on volunteering in general and on research reports written about the topic in other settings, for example, in the USA or the UK. Thus, you can review studies of volunteering in these countries and raise questions about the topic in the Caribbean setting. This could help to create the framework in which your research would be conducted.

While we must admit that identifying and locating literature can sometimes be frustrating, there are mechanisms to make the job easier. These mechanisms include indexes, and computer searches.

Indexes

An index is a major source of periodicals such as journals, bulletins, yearbooks and reports. There are several very good indexes that you will find quite useful. Many of them are available online, but there are also hard copies in libraries. In the field of education, these include the Education Index, Resources in Education (RIE), Current Index to Journals in Education (CIJE), the British Education Index (BEI) and Ingenta Services. Indexes in other fields include British Humanities Index, Social Sciences Index, Women's Studies Index and Sociological Abstracts. Some indexes provide full references for hundreds of periodicals, while others, along with the full reference, provide abstracts. While you will find that using indexes poses very little challenge, be prepared though, you might be overwhelmed by the number of references you may find that are related in some way to your problem. As with any index, entries are listed by subject, author and titles. To use an index, follow these few simple steps:

1. Work out key word(s) that are central to your problem and use them to search for the references. If you are investigating factors influencing students' academic performance, it would be a good thing to have an idea of some possible factors. So let us say that one factor is streaming, then, streaming can be used as a key word. It is also a good idea to come up with synonyms to your key word since different authors may use different words to refer to the same thing. Tracking or ability grouping are often used interchangeably with streaming. Don't be disheartened!

Even arriving at synonyms is painless. Many indexes have an accompanying thesaurus that you can consult for synonymous key words or descriptors as they are called by some.

2. Start with the most recent issue and look under the key word(s) that you identified. You will find a list of references under the key word(s) listed alphabetically.

3. You then need to determine which of the references listed under the key word(s) are directly related to your problem. Some of the indexes provide abstracts which will certainly assist you in coming to a decision as to whether the references are related to your research problem.

4. Once you have made the determination that a reference is related to your problem, you should record it. Make sure you record the complete reference. This will save you the effort later, since you may need this same reference for your bibliography.

5. Repeat steps 2 to 4 for previous issues of the index.

6. Your job now is to locate the materials in the library.

As we said earlier, the indexes can certainly make things substantially easier for you. The hardest thing might be to determine what is or is not relevant.

Computer Searches

Like indexes, computer searches should make the process of identifying and locating literature quite easy. In fact, computer searches will definitely speed up the review process. There are hundreds of databases available with information on much of the literature that you will need to use during your research career. One fairly well-known database in education is the Educational Resources Information Centre (ERIC). Other online databases in other fields include PsycINFO (psychological abstracts), JSTOR (multidisciplinary journals) and CARINDEX (literature published in the Caribbean). There are many other online journals and databases. Library staff at most educational institutions can give you advice on how to gain access to them to search for literature. Just remember that like the indexes, for best results, you need to come up with precise key words. For a basic search, all you have to do once you have access to the database is to type in a key word or phrase, click on the search button. This should allow you access to full references, abstracts and in some cases, full text documents. Depending on the database you are using, you can refine your search to specific journals, dates and even authors. When you are searching for literature for your review, it is certainly worth your while to become familiar with online databases and journals.

The convenient thing about computer searches is that they can be done from any computer with an Internet connection. It is also useful however, to check with your institution's library to find out whether they have access to any databases by subscription. Usually in such cases user names and passwords are required and the library staff would be able to supply these along with other useful information about usage. In addition, some libraries have a collection of indexes stored on CD-ROMs that you can use in the library.

Other sources of Literature

Although indexes and computer searches are extremely useful in locating literature, the activity of manually slugging through reading materials such as journals should not be underestimated. You might find it useful if you have some spare time on your hands to visit the journal section of the library, select a journal related to your field and browse through the articles. It is often when you are engaging in this somewhat unfocused quest that you stumble upon some invaluable gems of literature.

While the suggestions offered thus far could get you going in your search for literature, you do not have to restrict your activities to these. You need to be creative in your search. There will more than likely be other resources that you can tap into around you. There may also be persons knowledgeable in the area that you know who can direct you to either primary or secondary sources of literature. Ask them for help, but do not expect them to do it all for you. Be prepared to take whatever suggestions they may offer and follow them up on your own. Think of it as a treasure hunt and you are the detective following trails until you locate what you are looking for. Indeed, locating literature relevant to your research is like finding a pearl of great value!

READING RESEARCH REPORTS

Having determined that a research report is relevant to your problem, your task now is to read it. We expect that you would have already consulted some secondary sources and they would have pointed the way to the primary materials. We are stressing that you should strive to use mainly primary sources in your literature review. Thus, the information we will provide here is about reading research reports, the most common form of primary sources with which you will interact in research. Our job here is to help you to read such reports with a critical edge. In so doing, we are going to help you to identify the major components of a report. We will also show you how to evaluate the study using the various components as a guide.

Components of a Research Report

All well-written reports have the following parts: rationale, purpose, method, general procedure, results and discussion. Most of these components are often stated explicitly as headings in the report in an effort to guide you through your reading. However, be prepared, you will find the odd study where the various parts, though present, are stated implicitly.

The rationale lets you know what drove the researcher to conduct the study. The interest could have arisen from inconsistent or contradictory findings in previous studies, curiosity and/or some previous experience. The rationale normally will be expressed very early in the report. Like the rationale, the purpose of the study is stated quite early in the paper and it often comes just after the rationale. However, there is no hard and fast rule and in some cases you will find the purpose of the study stated before the rationale. It lets you know exactly what the investigator intended to accomplish. It is often stated in terms of the hypotheses, research questions or objectives. The next section, methods, focuses on the participants of the study. It indicates who they are, how they were recruited, selected, assigned or matched and how they were tested. This section should also provide information about the tests used. The procedure focuses on what was done to the participants or what they were required to do. In many reports, both the methods and procedure are combined to form one section. Next are the results. The results focus on the analyses of the data generated from the study. The analyses may be qualitative and/or quantitative. The final section, discussion, is where the researcher expresses the conclusions reached.

Evaluating the Study

You now know how to identify the different components of a research report; thus, your job now is to consider them as you evaluate a study. In evaluating a study, we are suggesting that you read it several times. Quite honestly, many research reports are difficult to read and you may need the rereading to pick out all the strengths, limitations and inconsistencies of a study. However, the more involved you become in research and the more reports you read, the easier it will be to work through an article. You will be able to cope with the esoteric nature of research only if you commit yourself to consistently reading such reports.

In evaluating a study, you need to consider each component of the report individually and collectively. For example, not only should you be able to identify the purpose of the study, but you should also discern a logical connection between that and the other components of the study. Thus, you may ask questions such as does the stated purpose match the rationale for conducting the study? Is the literature review related to the purpose of the study? Does the methodology adopted reflect the purpose of the study? Although this example begins with the purpose of the study, you can go through the same process beginning with any of the other components.

Practically then, if you have a study with the stated purpose 'to assess students' attitudes to the use of computers in essay writing,' you should check to see if the methods used by the investigator allow access to the type of information that would facilitate the assessment of student attitudes. You would perhaps expect the researcher to use some form of scale relating to the attitudes being assessed. It would not however be enough for the report to just state that an attitude scale was used. There should be information provided about the reliability and validity of the scale. In essence, you are trying to ascertain how much confidence you can place in the data obtained from the instrument, as this would also have implications for the validity of the conclusions drawn from it. More will be said about reliability and validity of instruments in chapter 9.

Another example pertaining to methods relates to issues of sampling. The sampling technique used by the investigator cannot be separated from the various components of the report. In particular, special attention should be paid to how the sampling methods relate to the purpose of the study, the results and the discussion. If the purpose of the study was stated in terms of a hypothesis, then you may get an indication as to the expectation of the investigator. Paying attention to both the purpose of the study and the sampling methods employed can suggest whether or not there was bias in the investigation. Say the hypothesis was that students who are taught essay writing with the aid of computers will display better writing skills than those who use paper and pencil only, then the sampling methods could give some insights into the investigator's thinking. Thus, the researcher may have chosen a group of students to be the experimental group because they already had computer skills. But the students in the group may also be the brighter ones who were doing work with the computer in an enrichment programme. On the other hand, no specific information is given about how the 'paper and pencil' group was selected. It would be reasonable to speculate that the non-random assignment of students to the two groups led to a situation in which the students in the experimental group had characteristics that predisposed them to write good essays whether they used the computer or paper and pencil. In such a case, the results of the study would be flawed and any conclusions drawn would be questionable.

As a reader, you should be prepared to challenge the results and conclusions in a report. The important point to bear in mind is that all the report components should be linked and that your evaluation should consider their interrelatedness.

General Advice for Reading Research Reports

One thing we are urging you to do when you read is to record complete bibliographic references. Do not leave the task of recording for when you have finished your study. Just the act of writing up a number of references at one time can be tiresome. If you do, you will find it onerous since you may have to spend many hours relocating the materials. Worst of all, for whatever reason, you just might not be able to relocate some of the materials that you consulted. You must avoid being like the student who called a university library, frantic to locate a book used extensively for her thesis. When asked the name of the author and the title of the book, she admitted that she did not know. All she was able to tell the librarian was that it was a red book. Imagine the consternation of the librarian who was surrounded by red books.

If you keep good bibliographic references, you should have no difficulty if at a later date you want to verify something or seek additional information from an article. Whatever you read or consult then, be sure to record the author's name, the title and edition of the book, the year of publication, the place of publication and the publishers. If your source is in a periodical or edited book, be sure to record both the title of the article or chapter and page numbers, as well as the name of the periodical or book. For periodicals, you should also record the volume and issue numbers and in cases such as newspapers and magazines, you will also need the date of publication. In these days where much information is accessed online, you must ensure that you keep a record of the web sites from which you retrieve literature. It might also be useful to record the date on which the literature was retrieved.

Since there are different styles of presenting references, you need to consult with your institution about the referencing style that they require and follow it. Although your institution may be following the general format of a particular style, you should consult any thesis/project guide that they provide. Sometimes these guidelines do not conform strictly to the referencing manuals. In such cases, the thesis or project guide would take precedence over the particular referencing manual. This is only fair since it is the institution, not the manual's publisher who will approve your paper. Having said this, we will introduce the APA (American Psychological Association) style, which is widely used. Figure 4a below provides a sample of references that follow the APA format.

Figure 4a
Examples of References Using the APA Style*

1. **A Book (One author):**
   Author's Last Name, Initial. (Date of Publication). Title of book. Place of Publication: Publishers

   E.g.

   Roberts, P. A. (1988). West Indians and their language. Cambridge, UK: Cambridge University Press.

2. **A Journal Article (One author):**
   Author's Last Name, Initial. (Date of publication). Title of article. Name of Journal, Volume number, Page numbers.

   E.g.

   Nissen, P. (1988). Microcomputers in the Jamaican school context: A case study. Programmed Learning and Educational Technology, 25, 354–357.

3. **A Chapter from an Edited Book (One author):**
   Author's Last Name, Initial. (Date of publication). Title of chapter. In Editor's Initials. Editor's Last Name (Ed.), Title of book (Page numbers). Place of Publication: Publishers

   E.g.

   Simmons-McDonald, H. (2001). Competence, proficiency and language acquisition. In P. Christie (Ed.), Due respect: Papers on English and English-related Creoles in the Caribbean in honour of Professor Robert Lepage (pp. 37–60). Mona, Jamaica: UWI Press.

4. **An Article in a Daily Newspaper:**
   Author's Last Name, Initial. (Year, Month Day). Title of article. Name of the Newspaper, Page number(s).

   E.g.

   Bradshaw, M. (2007, August 19). Solar power way to go. Sunday Sun, p. 21A.

* According to the 5th edition of the APA manual published in 2001
See the most recent edition of the manual for the full range of referencing protocol

Along with recording the references, some researchers find it useful to make copies of articles. In so doing, they will have the source at their disposal to use as they see fit. In terms of a book, it is a good idea to record its call number from the library so that you will know where to find it again. We do not expect you to copy entire books. If you do, the copyright police may hunt you down. One of the advantages of making copies of articles and chapters is that you can scribble notes on them as you read. But a more efficient means of noting useful information from these sources is to make annotations.

To make annotations from an article is to comment on points of interest. These comments can be descriptive or analytical in nature. Several annotations may be made from a single article that addresses different features relevant to your work. For example, imagine that you have read an article entitled 'I hate mornings: Finding your optimum performance period' by Ima Smartperson in the *Journal of Caribbean Occupational Matters.* You may want to make an annotation commenting on the methodology of the research (as illustrated in Figure 4b) and another about its findings (as in Figure 4c). You can decide if you want to make your annotations on index cards or type them directly into a file on your computer.

Figure 4b
An Example of an Annotation Focusing on the Methodology of the Research

THEME:
Methodology of the research (survey)

SMARTPERSON (2002)
Smartperson conducted a survey among workers in the Eastern Caribbean. These workers were either self-employed persons working at home or people who worked 9–5 jobs in the public and private sectors. Self-employed participants were randomly selected from the small business registry in the various territories. The other participants were employees of one private firm and one public organisation randomly selected from those in the capitals of each territory. Data were collected by questionnaires, sent by post to the self-employed people and distributed by hand by research assistants to the other participants. Participants had to indicate whether they felt their period of peak performance was (a) early morning – before 9 a.m. (b) late morning – between 9 a.m. and 12 noon (c) afternoon – between 1 p.m. and 5 p.m. or (d) evening – after 5 p.m. **Areas of Concern:** The participants working in the public and private sector offices may not be representative of this population. (1) Using only one business is restrictive and (2) employees working in capitals often have to commute, sometimes long distances, and may feel differently from those working outside the capital.

Figure 4c
An Example of an Annotation Focusing on the Findings of the Research

> **THEME**
> Findings of the study
>
> **SMARTPERSON (2002)**
> Smartperson found that, contrary to existing literature, there was no significant relationship between the employment status of the participants and their perceptions of their period of peak performance.

Note some important features in the examples above. Each one has the particular theme of the study on which you are commenting. When you have annotated a number of studies, you should end up with several on the same theme from different studies. Thus, using our example above, you would end up with several annotations of findings from studies dealing with people's perceptions of their period of peak performance. These themes become organisational tools that remind you of which articles deal with particular issues. In effect then, this facilitates retrieval of information when you are writing your review.

The other important feature, also facilitating retrieval, is the author and date of publication. This retrieval system is only efficient if you follow our advice about keeping a database with complete bibliographic information for all literature located and read. Thus, when you are ready to use the information from Smartperson's article, you would go to your database which would direct you to the article by name and the publication in which it is located. For those who choose to copy the article, a trip back to the library would not be necessary.

A word of caution with annotations is that if you have more that one article by the same author published in the same year, you should remember to use a system of distinguishing between them. One proven system involves referring to them as say Smartperson (2002a) and Smartperson (2002b) both in your database and on your annotation.

WRITING THE LITERATURE REVIEW

Having decided on the purpose of your research and identified, read and critically evaluated relevant literature, your task now is to set it all down in a coherent manner on paper. This calls for planning. A good plan is to some extent comparable to having a blueprint for a building. The important difference is that you can modify your plan at any stage without application to any authority but yourself! While it is outside of the sphere of this book to teach you how to make an outline or plan, we would advise you to organise your materials around relevant themes that you can use as subheadings. You should also identify the literature that you are going to use in the discussion of each theme. Here is where your annotations can be especially useful (aren't you glad you spent time doing them now?). It would be a good idea when you write the introduction to inform the reader about the organisation of your review by outlining the subheadings that you are going to use, and why these issues are vital to your research.

Once you have a reasonable plan, you are ready to start writing. From the start, you need to pay attention to aspects such as cohesiveness, logic and style. You may find yourself agonising over the style that you should use, but bear in mind that a literature review should be formal and you should adhere to the conventions of formal writing. That means that you should avoid using contractions, colloquialisms, or unexplained abbreviations. The language should be formal Standard English. It is imperative then that you pay close attention to grammar and spelling. Regardless of how logical and cohesive your review might be, nobody will want to read it if it is riddled with distracting grammatical and spelling errors! Remember, your hard-pressed examiner will be forced to read it but may take a dim view of such errors.

Another area to which you need to pay attention is the manner of citing literature in your review. You should acquaint yourself with the conventions for making citations according to the particular referencing style that you are using, try to be consistent. Regardless of what style you use, there are some things you should bear in mind. For instance, if you have several writers who make a similar point, it is not necessary to try to paraphrase each piece separately. It would be better (and more economical) to formulate a statement that encompasses the general point they are making and cite these writers at the end (illustrated in Figure 4d below). Note in the example that this is done in two ways. The first way can be seen in the first sentence where the authors are cited up front followed by the general point. The second way is demonstrated in the last sentence where the point is made and the writers cited at the end. As you gain experience in reading and writing academic work, you will acquire a sense of the various techniques that can be used. However, a general guideline is that when there are many authors to be cited, it might be best to have them at the end of the point.

Figure 4d
An Example of Citing Several Authors who Make a Similar Point in Different Articles, Using the APA Style

However, **Besser (1993)** and **Sutton (1991)** suggest that, far from promoting equity in schools, computer use maintains and exaggerates existing inequities. Indications are that there are quantitative and qualitative differences in the computer experiences of children of different socio-economic, racial, gender and academic ability groups **(Becker, 1992; Besser, 1993; Emihovich, 1990; Kennewell, Parkinson & Tanner, 2000; Riffel & Levin, 1997; Sutton, 1991).**

You should also avoid using too many direct quotes. You should perhaps only use direct quotes in situations where the author's exact words best express the point you are trying to make. A word of caution: it is not acceptable to directly quote pages from a source and argue that the author said everything in exactly the way that you would have said it! Paraphrasing is a skill that you must acquire to write a good review.

You may be wondering how much you need to write for a good literature review. While there may be no hard and fast rules on length of the review, there is a limit for the study. Therefore your literature review should be long enough to adequately deal with the relevant issues, but short enough to allow words for the rest of the report. In some cases, your supervisor or even the thesis guide may specify a word limit either as a number or as a percentage of the length of the entire study. We would suggest, however, that your literature review could perhaps be no more than 20 per cent of the entire thesis or project.

Whatever the length of your review, you should not forget that you must demonstrate analytical involvement with literature relevant to your study. A major weakness of many literature reviews is that they are mere reports of who said what in relation to the various areas. This often contributes to repetition of information and a lack of coherence and cohesiveness in the review. A good review however, needs to be critical, where you engage in analytical discussion of issues. This can sometimes involve doing a critique of some studies, a task that should only be used for research reports that are germane to your work. To critique a study, you need to mention where the study was done, who were the participants, what procedure was followed, the data collection techniques used, the nature of the data collected and how it was analysed (illustrated in Figure 4e below). This information should be reported concisely, since anyone interested in the study cited can obtain a copy of the report to learn the details.

Figure 4e
An Example of Some Descriptive Information about a Study to be Critiqued

Another study (Aranha, 1985) that to some extent raises questions about reading interests was conducted in a school in the suburbs of Bombay to see how using SSR in India would work in practice. According to the author, the students in the school were representative of the student population of Goregaon and Bombay City. Two fourth grade classes were used in the study. Along with the regular language programme, one class was flooded with books and given the SSR treatment twice a week for a year while the other received only the regular language programme. Comparisons were made using a Cloze test to ascertain whether the SSR was more effective than the regular method in improving students' reading achievement (the ability to understand the meaning of a passage).

You should then present a critical analysis of the findings and conclusions of the study (illustrated in Figure 4f below).

Figure 4f
An Example of a Critical Analysis of the Findings and Conclusions of a Study

> It was found that the mean change in reading achievement scores significantly favoured the SSR group. The benefits stood out particularly for the high ability readers: their reading achievement accelerated significantly more than that of the low ability readers. One peculiar finding among the SSR group was that boys showed no significant change in mean achievement, but girls showed significant improvement in achievement scores compared with girls in the control group. From this finding, Aranha deduced that girls might have made the best use of the SSR periods to improve their reading ability. **While Aranha's reasoning is plausible, it could also be that the boys were not interested in the type of books provided for the programme.** Aranha did not describe the materials nor how they were selected for the programme so there is no way of knowing whether the issue is one of reading interests.

In the example in Figure 4f, the reviewer not only reported the findings and conclusions of the study, he also gave an opinion of these (shaded in the figure). You should not shy away from giving opinions about the studies that you examine. In fact, this strengthens your analysis since it shows that you are not merely reporting what was said, but that you are also mentally engaging with the material. Note that in the last sentence of the analysis above, the reviewer highlighted a major weakness of the study reviewed. If it were applicable, the reviewer might have also highlighted trends, strengths, inconsistencies and gaps in the study. These are things that you would have been noting in your annotations while you were reading the literature (we told you those annotations would be useful!).

When reviewing literature, you may sometimes wish to go beyond mentioning weaknesses in the data analysis reported in a study. You may decide to highlight how these weaknesses may be corrected as illustrated in Figure 4g below. In that example, the writer could later establish a link between the literature reviewed and the methodology by showing how this information influenced the analysis of data that was collected with a similar instrument (shaded in the figure). Making connections between your literature review and the rest of your thesis is very important. Remember, your literature review is not just a generic essay on a broad topic. It should reflect the major issues relating to your research problem and it should be clear how this literature is informing your actual research.

Figure 4g
An Example of a Critical Analysis of Literature and How it Informs the Reviewer's Study

> It is worth noting here that the analysis of the data from these two studies could call into question the usefulness of semantic differential scales for assessing computer attitudes. Or perhaps the question should be about the adjectives included on the scales. For example, knowing that girls were more likely than boys to consider the computer to be expensive does not really tell about their attitudes toward computers. Perhaps the data may have provided better information about the attitudes of the students in the sample if the factor analytic approach suggested by Ransley (1991) were applied. Ransley ran a principal component factor analysis on the items on a semantic differential scale and identified five dimensions. He suggested that these dimensions could be used to study differences in attitudes toward computers. Thus, instead of discussing the data in terms of individual items, the researcher could refer to dimensions of attitude as suggested by the responses on *groups* of items. **This seems to provide more useful information from data collected by semantic differential scales and therefore this approach will be adopted in this current study.**

We do not want to give the impression that your literature review should be one critique of reported research after another. There are many other pieces of work that you will cite that do not require the type of critique mentioned above. This does not mean that you should not use these works analytically. Figure 4h below demonstrates how such works may contribute to your analytic review.

Figure 4h
An Example of How Works Other Than Research Reports May be Used in an Analytical Review

> Still, not everyone holds extreme views about the use of computers in education. Some people are more moderate in their opinions and suggest that computers can be a force for good or bad in education (Borg, 1993; Healy, 1998; Oppenheimer, 1997). This seems to suggest that there may be some things that can be appropriately done with computers and others for which these machines would be inappropriate. It may thus be incumbent on educators to first examine what they want to accomplish with the education programmes that they offer, and then decide whether computers can contribute to the achievement of their goals and how. The fact is that this is no easy task.

In the above example, not only are the writers' views expressed, but also those of the reviewer. As mentioned before, this indicates engagement with the material.

A misconception held by many inexperienced researchers is that, when writing a literature review, you should avoid discussing works that contradict your viewpoint or that show some approach that you are proposing to use in a poor light. However, including such works in your review can add to the analytical quality of your discussion. You do not need to attempt to conceal contradictory views, as you should not be trying to *prove* anything. You are merely testing a situation and in fact your data might even end up supporting one of the contradictory views. If that happens and you have already acknowledged the existence of such views in your literature review, then you can gracefully concede that your expectations were not met but that others were supported. This of course reduces the temptation that some inexperienced researchers face to 'cook' their data so that it reflects the one viewpoint explored in their literature review.

SOME FINAL WORDS

Writing your literature review can be challenging, but it does not have to be burdensome. Remember that the purpose of the review is to explore issues related to your research problem. It should not be simply a report of who said what, but a primarily critical and analytical discussion of previous research done in the area or related areas. It should also form the platform from which your problem statement and research questions and/or hypotheses should emerge. The literature review also provides a 'mirror' through which you can explore the findings of your own research. This point is especially important since you want your findings to contribute to knowledge in the area: either supporting existing knowledge or raising questions about or extending current viewpoints. Develop your skills of reading and analysing research articles. You will find that with practice and experience, reviewing literature becomes less fear-inducing.

5
CHOOSING A RESEARCH DESIGN

INTRODUCTION

So far, we have discussed how you can select a topic for research, ethical issues that you should consider, and how to use existing literature to inform what you do. Now we will get into planning your research project.

Each piece of research should have a theoretical framework that guides its activities. This framework helps you to decide what approach you will adopt, who will be your participants, how you will collect and analyse data, and how you will report your findings. This is your research plan or design. In this chapter, we examine some commonly used approaches to social research and issues that you should consider when you are designing your study. We also offer some guidelines about how to report this information in your research report.

COMMONLY USED RESEARCH APPROACHES

There are several approaches to research that are commonly used in social settings. Among these are (quasi) experimental studies, causal-comparative studies, correlational studies, surveys, historical studies, and in more recent times, case studies and action research. We will briefly outline each of these research approaches here, but as said before, we have devoted an entire chapter to action research. So let us explore these research designs.

Experimental Studies

This research approach is often said to be the best way of establishing whether a given condition (cause) results in a particular observed outcome (effect). With this approach, which is grounded in positivism, the researcher formulates hypotheses about relationships and then sets out to test them. Using principles adopted from the world of natural science research, the researcher attempts to control certain conditions (independent variables), while measuring the effect on others (dependent variables). For experimental research, participants are randomly selected and assigned to different groups, often referred to as experimental and control groups, and then subjected to different treatments (for example different teaching methods).

In some fields such as education, it is generally not feasible to randomly select individual participants for experimental research. In this context, this could lead to upheavals that most Caribbean schools could not sustain and that no school principal (unless bereft of reason!) would allow. Thus, if you choose to use an experimental approach, you are likely to find that you must work with students in their existing class groups. When individuals are not randomly selected for involvement in an experimental study, this study is said to be following a quasi-experimental approach. It is therefore quasi-experiments rather than full (or true) experiments that are commonly used in educational research, since you do not have the same degree of control over the environment as natural scientists would have with their experiments.

Causal-Comparative Studies

Causal-comparative studies are those for which you are seeking to determine reasons (causes) for existing conditions (effects). For this type of study, you the researcher make no attempt to manipulate any of the variables. Indeed, in many cases you could not do so since these conditions have already occurred. This type of causal-comparative study is referred to as ex post facto (Latin for 'after the fact'). Second, there are instances where you may choose not to manipulate any variables, but may choose to study them in a natural setting. Finally, there are some independent variables that you cannot manipulate, even if you wanted to. These are also called organismic variables, and are characteristics of the participants (such as gender, age and race) that cannot be controlled.

There are two approaches to carrying out a causal-comparative study. First, you may decide to start with the cause and then try to identify the effect. This is called a prospective causal-comparative study. For example, you may have a hunch that the age at which people obtain a driver's licence (cause) contributes to the number of road accidents in which they are involved within the first ten years of driving (effect). To investigate this, you may identify people who obtained a driver's licence before 21 years of age and people who obtained theirs after this age. Then, you would check for the number of accidents each one had during the first ten years of driving.

With the second approach, you would start with an observed phenomenon (effect) and try to identify possible causes. A study of this type is a retrospective causal-comparative one. Using this approach to investigate the previously mentioned study, you identify drivers who had five or more accidents during the first ten years of driving and those who had fewer. Then you would find out what proportion of each group obtained their driver's licence before age 21 and after age 21.

Unlike experimental studies, causal-comparative studies do not establish cause-effect relationships, but can be used to identify possible causes or effects of observed phenomenon.

The limitation of causal-comparative research is that you cannot be absolutely sure about the identified cause-effect relationship. For example, because the independent variables are not controlled, it is possible that the observed effect was caused by some other unidentified cause. Thus, while causal-comparative studies are useful for investigating cause-effect relationships, any such relationships can only be at best tentative.

Correlational Studies

Like causal-comparative research, correlational studies seek to investigate relationships between variables. The difference between these two types of studies is that while causal-comparative studies identify tentative cause-effect relationships, correlational studies make no claims about existing relationships being of that nature. What a correlational study does is to establish that there is a relationship between two variables, without suggesting that the outcome on one of these variables is caused by the other. You should think about the difference between these two types of studies in this way: with a causal-comparative study, you might have an independent variable with two or more conditions (groups) and you separate the sample according to these conditions in order to compare their performances on the dependent variable. With a correlational study, you might have the same sample, but you do not separate it into groups. What you would do in this case is to examine the two sets of data for that sample to find out if and how they are related.

Before you start to worry, let us look at an example. Imagine that you wanted to carry out a correlational study to find out if there is a relationship between gender of voters and their preference of a certain political party. You would have to identify a suitable sample of individuals (that is, people eligible to vote) and collect data on their gender and their preference of political party. You would then examine these data to find out if there is a significant relationship between these two variables. While you may establish that there is a relationship between these two variables, with the results of a correlational study, you could not say that the voters' gender caused them to prefer one party or the other. The fact is that while the two variables may be correlated, there might be some other variable (for example, family background or age of the voter) that influenced the outcome.

If you were doing a causal-comparative study, you would perhaps use the gender of the voters (independent variable) to group them. You would then examine the preference of political party to find out if and how they were different. From this, you might tentatively conclude that a cause-effect relationship appears to exist. Don't forget that there was no controlling of variables and thus it is possible that some other variable may be causing the results obtained. The fact is that neither correlational studies nor causal-comparative studies can lead you to a definitive cause-effect relationship. As was said before, correlational studies seek only to establish a relationship between two variables, but stops short of labelling any identified relationship as of the cause-effect nature. While it is true that a causal-comparative study can be considered a step closer to establishing cause-effect relationships, you must remember that, in the absence of controlling of variables, it is quite possible that some other factor might be causing the observed effects. For instance, in our example above, a factor such as the voters' age might be moderating their preference of political party!

The point to remember is that, correlational studies seek to investigate relationships between variables, but unlike causal-comparative studies, no cause-effect relationships are implied. Further, as with causal-comparative studies, any identified relationships suggest the need for more rigorous investigation of the phenomenon.

Survey Studies

Survey studies involve the collection of data from a selected group of persons in order to test hypotheses or answer questions about the feelings, beliefs and opinions that are held about some topic or issue. This form of research is often used to describe the status of a phenomenon at a particular time. It is like obtaining a snapshot of a particular situation at an identified time.

In survey research, data are collected from members of a population in order to ascertain the status of that population with respect to one or more variables. When data are gathered from every member of the population, the procedure is called a census survey. Census surveys are carried out periodically by government departments who are interested in learning about the status of the nation's people with regards to births, deaths, marriages, employment, and such variables. In many social settings however, it is not necessary (and often not feasible!) for us to gather information from everyone involved in the sector when we are doing research. Thus, for social research purposes, we tend to include only a sample of the population when conducting survey research. Such a survey is called a sample survey.

In survey research, the group of participants involved is very important, and hence by extension, so is your sampling technique. You must ensure as much as possible that the sample is a good representation of the population from which it is selected and about which you want to learn. In a similar vein, the instrument that you use to collect your data is also important. It must be designed in such a way as to persuade the participants to complete and return it to you. Typical data collection techniques for surveys include administration of structured questionnaires, attitude scales, interest inventories, rating scales and checklists. These can be administered face-to-face in an interview-like setting or can be sent to the participants who complete them and return them to you. Because survey research tends to involve comparison of data from participants with different characteristics, when you design your instruments, you should include items that would allow you to group your sample according to several different independent variables, for example gender, age, professional status and types of attitudes, to name a few.

By now, you may have become aware of one of the shortcomings of survey research: the fact that self-report instruments are often used. This may lead to the collection of data that is distorted by perception, personal experience, the passage of time or outright deliberate misrepresentation of the facts. It is therefore advisable to use other complementary data collection techniques to corroborate the data collected by means of self-report methods. Complementary methods may include observation of some members of the sample or by conducting more in depth interviews with some of them.

Survey research is similar to causal-comparative and correlational studies in that there is no manipulating of variables. In fact, data for use in causal-comparative and correlational studies are often collected by means of survey techniques!

Historical Studies

Historical studies investigate events of the past. The aim of such studies is to describe causes, effects or trends related to these events through the systematic collection and analysis of data. The data should allow you to explain current events and to anticipate future ones. Since historical research delves into occurrences of the past, data tends to be accessible from sources such as diaries, journals, legal papers, organisational records, minutes from meetings, personal letters and people. Such sources may be described as either primary or secondary sources.

Primary sources are first hand accounts related to the phenomenon that you are investigating. An example is if you were investigating events relating to the evolution of the social security scheme in Dominica, you may interview some of the founders (if they are alive) of the system to find out from them what prompted them to set it up. These people would be giving a first hand account of the events since they were involved in them. These participants would be classified as primary sources. Other examples of primary sources include original documents, personal diaries, letters and journals containing eyewitness accounts of events. On the other hand, secondary sources are second hand accounts of events. These accounts are reported by others and can typically be found in reference books, reports in newspapers and any other accounts of the event written by people who were not eyewitnesses. Secondary sources may also include relatives of people who participated in the events being investigated.

If you are conducting a historical study, you must take special care to check your sources. These must be examined for authenticity and accuracy. To check for authenticity, you must answer the question is the data source what it is said to be? To answer this question you must verify characteristics such as its authorship, the time period and the location. This activity is referred to as external criticism. For instance, you may discover a box of documents tucked away in a vault in the Ministry of Finance building in which references are made to the establishment of the social security scheme. Your job would be to ascertain the authenticity of these documents. For instance, you may try to find out who wrote them and when were they written? You may very well discover that they were written five years previously by a creative student as part of a history project. You may eventually find out that the teacher was so impressed that the project was stored away for safe keeping and that the yellowing of the paper was not from age, but because of the musty environment inside the vault! In other words, your exciting find might turn out to be lacking in authenticity and therefore be of little use to your research.

Accuracy of sources of data in historical research refers to the extent to which the information from the source is a reflection of the truth. To make a decision on this, you must consider issues such as the knowledge and competency of the author, the amount of time that elapsed between the occurrence of the event and its being recorded, and whether the author might have had a personal agenda that might have affected what was recorded. You may also want to ascertain to what extent the information is consistent with what is gathered from other sources. When you engage in such activities, you are submitting the source to internal criticism. Again using our social security scheme example, you may discover that the documents found in the vault were in fact written by one of the founders of the scheme. But her account of the meeting in which the first director was selected may differ from what was recorded in the official minutes of the meeting. You may later find out that this founder disapproved of the choice and her description of what was said at the meeting reflected her disapproval rather than what actually occurred.

Historical research tends to yield a large amount of textual data that is analysed by qualitative techniques and hence it is often labelled as qualitative research. But the fact is that historical research may also yield numerical data that can be analysed by quantitative techniques. The type of data collected will depend on what questions you are asking. Having said that however, we must reiterate that historical studies are predominantly qualitative in nature.

Case Studies

A case study is an investigation of a contemporary phenomenon in a specific context. The phenomenon or case can be an individual, a group, a policy, an innovation, or any entity that can be bounded, that is, an entity that can stand on its own. To study the entity, you collect as much data as you can using a variety of sources and data collection techniques and then analyse them to learn about the case. Case studies can take on a qualitative or quantitative face, depending on the entity being studied and your purpose for conducting the study. Case studies are appropriate under certain circumstances. Such a study is appropriate when the phenomenon to be studied is a unique or extreme case, a revelatory case or a critical case. It can be the case that in a climate of social upheaval, one community remains stable and flourishing. A case study of this phenomenon can be carried out to find out why, in the face of turmoil, there is this oasis of calm. A case study would also be appropriate if you were interested in studying the implementation of a new policy in an organisation.

Though traditionally not seen as a research design in its own right, some writers provide compelling arguments for case study as a legitimate design. For example, Yin (1994) introduces the idea of single case study (where one case is studied) and multiple case studies (where two or more cases are studied and the findings compared). He also presents the concept of a holistic case study (the case is studied as a single entity) and embedded case studies (sub-units within the case are studied). This approach to case study can be very exciting and rewarding. The key is to ensure that your case is a well defined entity and that you are clear about why you are investigating that particular entity. If you think that case study might be appropriate for your investigation, then we recommend that you have a closer look at the work of Yin (1994).

General Qualitative Designs

Quite often, when inexperienced researchers think about qualitative research they may think solely of research where narrative data are collected by means of a questionnaire. However, this is a somewhat narrow view. There is in fact a range of research designs where narrative or textual data are gathered. Generally, the purpose of these designs is to shed light or foster understanding (verstehen or enlightenment) of a phenomenon within a particular context. These designs are predicated on the notion that interpretation of events and phenomena that leads to what people call 'truth' or 'knowledge' is subjective, influenced by factors such as culture, past experiences, and context. With these qualitative designs, the researcher seeks to understand how individuals and groups interact with and interpret their environment; how they develop rules by which they live; and generally how they operate within their social systems. There are several different approaches that fall into the category of qualitative designs. Among these are phenomenology (the study of individuals' or groups' experience of a phenomenon); ethnography (the study of communities); ethnomethodology (the study of how social order is produced and shared); and hermeneutics (the study of the interpretation of text). Fully exploring each of these approaches is outside the scope of this book, but if you are interested, you might want to explore the works of writers such as Layder (1998), Patton (2002) and Miles and Huberman (1994) who offer theory and advice that would be very helpful to you.

In this section, we briefly presented some types of methods commonly used in social research. There are of course, other types and, no matter which one you choose, there are some factors that you need to consider. In the next section, we discuss some of these factors.

FACTORS TO CONSIDER WHEN SELECTING A RESEARCH APPROACH

There are many factors that you should bear in mind when selecting an approach to use for your research. These include the general philosophy guiding your research, the nature of your research questions, and the availability of resources. Let us briefly examine how each of these considerations might influence your choice.

General Philosophy

In chapter 1, we mentioned that there are several views about what constitutes knowledge and how we come to know. Research can generate knowledge and the particular philosophy that underpins your research will influence what approaches are appropriate for doing so. If you adopt a positivist perspective, then you might select a research design in which measuring characteristics and other quantifying procedures are used. On the other hand, if you adopt a more interpretivist approach, then you might select a design that relies mainly on qualitative data. It is important to remember though, that unless you are a purist, it is likely that you may find yourself drawing on non-conflicting approaches from both camps.

A good demonstration of how a researcher may draw from the approaches appropriate for a positivist paradigm and also those appropriate for the interpretivist, can be seen in action research. Many proponents of action research tend to adopt a critical theorist philosophy. Adherents of this philosophy believe that the purposes of both the positivists and the interpretivists all have some merit, but that neither group does enough to ensure that their research makes a difference in the lives of the participants. Thus, if you adopt a critical theorist philosophy, you would use whatever approach you deem necessary and appropriate, whether quantitative or qualitative, as long as outcome of the research has a positive impact on the participants.

While the level of your programme of study may not require that you devote time and space in your thesis/project to a philosophical discussion about your research design, you may want to keep it in the back of your mind. However, if you decide to work on a Master of Philosophy or doctoral degree, then in your dissertation you should defend your research design on philosophical grounds, showing how the philosophical perspective that you are adopting influenced your choice of design.

The Nature of the Research Questions

Some researchers might be heard saying, 'I am a quantitative researcher' or 'I am a qualitative researcher,' and they may attempt to force each piece of research they carry out into their preferred mould. But as inexperienced researchers, you do not want to follow their example. The fact is that more often than not, the nature of your research questions will suggest what approach you ought to take. Let us say that you were investigating the attitudes of Caribbean teachers towards use of Creole in the classroom, and one of your research questions asked, 'Are there differences in attitudes towards the use of Creole in the classroom among teachers in islands with an English-based Creole and those in islands with French-based Creoles?' This question suggests that a survey ought to be carried out, with samples of teachers selected from among the teaching fraternity of islands that meet these two conditions, and that statistical procedures should be used to analyse the data collected.

On the other hand, you may be investigating individual differences in the operations of organisations, examining the characteristics of successful organisations and those that are less so. Your question might be 'Why is Corporation X so successful while Corporation Y is experiencing crippling problems?' This question suggests a case study approach, with two cases involved. Here you may collect data on the two 'cases' by whatever means are deemed appropriate and necessary. Thus you may collect data on features such as management style, work climate, and staff satisfaction, using for example observation, interviews, and attitude scales. These are ways in which the nature of your research problem and or questions could influence the research design that you choose. The point to remember is that whether you do a correlational study, a survey or a quasi-experimental study, this should be determined by the appropriateness of the approach for finding answers to your research questions or for allowing you to test your hypotheses.

Available Resources

It is said that it is a foolish person who starts a project without first considering if the resources needed to bring it to a successful completion are available. This is certainly true when you are selecting a research approach. From the beginning of your planning, you should bear in mind what resources you have available to you. You should be aware of the availability of resources such as time, funds, sources of data, people with technical skills, and your own skills. If you have three months to produce your research paper, then you would not want to select a design that requires weeks, even months in which to collect, collate and analyse all the relevant data. Nor would you want to conduct many long interviews that would take weeks to transcribe. This would clearly not be appropriate for the time available to you.

In the same vein, if, like most student researchers, you have very little money, then you would select an approach that matches your budget. Avoid carrying out a large-scale survey if you do not have money to purchase paper, envelopes and stamps to distribute your instruments. You may have to find another means of collecting relevant data or adjust your research questions so that a smaller survey would be satisfactory. In the latter case, you might confine your sample to a particular geographical location, making it easier for you to deliver and collect your instruments by hand. Now, if you are fortunate enough to acquire funding from some source, this could influence how you design your research.

The point being made here is that you must be practical when designing your research. It is not helpful to have an elaborate research design and no means of executing it. It is far better to have a modest but rigorous design that is 'doable' with the resources available to you.

Reporting Your Research Design

When you are preparing to conduct a piece of research, you may be required to submit a proposal in which you outline what you intend to do and why. But while you are carrying out the research, you may be forced to make decisions and changes based on what is happening at the time. This is not unusual, since at the time of planning, researchers cannot foresee every situation that could possibly affect their research as it is executed. It might help as you plan your research to ask yourself, 'What could possibly go wrong with this?' and have a contingency plan (a plan B), just in case one is needed. While there is no guarantee that what you anticipate will actually happen, or that your back up plan will be adequate, you will feel a whole lot more confident and are likely to be better able to cope with unforeseen circumstances. But, whatever you do, you should report it in the 'design' chapter or section of your research report. So then, what do you report in this chapter or section?

In your 'design' chapter or section, you should explain your research approach and justify its use, for example, why a case study and not a historical study or some other approach? You should explain why, in your opinion, the design you selected is appropriate for your research. You should highlight the strengths of your selected approach, while acknowledging its limitations, and discussing what steps you took to minimise the effects of these limitations. Naturally, you would support your arguments with appropriate literature. In this chapter, you should also discuss issues related to the research design, such as sampling, data collection and analysis.

When you report your design, you should describe the participants and how they were selected, again justifying your actions. This is important because sometimes you start out with one plan for selecting a sample, but in the course of the research, real-life situations may force you to make certain decisions that alter these plans. It is here that you may want to mention these situations and defend the choices you made. It is also here that you could mention your awareness of the effects of your sampling technique on the outcome of your research, and what steps you took to lessen any negative effects. You should also discuss your data collection methods in this chapter or section. Here you could again defend your methods, highlighting their strengths and explaining what was done to eliminate or minimise the effects of their limitations. You should also describe any instruments that you used for collecting data, and give information about how they were constructed and validated for the research. Finally, you should report how the data were compiled and analysed, justifying techniques of analysis that you selected.

By now, you would have picked up that this chapter is a mixture of theory and practice. Here you present the theoretical frameworks on which your research is based, along with the practical actions that you took in executing your plan. Fundamental to all this is your justification for your choices. Often in research, there is no 'right' way of doing things, but whatever choices you make should have some theoretical support. Remember, some people may question your research because they do not agree with your choices or subscribe to the theories that guided them, but no one should be able to accuse you of not having any basis for what you do. In your 'design' chapter or section, not only should you clearly state your actions, but you should also, just as clearly, present the underlying principles that informed your choices.

WHY PAY ATTENTION TO YOUR DESIGN

You might be wondering why we are admonishing you to pay careful attention to your research design. The fact is that if your research is to be useful in any way then you should try as much as possible to safeguard the quality of your work. To this end, you must be aware of issues of validity and reliability of your research. Let us explore what this means for you.

VALIDITY OF RESEARCH

Validity of research relates to the extent to which your research findings and conclusions are based on fact or evidence. In other words, can your conclusions be justified based on the evidence collected? When doing your research, you need to pay attention to both internal validity and external validity. Internal validity is concerned with the extent to which the results of the research can be interpreted accurately and with confidence. If your research design was poor or inappropriate, then your conclusions may be invalid. You may conclude after carrying out a piece of research, that young people are more likely to vote for Party X than are older people. The validity of this conclusion can be called into question if it is based on the fact that on the Friday afternoon that you collected your data, more young people waiting for the bus in the terminal wore red (Party X's colour) than did older people. How accurate is this conclusion and how much confidence can we place in this interpretation? There may have been some other reason for many young people wearing red, other than political affiliation! For example, Valentine's Day may have been falling over the weekend and many workplaces celebrated it that Friday by wearing red! Thus, the colour the young people were wearing had nothing to do with party preference, but with Valentine's Day celebrations! Hence, your research would lack internal validity.

On the other hand, external validity is concerned with the extent to which the research results can be generalised to other populations and conditions. Again, a poor or inappropriate design can limit the generalisability of your research, if indeed this was your aim. Let us say that you wanted to investigate workers' levels of job satisfaction and you decided to do a case study of a unique bank known for advocating total employee participation at all levels. Based on your data, you conclude that bank employees have high levels of job satisfaction. Your research findings may again be called into question as lacking external validity. You cannot extend findings based on evidence from a unique situation to a general population. Your findings can, at best, only be applicable to the employees of that unique case! Hence, your research design would be inappropriate for the purpose of your research.

The point here is that when you are planning your research, you must select a research design that would allow you to be confident that your conclusions are accurate and evidence-based. In addition, if generalisability is your aim, then your design should be such as to allow you to generalise.

Validity of research is particularly important to experimental research. Since experimental research is used to confirm cause-effect relationships, then a high degree of certainty is desirable, that is, the research must be seen as valid. Campbell and Stanley (1971) identified a number of conditions that can threaten the validity of experimental research. These are summarised in Figure 5a below. Although these threats are related primarily to experimental research, and the various experimental designs control for these threats to varying degrees, the concepts may also be applied to other types of research. Therefore, when selecting a design, you should ensure that you do all you can to eliminate threats to validity or at least to minimise their effects.

Figure 5a
Threats to Validity of Experimental Research (Campbell & Stanley, 1971)

Threats to Internal Validity
- *History* – occurrence of events not part of the experiment that can affect the outcome;
- *Maturation* – physical or mental changes in the participants over time that may affect the outcome;
- *Mortality (attrition)* – participants fall out of the study in ways that may alter the characteristics of the experimental group;
- *Testing* – improved scores on post-test as a result of participants being pre-tested (test wise-ness)
- *Instrumentation* – unreliability of measuring instruments can produce invalid assessment data;
- *Statistical regression* – occurs when participants are selected based on extreme scores; is the tendency for those who score highest on pre-test to score lower on post-test and those who score lowest on the pre-test to score higher on the post-test.
- *Differential selection* – occurs when participants are selected in existing groups and may already be different in ways that affect the outcomes;
- *Interaction of selection and other factors* – if existing groups are used, one group may profit more from (or less) from a treatment or have an initial advantage (or disadvantage) because of maturation, history, or testing factors.
Threats to External Validity
- *Pre-test treatment interaction* – participants perform or react differently to the treatment because of having been pre-tested;
- *Post-test sensitisation* – treatment effects influenced by the pre-test (pre-test provides info that affects post-test results;
- *Multiple-treatment interference* – when same participants receive more than one treatment in succession and carry over effects from an earlier treatment influence results of a later treatment;
- *Specificity* – treatment variables not properly operationalised making it unclear to whom the results may be generalised;
- *Experimenter's bias or expectations* – when the researcher affects participants' behaviour or is unintentionally biased when scoring different treatment groups

Reliability of Research

Reliability of research is concerned with its consistency and replicability. When you carry out a piece of research, you must do all that you can to ensure that, should you repeat it at another time in a similar context, the outcome would be similar. This speaks to consistency or internal reliability of the research. For example, suppose you were carrying out an observation study to investigate drinking habits of university students, and you collected your data by observing the activity at the university bar. However, you collected your data during the two weeks of examinations when most students spend more time in the library than anywhere else. You may conclude that university students are not heavy drinkers at all! The question is, would you have obtained the same results if you had collected your data during Carnival Week or over a longer period? This speaks to the consistency or internal reliability of your research.

The value of research is often linked to the replication of the results by independent researchers. The extent to which this can be done speaks to the external reliability of your study. If your research design is so complicated or involves such unique conditions that no one else can replicate it, then there may always be doubt about your findings. When you report your research therefore, you should take care to explain your design clearly so that readers can understand what you did, and if they wish, can replicate it.

You should be aware that a study may be reliable but invalid, since validity is not a necessary condition for reliability. However, reliability is a necessary condition for validity. If a study is valid, then it is also reliable. Both these concepts are measured on a continuum that ranges from low to high. Thus you may speak of a study having low reliability or high validity. When you plan your research, when you select a research design, keep the concept of validity foremost in your mind. The extent to which your research is valid and reliable is related to the sources of your data (sample), the nature of your data (data collection) and the manner in which you manipulate the data (data analysis). These concepts, all linked to your research design, will be discussed in later chapters of this book.

In this chapter we discussed issues related to choosing an appropriate design for your research. We briefly considered several designs from which you can choose. Of course, there are others. In fact, there is another research design that we feel should be given more in-depth consideration, action research. In the next chapter we explore this form of research.

6

ACTION RESEARCH:
A DESIGN FOR BRINGING ABOUT CHANGE

INTRODUCTION

This chapter is specially included in this book as a labour of love for a field that is dear to our hearts. As educators, we have noticed over the years that many of the challenges faced in the field are tackled by people with good intentions, but insufficient information. Solutions are applied to problems in a one-size-fits-all manner that often leads to disaster. We believe that each Caribbean territory, each school, each classroom, each student is sufficiently different for unique solutions to be sought to the many challenges in education. We further believe that teachers and other practising professionals have a lot to contribute to identifying these solutions through research. We are aware that many of these professionals may not have the time or the technical skills to pursue this research on their own. However exposure to research practice would go a far way in helping them to know the kind of help they need, and the kinds of partnerships they need to foster. The purpose of this chapter is to increase the readers' awareness of a form of research that we believe is vital to the development of educational policy and practice in the region.

Lest we be accused of being bias, we want to stress that the principles and practices espoused here can be applied in other social settings where improvements seem necessary, and the best way to bring about sustainable change is to involve all the stakeholders in the solution. So then, let us explore action research together.

DEFINING ACTION RESEARCH

Action research is not only a means of solving problems and bringing about meaningful change, but also a legitimate research methodology. One of the key features of action research is that unlike other methodologies, it actively involves the participants in the research or change process. Thus, participants are not just seen as subjects to be manipulated or surveyed. Burns (2000), in summarizing the action research process as it happens in schools, defines it as:

> the application of fact-finding to solving practical problems. It is situational, collaborative and participatory. Action-research involves teachers as generators of knowledge in a bottom-up approach to professional development with the professional researcher as the resource person for the teacher (p. 458).

Because action research is situational, it authenticates the research process. There is nothing artificial about it as some of the other methodologies can sometimes appear to be. It takes place at the site of the problem and importantly, it is not just a professional researcher calling the shots, but there is collaboration and active participation by all involved. In the end, all involved can claim ownership to the knowledge generated because of the collaborative and participatory role that they played throughout the research. Though Burns overview suggests that a professional researcher should always be involved in the research process, it is quite feasible for a school or even a single teacher to embark on action research in an attempt to improve a school or classroom situation.

Due to the nature of action research, its worth cannot be measured in the same way as other methodologies. Since its major aim is to solve practical problems, the validity of the knowledge it generates cannot be solely dependent on 'scientific' tests, but more so on the usefulness in helping the participants to function efficiently. Therefore in a classroom setting, it is expected that action research will result in an improvement in practice. Unlike other approaches where theories are tested independently and then applied to practice, action research is validated through practice. Remember that problems are solved as the participants, during their normal practice, strive to improve their situation. In conducting action research in schools there are several possible results that can help to validate the research process. Teachers may learn new pedagogical skills; they may become more aware of what they do in the classroom; teacher-student relationship may improve; teacher-parent relationship may improve; relationships among teachers may improve; teachers may come to see the value of allowing their practice to be guided by research; the school's organisation may improve and the overall atmosphere of the school may improve.

It should be noted that this same utilitarian feature that we acknowledge as validating the knowledge generated is what most critics note as the major weakness of action research. They argue that those who conduct action research actually confuse social activism and development with research. Action research, they argue is just a process to help people, but lacks the scientific rigour necessary to survive the scrutiny of 'real' research. We, like other proponents of action research are however arguing that it is both scientific and helpful in improving people's lives. The problem as we see it is that too many studies have been done without sufficient consideration on how they can be helpful. Even where their usefulness is considered, often, the mechanism is not put in place for the study to affect the lives of those it is intended to benefit. Action research is not presented with any such problems since along with the process of research, it seeks to directly help.

THE ORIGIN OF ACTION RESEARCH

The social psychologist, Kurt Lewin, is generally credited for the birth of the action research movement. It is felt that it is because of Lewin why many researchers can now envisage their roles as not being that of a distant, 'objective' observer, but as being involved in a problem solving process. While action research today has evolved into a much more sophisticated process than Lewin's model, to gain an understanding of how it works, it seems an excellent idea to return to his conception.

The first stage in Lewin's model starts with the dismantling of former structures (unfreezing). At this stage the role of the researcher is to identify the problem and set the stage to finding a solution. The next stage is changing the structures (changing). Here, the researcher actively seeks to solve the problem through his/her investigation. In the final stage the researcher, having succeeded in solving the problem, locks the new structures permanently in place (freezing).

Lewin's 1943 seminal study that investigated the use of tripe in daily diet of American families is illustrative of his model. The study, conducted in the early stages of the Second World War, was commissioned by the US authorities because beef was scarce and was destined primarily for the troops. He sought to answer the question to what extent American housewives could be encouraged to use tripe rather than beef for family dinners (unfreezing). His approach to the study was to train a limited number of housewives in the art of cooking tripe for dinner (changing). He then surveyed what effects the training had on the cooking habits of the families. With the success of the study, the next step was to reorient American housewives to adopt tripe on their dinner menu (freezing).

There are those who have criticised Lewin's model on the grounds that it is synonymous to a so-called natural experiment where the researcher in a real-life setting invites or forces participants to take part in an experimental activity. While modern proponents of action research recognise the value in Lewin's work, it is generally felt that his model gives too much authoritarian control to the researcher. Thus, the trend in action research is that the researcher and all participants of a study should work together as equal partners in solving problems. In the next section, we present a more modern interpretation of action research.

THE ACTION RESEARCH PROCESS

There are many approaches to conducting action research in educational settings. We cannot describe all these approaches here, so instead, we will try to present a broad overview that we believe can help you as you embark on your research.

In conducting action research, you must first of all understand where you are situated in the process. That is, you may be conducting action research as a professional researcher (outsider) or as a practitioner in the school (insider). It is important to pay attention to your position, because it is likely that you will affect the research process differently according to whether you are an insider or outsider. We will discuss this insider versus outsider role a bit later in the chapter.

Remember that a major aim of action research should be to improve the lives within a specific situation. Thus, anyone embarking on action research needs to be diagnostic in their practice right from the start. As a researcher, you have to identify and understand the problem at hand. Without a proper understanding of the problem, you would not be able to effect any change in the lives of the participants of the study. Thus, the first thing we will address in this section is the issue of how you can come to understand a problem.

Steps in Understanding a Problem

The first thing we must emphasise is that you should not take anything for granted. Do not assume that you know all there is to know about the problem. For example, because you are the teacher of the class in which you are conducting the research does not mean that you understand your students. You may have biases that can cloud your judgement, or the students for whatever reason may not be open or forthright to you. Regardless of how familiar you consider the context, you should spend time trying to diagnose the problem.

To diagnose a problem, you will have to enter into dialogue with all directly involved in the study. Action research as we see it requires collaboration. As the researcher you must forge a relationship with the participants. Along with you conducting yourself in a manner that will gain the trust and respect of the participants of the study, you must engage them in dialogue. They must be made to feel that you value their opinion and that they are in fact equal partners in everything that is done in the study. Such a relationship will improve the chances of the participants opening up to you. We strongly believe that only through such consultation you will ever get to the root of a problem.

We need to emphasise that with action research you do not stop at your initial understanding of a problem, but your understanding should evolve as you interact and consult with the participants. This whole action research process as we see it is an emergent one. It continues to be emergent until the problems have been resolved at least to the satisfaction of the local participants, the finances or energy have been exhausted, or some other event intervenes to change the direction of the process or to end it. Thus, initially, you and the other participants may perceive the problem in one way, but as you go along your understanding may change. For example, you may be conducting a study into the possibility of improving reading at a secondary school. Through dialogue, initially, the students, teachers and you may have concluded that many of the students came from the primary schools as struggling readers. However, at some point during the study you discover that your understanding of the problem is not accurate. The students may all be good at narrative reading (the type that is commonly practiced in primary school) but are struggling with content reading (the type mostly required of secondary schools). Thus, armed with this new information there will have to be a re-conceptualisation of the approach to solving the problem.

Importantly, the collaboration throughout the research process must continue. So in the case where the approach to solving a problem must be reconsidered, the participants should again be consulted. At all stages of the process, decisions about the direction a project should take are made through dialogue between the researcher and the stakeholders. You should try to bring together the stakeholders on a regular basis to allow for collaborative planning and designing of actions aimed at solving their problems. Staff meetings, class meetings, or any other forums could be used as platforms for such dialogue.

Conducting the Study

It is worth noting that action research is very much in keeping with the scientific approach. It would be a good idea for you to read up on the scientific approach if you have not yet done so. Thus, in this section we are not going to present you with a template for conducting this type of research, rather, we seek to sensitise you to the particular features that will help to classify it as action research.

First of all, where action research is different from other models that follow the scientific approach is that, as we mentioned before, throughout the process there is 'action.' Remember, this type of research, unlike others, actively seeks to improve the lives of participants by involving them directly in the process. The participants will help in 1) the planning of the research, 2) the analysing and interpreting of any information gathered and 3) directing the path that the research takes. In effect, the participants should have ownership of the project and be thoroughly involved in all decision-making since as we mentioned earlier, it is their lives that will be ultimately affected by the study. You as the researcher must bear in mind the importance of giving the participants a voice in the process, and hence, provide opportunities to actively involve them at all times. Do not underestimate the power of having a sense of ownership. In most cases, for a change implemented because of a research project to survive after the research has ended, the stakeholders must feel that they have ownership of it. We must reiterate that this sense of ownership comes through active involvement.

Additionally, you must be aware that action research is not restricted by technique. In conducting your study, you can for instance, survey your participants, interview them and observe them. Likewise, you can collect data from several sources. In a school setting, data sources might include teachers, students and parents. In fact, like other forms of research, the employment of multiple perspectives (triangulation) in an action research project is viewed as a strong point. Triangulation helps a researcher to measure the quality of the data gathered. However, triangulation in an action research context has greater significance. Triangulation can help to promote dialogue between the researcher (especially when the researcher is an outsider) and the stakeholders of the study as well as among the stakeholders themselves. Action research encourages the researcher to bring together stakeholders with different interests to discuss a problem. Thus, while information is being gathered from the various sources, the researcher should also be encouraging dialogue among all the different parties in an effort to solve the problem at hand.

One thing about action research that we particularly stress is the practice of reflexivity. This is generally a good habit to develop, regardless of whether or not you are engaging in action research or some other approach. As a researcher, you need to reflect on your research experience. It is quite likely that with reflection you will come to a deeper understanding of a phenomenon. For example, during data collection, even the most seasoned researchers tend to have their judgements clouded. Do not forget, judgements are subjective. With reflection though, often you will be able to see among other things where you came to premature judgements, how you should have approached a particular task and consider whether or not you want to reattempt that task. Where action research is different from most other approaches to research is that it encourages the stakeholders to also be reflexive. They, for example, may also have made conclusions that with reflection they would revise. Importantly, as part of being reflexive in your research you should try to keep aware as to your place in the study, that is, whether you are an insider or an outsider. Your place can bring much to bear on how the study turns out.

The Insider (practitioner) versus the Outsider (professional researcher) in Action Research

The notion of research being conducted by a practitioner or a professional researcher has been a point of debate for many years now. We certainly will not get involved in that debate since we believe that both can play a role in the research process. We are instead going to present what we consider the advantages and disadvantages of conducting action research from either position. We hope that by taking this approach, you would become sensitised to issues related to your positioning in the research process, and as such, you would become more reflexive in your practice. We must admit that much of what we present in this section will be applicable to any type of research. However, this seems a very good place to deal with it since we are encouraging action research and we expect you to grapple with some of these same issues during the course of your project.

In the context of education, we describe the insider as one who works in a school and at the same time carries out systematic enquiry in an effort to bring about change in the school. The insider here could be a teacher, librarian, guidance counsellor or even the principal. For example, a principal may conduct action research to find out what is causing the high rate of absenteeism in the school and then seek to reduce it. Similarly, a teacher may want to introduce a new teaching strategy to try to improve classroom learning. To do this, the teacher would first have to systematically try out this strategy on a small scale to measure its effects on students' learning. The key is that with both examples, the aim is to improve a situation (absenteeism and learning).

Action research done by insiders has its distinct advantages. First, as an insider, you will have knowledge and experience about the situation and the people involved in the study.

This pre-existing knowledge and experience can help the researcher to guide the course of the study. Secondly, because as a practitioner you are stationed at the school, you are in an excellent position to observe and guide the course of the study. By just being there, coupled with the pre-existing knowledge of the situation and the people, there is likely to be a substantial reduction of problems related to implementation. Finally, you more than likely have practical knowledge which, you can apply to all aspects of the research process – designing the study, implementing the study, analysing the findings and drawing conclusions from the findings.

There are however some disadvantages to conducting research as an insider. Heading the list is the fact that as a practitioner you are likely to be very busy. Thus, you may find it difficult to make the time for an additional activity – research. Second, it is also not easy to balance the psychological demands of research and work. It is possible that your action as a researcher may be at odds with your work and you may have to make decisions as a researcher that is contrary to your normal practice. Such decisions, though sound scientifically, may send you in a state of dissonance because they go against your long held beliefs. Thirdly, the same knowledge and experience that can place the insider at an advantage can also be at times disadvantageous. This pre-existing knowledge may be the source of preconceptions that can cloud your judgement. Also, as a practitioner, you may not have the skills needed to do research, whether it be action research or otherwise. Very often, while practitioners have some research skills, it is limited because their training was more than likely devoted to issues related to their practice. If you find yourself in this situation, even a well-intentioned research effort may turn out to be a disaster. Finally, even when you possess the necessary skills to conduct a well-designed study, your advice and suggestions coming out of the research may not be accepted by your peers and other interest groups. Many people prefer to take advice from the outsider – the professional researcher.

If you are an outsider you also have your share of advantages and disadvantages. Along with the fact that many people may prefer to take your advice just because they see you as a professional, they are also more likely to trust your judgement because of your limited knowledge of the research context. Once they establish that you are not very knowledgeable about the context, they will come to the conclusion that you are likely to be objective. Secondly, professional researchers normally have the training, skills and confidence needed for action research. They normally would have taken in depth courses in research methods and may have experience conducting similar studies. Finally, as a professional researcher, you would have dedicated time for research projects. Therefore you can devote sufficient time to a project without having to worry about the challenges, such as job demands, that the practitioner will face.

The major disadvantage that you will face as an outsider, results from your limited knowledge of the research context. Due to your limited knowledge of the context, you may find it difficult to gain the confidence and trust of the participants, who see you as a stranger. This in turn may make the building of structures for dialogue difficult. Remember, it is not always easy to talk to someone you do not trust, and as pointed out earlier, dialogue is vital to the change process.

So far we have presented the information in a dichotomous way about the researcher as practitioner and the researcher as a professional, however you need to become aware that it is not always that simplistic. Many researchers find themselves in a hybrid situation where they are both practitioner and professional researcher. For example, you may be a part-time post graduate student who is teaching in a primary school. Part of your requirement as a student may be to do an in depth study of a problem in your school. Clearly, with your research training you are a professional researcher sent by your university to conduct the study, but you are also a part of the school and as such are not an outsider. In this case, you will have to be mindful of both the insider and outsider factors that can affect the study.

Additionally, by now you should have detected that what is an advantage for the insider may be viewed as a disadvantage for the outsider and vice versa. As such, opposite advice is often given to researchers in the two positions. One key advice that is given to the insider is to make 'strange' what appears to be 'familiar'. In so doing, the insider should try to think as an outsider who possesses limited knowledge of the research context. Therefore, as an insider you must at times ignore what you think you know about the context and try to carry out the investigation as someone who knows very little about what is being studied.

Conversely, if you are an outsider, the advice is to make 'familiar' that which is 'strange'. Therefore, the outsider has to try to see things through the eyes of the insider. You must become attune to factors such as the atmosphere of the research site, the routine ways that things are done and the jargon spoken by the participants.

Confused? Don't be. What you should get from this strange/familiar relationship is that both the insider and the outsider have important parts to play in the action research process. The key is to understand your position so that you will be aware of how you can affect the research process and how you can be affected by the context of the research.

CONCLUSION

Action research is often maligned by people who adhere to the more traditionalist approach to research. Indeed, some eschew it claiming that it lacks rigour because there are no 'control' groups. Do not be swayed by these arguments. The purpose of action research is not to show that one approach is better than another in all contexts. Its purpose is to find sustainable solutions to existing problems in a given context, not to generalise to any other setting. When you report your research, people with similar problems may obtain ideas for exploring their own solutions.

As a student, your supervisor may try to point you in the direction of a more traditional research design, for example, an experimental design. However, if you think that action research is the thing for you, then forge on! You will find that it can be a very rewarding approach as you apply a systematic, scientific process to finding workable solutions to problems that plague classroom, schools and many other work environments.

For an example of action research conducted in the Caribbean, consult the article 'Action Research: A Viable Option for Effecting Change' by Warrican (2006), published in the *Journal of Curriculum Studies*, volume 38, no.1. Warrican introduces the article by stating:

> Using a literacy project as illustration, I make a case for action
> research as an approach for external innovators who seek to effect
> educational change. Collaboration between the innovator and
> those for whom the innovation is intended, rather than power,
> is the key ingredient in bringing about change. Clients must be
> actively involved at all stages of an innovation (1).

7

SELECTING SOURCES OF DATA

INTRODUCTION

A very important aspect of your research is the concept of sampling. This is where you select people and ask them to participate in your research. Your selection of participants is dependent on several factors, including the purpose of the research, the design you are using, access to people and funding. In this chapter, we will explore some of the concepts related to sampling and the types of decisions you are likely to have to make. Areas considered include deciding on a sample size, types of samples and techniques for selecting a sample. We also examine factors such as sampling error and sampling bias that can influence the credibility of your research.

POPULATION AND SAMPLE

When you undertake a piece of research, it is about some entity or group of people. You may want to explore nurses' perceptions of a new regional health care policy. The thing is, you are examining some entity or group with particular characteristics. All the things or people that possess the characteristics in which you are interested make up your population. Thus, using the examples above, all of the nurses in the region would be eligible for inclusion in your study. These are the ones about which you would want to make statements when you have collected and analysed your data. But clearly, it would not be feasible to collect data from them all. Even if you are only interested in the phenomenon as it relates to your territory, it can still involve large numbers. You must select some of the population with which to work, that is, you must select a sample. A sample is a subgroup of the population that reflects the characteristics of that population.

Often, as a researcher, your task is to observe your sample in order to learn something about the population in general. This means that the sample you select should be representative of the population of interest. This can sometimes be difficult to accomplish, but there are techniques that you can use that would ensure that your sample very closely matches your population. As mentioned before, the population about which you want to draw conclusions includes all with the particular characteristics of interest. This group is referred to as the target population. However, you might recognise that this group may be any size and not all realistically available to you. The population from which you can realistically select your sample is called the accessible population. Therefore, ideally the target population of a study about the new healthcare policy might be all the registered nurses in the region. Realistically however, you may only have access to the ones who are rostered to work at the main healthcare facility (national hospital) and district clinics in your territory. These would be your accessible or available population, and it is from among them that you would select your sample. Thus, in most cases, the definition of your population tends to be realistic instead of idealistic.

Before going any further, it would be good to get familiar with some terminology. As mentioned above, your population is a group that possesses certain characteristics. When the characteristics are measured within a sample, they are called statistics. The measures of these characteristics within the population are called parameters. One of the tasks that you might face as a researcher, especially when undertaking quantitative research, would be to collect statistics from your sample and then use them to make inferences about the parameters of the population. This should help you to recognise how vital it is for you to select your sample with care, since an inappropriate sample could yield statistics that could lead you to erroneous conclusions about the population. Such errors are to be avoided at all costs as they have a way of rearing their ugly heads at the most inconvenient times and biting you in a most public and embarrassing way.

When you are thinking of avoiding embarrassing errors, you might want to give some consideration to some sources of error related to sampling: sampling bias, random sampling error and sample size. Let us briefly examine these before we explore types of samples and sampling procedures.

SAMPLING BIAS

This source of sampling error occurs when the sampling procedure is flawed. This means that the sample was selected by an inappropriate procedure, resulting in a group that is not representative of the population. If representativeness is vital to your research, then you can see how this could be a problem. If you use such a biased sample to draw conclusions about a population, then clearly those conclusions could be flawed. Let us say that you wanted to draw conclusions about workers' attitudes towards colleagues with physical disabilities. Let us say, to collect your data, you administered an attitude scale to a group of workers at a supermarket known for its success at hiring and retaining people with disabilities. Could you then draw conclusions about attitudes of workers in general? Not really, because such a sample may be biased. It is possible, that the supermarket's hiring policy has measures in place to facilitate their disabled employees and to integrate them and their more-abled co-workers into one happy family. This environment may have a positive impact on the workers and may have shaped their beliefs and attitudes. Other workers not employed by that supermarket may have different attitudes and beliefs. Therefore, when you draw conclusions from your data, it would be wrong for you to generalise them to all workers.

Sampling bias cannot be measured and cannot be corrected once your data is collected. So if generalising is important to your research, you must pay attention to your sampling techniques. You must use a sampling procedure that allows you to select an appropriate sample from among the target population. Some of these procedures are presented later in the chapter. Remember that sampling bias is a flaw, a fatal error made by the researcher that should be avoided at all costs. However, if by chance you collect data from a sample that is biased in some way, you must make a decision as to whether that bias is acute enough to render the research useless. If you decide to press on with your research, be sure to make a comprehensive report of the bias in your write-up defending your decision to continue. Then, persons who read your research report can decide for themselves about the severity of the bias and whether or not they will accept your findings.

RANDOM SAMPLING ERROR

Unlike sampling bias, random sampling error does not occur as a result of flawed actions on the part of the researcher. It is in fact the result of the nature of the act of selecting a random sample from a population. When you as a researcher select a sample from the population, you are getting only one of the possible samples. There are several other different samples of the same size that can be selected from the population. Sampling error is related to the fact that you are selecting and using only one of these possible samples or one part of the population instead of the entire population.

Pretend that you were observing a particular characteristic in a population of N persons and that the population mean (μ) was known to you. Let us say that you selected a sample of n persons from the population, the mean of the sample would not be the exact value as the population mean. By chance, it would be higher or lower. If it were possible for you to find all the different samples of n that could be had from your population and calculate the mean for each one of them, you could construct a frequency distribution for those means. If you were to draw a frequency polygon to represent these values, you would obtain a normal curve with a mean that would be the same as the population mean. The standard deviation for those means is an indication of the random sampling error. It is also called the standard error of the mean or simply the standard error. Let us see how this works by taking an unlikely population and sample. The numbers are unrealistically small, but it makes the point.

Figure 7a shows the scores of a population of six people from which a sample of three scores must be selected. The figure also shows all the possible samples of three that can be selected. There are 20 of them. Notice that the population mean is 3.5, but that none of the sample means are exactly that. Some of them are closer than are the others. However you can see that the mean of these sample means is the same as the population mean.

Figure 7a
A sampling frame of six people with all the possible samples of three that can be selected

Names of Population	A	B	C	D	E	F	Population Mean*
Scores of the Population	1	2	3	4	5	6	3.5
Possible Samples of 3							Sample Means
Sample 1	1	2	3				2.0
Sample 2	1	2		4			2.3
Sample 3	1	2			5		2.7
Sample 4	1	2				6	3.0
Sample 5	1		3	4			2.7
Sample 6	1		3		5		3.0
Sample 7	1		3			6	3.3
Sample 8	1			4	5		3.3
Sample 9	1			4		6	3.7
Sample 10	1				5	6	4.0
Sample 11		2	3	4			3.0
Sample 12		2	3		5		3.3
Sample 13		2	3			6	3.7
Sample 14		2		4	5		3.7
Sample 15		2		4		6	4.0
Sample 16		2			5	6	4.3
Sample 17			3	4	5		4.0
Sample 18			3	4		6	4.3
Sample 19			3		5	6	4.7
Sample 20				4	5	6	5.0
Mean of Sample Means							3.5

* All means are approximated to one decimal place

Figure 7b shows a sample distribution for all the sample means. If we plot this data on a frequency polygon (Figure 7c below), we would get a normal curve, with the mean at 3.5 (as we would expect from our data in Figure 7a) and a standard deviation of 0.78.

Figure 7b
Frequency Distribution for the Sample Means Above

Sample Mean	Frequency
2.0	1
2.3	1
2.7	2
3.0	3
3.3	3
3.7	3
4.0	3
Total	20

Figure 7c
Frequency Polygon for the Distribution of Sample Means

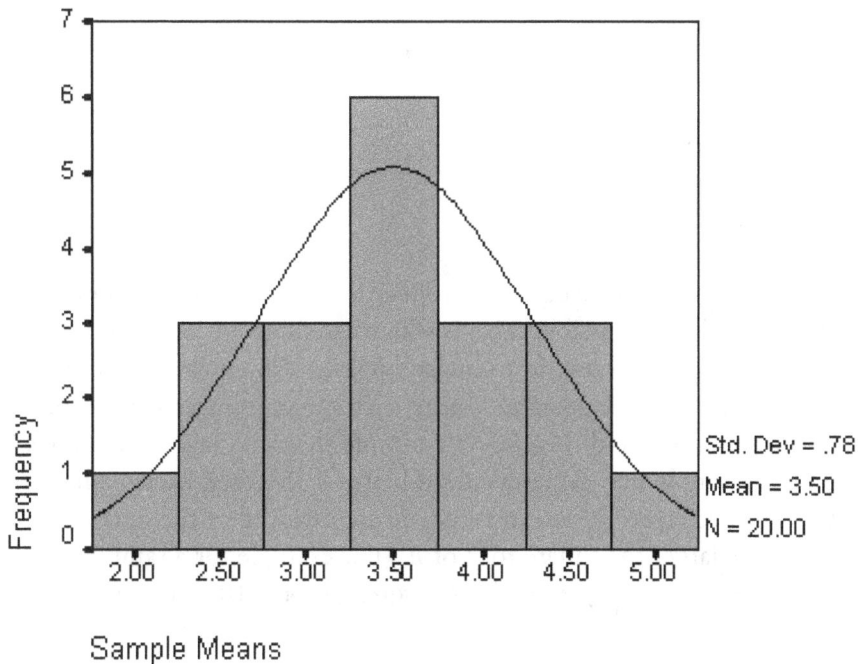

Std. Dev = .78
Mean = 3.50
N = 20.00

Sample Means

Using the properties of the normal curve, this tells us that 68 per cent of sample means fall between −1 and +1 standard deviation from the mean, that is between 2.72 (3.5–0.78) and 4.28 (3.5 + 0.78); 95 per cent of them fall between −2 and +2 standard deviations from the mean, that is between 1.94 (3.5 - 0.78 x 2) and 5.06 (3.5 + 0.78 x 2); and 99 per cent fall between −3 and +3 standard deviations from the mean, or between 1.16 (3.5 - 0.78 x 3) and 5.84 (3.5 + 0.78 x 3).

You might recall from your statistics classes in Mathematics that the standard deviation is an indication of the spread of a set of scores. A large standard deviation is an indication that the scores are spread widely from the mean, whereas a small standard deviation indicates that the scores are clustered closely around the mean. Remember, the standard error is the standard deviation of the sample means (0.78 in our example above). It tells you the extent to which you can expect the means of samples selected randomly to differ from the population mean. Hence, if the standard error is large, that suggests that the sample mean differs greatly from the population mean. If it is small, then the sample mean more closely estimates the population mean. You should therefore aim to keep the standard error as low as possible. This is important because it can affect the conclusions that you draw.

However it is not as simple as it was with our example to select all the possible samples in order to work out the standard error. Think what a mammoth task it would be if you had a population of 5,000 11-year-olds from which to select a sample of 100! Does that mean that we cannot find the standard error? Not at all! We can in fact obtain a very good estimate of the standard error with a relatively simple formula, shown below.

$$S_{\overline{X}} = \frac{s}{\sqrt{n}}$$

Where $S_{\overline{X}}$ = Standard error for the sample
s = standard deviation for the sample scores
n = size of the sample

As mentioned before, when you are doing your quantitative research, your aim then is to keep the standard error as low as possible. This is where careful attention to your sampling procedure is vital, especially if you intend to make inferences about the population based on the statistics collected from the sample. Under such circumstances you should use a probability sampling procedure and then select a sample that is as large as possible. This notion of using a large sample may be understood better if you look back at the formula for calculating the standard error. As you can see, you are dividing by the square root of n. The larger n is, then the larger the square root of n. [For example for a sample of 50, the square root is 7.1 whereas for a sample of 100, the square root is 10.] You may know that the bigger the number you are dividing by, the smaller the answer. Hence having a large sample size could reduce the size of the standard error.[7] Thus, before selecting a sample, it would be a good idea to determine an adequate sample size.

DETERMINING A SAMPLE SIZE

When deciding on a sample size that would suit your research, you must be aware of several things. You must be clear on the purpose of your research. You must also determine how you intend to use the data collected. For instance, do you want to use quantitative procedures to make generalizations about a population based on your sample statistics or do you want to do an in-depth qualitative study of a particular phenomenon? In the first case, you would want a larger sample than you would in the second case.

Why should you make your sample as large as possible for quantitative research? First, this would increase the chances of the sample being representative of the population, and confidence in your findings would be high. Second, a large sample increases the chance of rejecting the null hypothesis if it is false, that is, finding a significant difference or relationship that really exists (this concept is discussed in chapter 11). Then as explained above, you can reduce the sampling error, making your inferences firmer. In reality though, student researchers are seldom in a position to make their sample extremely large. Limited time, finances and other resources impose restrictions. However, there are some guidelines that can assist you in deciding on an adequate sample size. For example, it can be shown that increasing the sample size beyond a certain point results in very little reduction in random sampling error. In fact, some writers suggest that no matter how large the population, a sample of about 400 would be adequate (Gay, Mills & Airasian, 2006). Before you start to worry, you should note that the general rule is that, for most types of research (correlational, causal-comparative, and experimental), a minimum sample of 30 would suffice (Burns, 2000). For survey research, a minimum number of 100 would be adequate.

There are other considerations that you must think on when deciding on a sample size for quantitative research. You must bear in mind whether or not you want to do subgroup comparisons. Do you want to compare characteristics along the line of gender? If so, then you must ensure that you have adequate numbers of these groups in your sample. In such a case, a stratified random sampling technique (explained below) would be useful. Secondly, you must bear in mind that for whatever reason, some of your participants may drop out of the study. One recommendation for lessening the effects of this attrition is to increase the sample size by a certain percentage (Gall, Borg & Gall, 1996). It is important for you to remember however, that no matter how large your sample might be, if it is not selected by an appropriate technique, your sample could still be biased and hence, your findings suspect.

As mentioned in chapter 5, one characteristic of qualitative research is that it usually involves a small number of participants. Your sample size could depend on who has relevant information and whether you can persuade them to share it with you. However there are other considerations. You must take your resources, especially time, into account. A common method of collecting data in qualitative research is by conducting interviews. The number of persons interviewed could yield hours and hours of audiotapes or field notes to transcribe. It is estimated that a one-hour interview could take as much as eight hours to transcribe. If you interview 20 people for one hour, well you can see how much time you'll be spending transcribing!

The thing is, while there may be no hard and fast rule for determining a sample size for qualitative research, you should be guided by these tips:

1. Ensure that you have enough people so that you get the information that you want.
2. Make sure that you have enough people so that you can corroborate information. If one person says something, it is a good idea to hear what other people have to say on the matter. One opinion is hardly the basis for sound conclusions. This concept of corroboration through triangulation (discussed in chapter 5) is basic to qualitative research.
3. The number of people in your sample should allow you enough time to spend with them to obtain in-depth information, and to transcribe your notes and interviews.

So, now that you know how many participants you need for your research, the next step is selecting them. How you do this depends on the purpose of your research and the types of questions you are asking. Next then, we shall explore ideas about types of samples and techniques for selecting them.

TYPES OF SAMPLES

As previously mentioned, the way in which your sample is selected often depends on factors such as the purpose of your research and the philosophical perspective on which you base your work. But samples tend to fall into two broad categories; probability samples and non-probability samples.

Probability sampling involves techniques where the chance of the selection of each participant is known. This usually involves some form of randomisation that results in a sample that is representative of the population. That means that the sample that you use in your research possesses the same characteristics in the same proportion as they exist in the population. Non-probability sampling relies on techniques where the probability of selecting each participant is unknown. Such techniques tend to produce non-representative samples, making it difficult, even impossible to make inferences about the population. Perhaps these types of sampling and the corresponding concerns could best be understood with an example.

Suppose you were conducting a study about the reading habits of primary school students in the 8–9 year-old age group and you determine that your population would include all the primary school students in that age group in your territory. Now, if you include only your class of 8–9 year-olds in your research – you use a non-probability sample – the conclusions that you draw and statements that you make would be applicable only to your class. You might not be able to say that any of it applies to students in other schools in the territory. In fact, you might not even be able to apply them to 8–9 year-olds in other classes in your school! But if you include a random selection of 8–9 year-olds from a number of schools within the territory – that is you use a probability sample – you can be more confident that your conclusions and statements could be applied to the wider

8–9 year-old community in your territory. Hence, your method of sampling affects the confidence with which you can make statements and the groups to which those statements can be applied.

There are many techniques for selecting both probability and non-probability samples. Some of these will now be presented.

PROBABILITY SAMPLING TECHNIQUES

The most commonly used probability sampling techniques are simple random sampling, systematic sampling, stratified random sampling, cluster sampling and multi-stage sampling.

Simple Random Sampling

This might be considered as the purest form of probability sampling. With this technique, a list of the population (called a sampling frame in survey research) is compiled and the determined number of persons or objects to be included in the sample is randomly selected. One approach to choosing a random sample is to put the names of all the population in a container, say a hat, and pull out the sample one by one. It is important to remember that each selected name must be replaced in the container before the next selection is made. This is necessary to meet the requirement that all the selected names have the same chance of being drawn. If a name is selected a second time, just put it back into the container and make the selection again. You repeat this process until you have the required number for your sample.

Now if you think about it, you would recognise that, with its repetitive nature, the above approach could become tedious if the desired sample is large. But fear not! In this technological age, less daunting approaches are available. You can for instance take your population list and assign each member with a number. You can use computer software to do this. Then you would generate a list of random numbers, each of which corresponds to a member of the population. These members would then be included in your sample. Let us consider an example.

Suppose you had a population of 100 textbooks from which you wanted to select a sample of 15, you would take a list of the names of these texts and number them from 0 to 99. You can then use a table of random numbers, a calculator or a computer to generate a list of 15 random numbers, and textbooks that correspond to these numbers would be included in your sample. If you use a table of random numbers, each selected number may have up to five digits. For our example, you would consider only the first two. So if the number 03164 is in your list, then the book numbered 03 or just 3 would be in the sample. Calculators on the other hand tend to generate random numbers in decimal form, hence your calculator may generate say 0.305. For our example, you would use the first two digits after the decimal point. Therefore the book numbered 30 would be in the sample. Computers can be programmed to generate only numbers within the required range and so would produce only whole numbers from 0 to 99.

The approaches described above are the most common means of producing a random sample. You may be wondering why go through all that trouble. But there are some advantages that make it all worthwhile. If your aim is to make generalisations about the population based on sample statistics, then a representative sample is desirable. Simple random sampling is the most basic way of selecting a sample that is representative of your population. In fact, many of the statistical tests carried out on the data collected from the sample to make inferences about the population are built on the assumption that the sample was randomly selected.

A major disadvantage of simple random sampling is that, often in social research, it is not a practical option. The population may be so large and scattered that it might make it difficult to access a sample chosen through this method. Indeed, it might be difficult, if not impossible, to obtain a complete list of the entire population. But more troubling is the fact that the population may be so diverse, there is the danger that small subgroups within the population may be under-represented or not represented at all in the sample. Some Caribbean populations have indigenous peoples who are in the minority (for example, the Caribs in St Vincent). A group selected through simple random sampling might produce a sample in which these individuals are under-represented. In such situations, other sampling techniques might be more appropriate.

Systematic Sampling

Systematic sampling is usually more appropriate when large populations are involved, and complete lists of the members are available. It is a procedure in which the selection of the first member of the sample influences the entire sample. With this technique, the first member of the sample is randomly chosen from a numbered population list. Then starting at that point, every nth object or person is selected. To determine the interval, that is, the value of n, first decide on the required size of the sample and then divide the number of members in the population by that sample size. Let us consider an example.

Imagine that you want to select a sample of police officers from among all those in the service in your territory. Your first step would be to obtain a list of all the names of these people from the Police Headquarters and assign a number to each of them. Let us say that there are 800 names, numbered from 0 to 799. Let us say that you have determined that a sample of 260 would be adequate for your research. To determine the value of n, you would divide 800 by 260. This gives a result of 3.08, or 3 to the nearest whole number. Thus, you are going to take every 3rd member of the population from the starting point. So, if your randomly selected number is 471, then your next selected number would be 474, then 477, 480, 483 and so on. When you reach the end of the list, you would go to the top and continue. This would be done until 260 members of the population are chosen.

The major problem with systematic sampling is that all the members of the population do not have an independent chance of being included in the sample and this could produce a biased sample. As mentioned before, the random selection of the first member automatically excludes some members of the population from the sample. It is possible that the order of the population list could be such that every nth person has some characteristic that introduces bias to the sample. It is also possible for the excluded members to possess characteristics that are important to the research. One way of reducing the possibility of a biased sample when this technique is used is to ensure that the population list is randomly ordered.

Stratified Random Sampling

Sometimes a population may include several subgroups that you the researcher want to have adequately represented in your sample. When this is the case, you may adopt a stratified random sampling technique to select your research participants. Stratified random sampling involves dividing the population into its component groups [called STRATA] and randomly selecting a sample from each group to be included in the research.

Once you have identified the subgroups in the population, you must decide the number of each group to be included in the sample, that is, you must decide on allocation. One approach to allocation is called equal allocation. With this approach, equal numbers are selected from each stratum. Thus, if the sample size is 100 and there are five strata, then you would randomly select 20 members of each stratum for the sample. Another approach to allocation is called proportional allocation. Here, each stratum is represented in the sample in the same proportion in which it exists in the population.

There are two methods of selecting a proportional sample. One of these involves the concept of the sampling fraction. This is the ratio of the sample size (n) to the population size (N), expressed as n/N. With this approach, the ratio of the size of the sample of each stratum to its size in the population is the same as the sampling fraction. Before you throw up your hands in total horror, let us consider an example. Suppose you had a population (N) of 1600 police officers from among whom you want to select a sample (n) of 240. The sampling fraction therefore would be n/N or 240/1600, which is 3/20 or 0.15. Now let us suppose that you divide this population in three strata: Non-Commissioned Officers (Stratum 1) with a size (N_1) of 800, Auxiliary (Reserved) Officers (Stratum 2) with a size (N_2) of 600; and Commissioned Officers (Stratum 3) with a size (N_3) of 200. The sample sizes of these strata can be represented by n_1, n_2 and n_3 respectively. This means that $n/N = n_1/N_1 = n_2/N_2 = n_3/N_3$, where $N_1 + N_2 + N_3 = N$ and $n_1 + n_2 + n_3 = n$. Therefore, the size of each stratum in the sample can be worked out by multiplying its population size by the sampling fraction as follows:

Stratum 1	800 x 0.15 =	120
Stratum 2	600 x 0.15 =	90
Stratum 3	200 x 0.15 =	30
TOTAL	1600 x 0.15	240

ßThus your sample would consist of 120 Non-Commissioned Officers, 90 Auxiliary (Reserved) Officers and 30 Commissioned Officers. Now that wasn't so difficult, was it?

The second method involves ascertaining the size of the population and the size of each of the identified strata in that population. Then you must determine what proportion of the population constitutes each stratum and calculate the same proportion of the desired sample size for each of them. Again, an example will help you to understand this. Let us use the same information given above. There is a population of 1600 police officers that is divided into three strata: Non-Commissioned (Stratum 1) with 800 officers, Auxiliary (Reserved) (Stratum 2) with 600 officers and Commissioned (Stratum 3) with 200 officers. From this population, you want to select a proportional sample of 240 officers. Now the proportion of each stratum in the population can be worked out as follows:

Proportion for Stratum 1 $800/1600 =$ ½

Proportion for Stratum 2 $600/1600 =$

Proportion for Stratum 3 $200/1600 =$

To find the size of each stratum in the sample, you must calculate similar proportions of the 240 needed as follows:

Size of Stratum 1 in the sample $½ \times 240 =$ 120

Size of Stratum 2 in the sample $\times 240 =$ 90

Size of Stratum 3 in the sample $\times 240 =$ 30

Total size of sample $=$ 240

As before, your sample would be made up of 120 Non-Commissioned Officers, 90 Auxiliary (Reserved) Officers and 30 Commissioned Officers just as before. That too was relatively painless, wasn't it?

The decision to adopt or not to adopt a stratified random sampling technique may be influenced by several factors, such as the nature of the population and the purpose of your research. Likewise, whether you use equal allocation or proportional allocation depends on your purpose. For example, the equal allocation method is appropriate when you want to do comparisons among different groups in the population. Thus, if you were interested in comparing the perspectives of boys with those of girls, you would stratify your population along the line of gender and randomly select equal numbers of girls and boys to participate in your research. Proportional allocation is suitable in instances where you want to learn something about the population and you need the sample to reflect certain characteristics of that population. It is important to note that the purpose of stratified random sampling is to guarantee that subgroups within the population are adequately represented.

Cluster Sampling

So far, all the sampling techniques involved selecting individuals to participate in research. Cluster sampling is different in this respect. With this technique, groups are randomly selected for the sample. All the members in the groups possess similar characteristics. A cluster may be a classroom, or a school, or a group of schools in a parish. Thus, when using cluster sampling, instead of selecting individual 9–10 year olds, you would select classrooms of 9–10 year olds and all the students in those classrooms would be included in the sample. Cluster sampling is appropriate when the population is extremely large, when no list of the members of the population exists or when the population is scattered over a wide geographical area. It is also very useful when the population members naturally exist in units that can be convenient to use. There are definitely some circumstances where it is more practical to select groups for a research project than to select individuals. For instance, it would be more convenient to administer 150 questionnaires to five classes of students as groups or clusters than it would be to administer them to 150 randomly selected students scattered across many classrooms in several different schools.

To carry out a cluster sampling exercise, you would first need to identify and define the population, and determine the desired sample size. Then you would have to identify and define a logical cluster and make or obtain a list of clusters that make up the population. Next, estimate the average number of population members per cluster and determine the number of clusters needed to obtain the desired sample size. This is done by dividing the sample size by the estimated average size of each cluster. Once you know the number of clusters needed, you can go ahead and select them using a random sampling technique. You would then include all the members of selected clusters in your study. Now let us consider an example.

Let us say that in your territory, the primary schools are small and tend to have only one class at each grade level. You want to investigate some phenomenon among Grade 4 students (9–10 year-olds). According to information from the department of education, there are 3,000 Grade 4 students in the territory, and you decide on a sample of 300. A logical cluster would be a classroom. Again from the department of education, you learn that there are 120 Grade 4 classes across the territory, and you obtain a list of these. You would then need to estimate the average number of population members per cluster. Although there may be varying numbers of students in each class, the average number per classroom here is 25 (3,000 ÷ 120). If there is an average of 25 students in each class, how many classes (or clusters) would you need to make up a sample of 300? Yes, you have it! The answer is 12 (300 ÷ 25). You would then randomly select 12 of the 120 Grade 4 classes for your research. All of the students in those classes would be in your sample. You should note that the actual sample size might differ from your desired size because some of the classes selected may actually contain fewer or more than 25 students.

The advantages of cluster sampling are no doubt apparent in the above example. If the above sample were selected using a simple random sampling technique, you might find yourself visiting all 120 Grade 4 classes, sometimes just to collect data from one student. Visiting 12 classrooms is infinitely more convenient and would certainly save time, money and energy! Sounds good, doesn't it? But there is a saying that there is some bad in all good things, and this is certainly true about cluster sampling, as it has several drawbacks.

One disadvantage of cluster sampling is that you stand a greater chance of selecting a sample that is in some way not representative of the population. For instance, in the example above, the 300 students in the sample are from a relatively small number of classrooms. It is possible that these classrooms differ significantly from the other 108 classrooms that were not selected. For example, it is possible that none of the 12 classrooms were from a district where things are viewed differently from the rest of the population. Some writers suggest that you can compensate for this drawback by selecting a larger sample, that is include more classes, which would increase the chance of adequately representing all the classes. If you choose to do this however, you must bear in mind the suggestion by other writers that using too large a sample can lead to erroneous conclusions.

Another drawback is that frequently used inferential statistics may not be appropriate for analysing data collected from samples that are selected by cluster sampling. Such procedures often assume that more equitable means such as simple random sampling were used. In experimental research, some try to get around this by randomly assigning existing clusters to the different treatments, but this is not enough. Since the clusters are not randomly formed, one cluster might be sufficiently different from the other(s) in ways that could affect the outcome of the treatment. This could lead to erroneous conclusions.

One way of addressing this problem is to use a pre-test/post-test design so that you can ascertain to what extent the groups were different before treatment was administered. There are statistical procedures that can compensate for any differences found. Another way of addressing this problem is by using other statistical procedures that do not assume approaches such as simple random sampling. However, these tend to be less sensitive to differences that may exist between groups. You should not, however, be put off by these drawbacks. Carefully consider the advantages and disadvantages of cluster sampling before choosing. If it is appropriate for your research, then do all that you can to capitalise on the advantages and minimise the disadvantages.

Multi-stage Sampling

Some may consider multi-stage sampling an extension of cluster sampling. It involves selecting a sample in stages or getting a sample of a sample. Again, this is best explained by taking an example. Let us suppose that there are 25 constituencies in your country. For manageability, you may decide to randomly select five of those constituencies from which to select a sample of eligible voters. From within each of the five constituencies, you may then randomly select two districts for your study. Thus you would have 10 districts in your sample. You could then include all the eligible voters in these 10 districts in your study. If these numbers are unmanageably large, you may decide to select a sample from each district, perhaps using a voter's registration list and a systematic sampling technique.

Note then, that techniques other than cluster sampling can be used in multi-stage sampling. Perhaps you may want to randomly select a number of constituencies, stratify the districts in each one according to socio-economic status (SES) and then randomly select one district from SES group. Thus, each constituency can be divided into Upper SES districts, Middle SES districts and Lower SES districts. Then, you can randomly select one district from each SES group, from within each constituency. As you can see, this approach to selecting a sample can be done in different ways. The common thread is that selection is done at various levels and possibly in different ways. Always bear in mind that though multi-stage sampling may be practical and convenient, there may be consequences to the generalisability of your research findings. For example, if you randomly select three constituencies from which to select your stratified sample of voters, depending on the characteristics of the constituencies selected, you may not be able to make generalisations to all the constituencies in the country.

So far we have presented probability sampling techniques, that is, techniques that involve randomisation on some level. These sampling approaches tend to be used more commonly in quantitative research, where generalisation is desirable. But there are other techniques that may be used to select a research sample, in which randomisation is not involved. We will now examine the most frequently used of these.

NON-PROBABILITY SAMPLING TECHNIQUES

Some inexperienced researchers may hold the belief that the only worthwhile sampling techniques are those that involve randomisation. Indeed, even experienced researchers may feel this way. However, there are some instances in which a random sample is the last thing that you need for your research, or circumstances may make it impossible for you to obtain a random sample. Does that mean that you should abandon your research? Not necessarily! In this section, we will introduce you to four alternative approaches to sampling that can be extremely useful to you: purposive sampling, convenience sampling, snowball sampling and quota sampling.

Purposive Sampling

As mentioned earlier, there are some instances when a random sample is the absolute last thing you need. Some research projects require specific participants. When this is the case, you may want to use purposive (or purposeful) sampling. Purposive sampling is the process of deliberately selecting a particular sample because you believe it to be a source of rich information about the phenomenon that you are investigating. For example, you may select your sample from a particular location because it gives you access to people that exemplify the phenomenon you wish to study. You may select specific individuals because they possess some characteristic(s) that you wish to study. In such instances, if you select a random sample from the general population, you may end up with participants who cannot provide the data you need for your research. Thus, if you are interested in studying the experiences and views of people living with diabetes, it would be prudent to go to a medical facility that would allow you access to diabetics, and then from their records, to deliberately or purposefully select individuals with this condition.

Purposive sampling is especially useful to researchers engaging in qualitative research for which rich textual data from a relatively small sample is needed. It is particularly useful for case studies, where you would carefully select a case with the characteristics in which you are interested. In order to make a decision about who or what to select, you may first want to carry out an initial investigative study. Using techniques such as interviewing, observation, testing, examining records or administering questionnaires, you could identify potential sources of information. Based on the analysis of the data collected, you could then purposefully select a sample that you believe could best help you to understand the phenomenon you wish to study.

Convenience Sampling

One writer describes this approach as a 'cheap and dirty way of doing a sample survey' (Robson, 1993, p. 141). It involves selecting as the research sample whoever or whatever is available and convenient, and sometimes this may be the only option open to the researcher. No doubt you will read, or have already read, the report of a study in which the participants were 'first year psychology students' at the researcher's university. This is often another way of saying that the researcher grabbed a 'captive audience' and made it the research sample. A convenience sample can also result if you select people who volunteer for your research. For example, you may want a sample of 50 alcoholics to complete a questionnaire, and you may take the instrument to three Alcoholics Anonymous meetings and ask any attendees who happen to be there to complete it. Some may say yes, and others may decline. You may have your 50 completed questionnaires, but what population are your volunteers representing? Certainly not the people who were attending the meetings! The volunteers may be different from the non-volunteers in ways that are crucial to your research. Thus, you may end up with a biased sample. In the real world, this is sometimes necessary or some research projects would never get done, but if this approach can be avoided, then do so!

The absence of representativeness is one limitation of a convenience sample. Another limitation relates to the analysis of the data gathered from such a sample. In many studies that involve convenience samples, researchers run statistical procedures that assume random sampling. However, since this is not the case, any inferences made from such analyses are likely to be erroneous. So, is there no hope if all you can find for your research is a convenience sample? Fear not! There are some steps that you can take that can still result in worthwhile research.

If all you can find is a convenience sample, be honest about it when reporting your research. Then provide the best possible description of the sample. That does not mean that you must give characteristics of every individual in the sample, rather you should describe it as a group. If you have to carry out statistical procedures, choose those for which there are no assumptions of a random sample. Then, be careful not to make sweeping generalisations from your findings. Yes, convenience sampling may be 'cheap and dirty', but it has its uses. It can be especially useful if you want to get a 'feel' for issues involved in the particular area or if you are carrying out a pilot study.

Snowball Sampling

This approach to sampling is named after a phenomenon that may be somewhat foreign – though not unknown – to people in the Caribbean. Apparently in lands where snow is common and packing it into balls is the thing to do, these balls can be made bigger by rolling them in the snow. Thus, if one of these snowballs starts to roll down a hill, it gets bigger and bigger as it approaches the bottom (we've seen this in the cartoons, haven't we?). It is from this idea of growing bigger as it goes along that this sampling technique gets its name.

Snowball sampling calls for the researcher to identify and obtain the cooperation of at least one participant with the characteristics of interest. After interviewing that participant or using some other appropriate data collecting approach, the researcher asks that participant to identify and seek the cooperation of someone else with the same characteristics. This is repeated until there are no more willing participants or until the researcher has enough data for his/her purpose. Thus, the sample gets bigger and bigger as the research progresses, just like the snowball going down the hill!

Snowball sampling is appropriate when the research involves sensitive issues, such as those related to drugs, gang activity, violence and crime, sexuality and abuse or others that may border on the illegal or may have some stigma attached. Individuals may not want to openly identify themselves as being involved in such activities or having any knowledge of them and so you the researcher must take care in selecting a sample if your study involves such sensitive issues. If you were investigating the extent of drug abuse in schools and its effects on classroom activities, you may, perhaps through a guidance counsellor, identify one student who is willing to speak with you. If this student is involved in drug use in the school, he/she might also be aware of others who are involved. After talking with this student, you may ask him/her if he/she knows anyone else who is involved with drugs who may be willing to speak with you. Do not demand names, but note them if they are given. It might also be a good idea not to approach anyone unless you are reasonably sure that they are willing to participate. You could ask your participants if they would be willing to put you in contact with other individuals who might be willing to participate and then make such contact as discreetly as possible. Remember in such communities, invisibility is often desirable and people might not want to be seen with you if your purpose is generally known.

Using this sampling technique may involve ethical concerns that you must be clear on before you begin. So if you are dealing with a sensitive topic, be sure that you understand what your responsibilities are to the participants and to the general public. Make sure you understand the law! Do not attempt to increase the size of your sample by making promises that you cannot keep as this erodes any trust that the participants may have in you and essentially closes the door to the community that could best inform your research. Also, depending on the situation, it may put you or one of your participants in danger. Despite what might sound like dire warnings, snowball sampling has its advantages. For example, if you do it right, it could put you in contact with people who can best provide rich information about the phenomenon that you are investigating. It can allow you to develop a relationship with each participant that can foster trust and increase the chances of their being open and honest in their expressions. This in turn could help you to better accomplish your goal, which is to get an accurate understanding of the phenomenon you are investigating.

Quota Sampling

This sampling technique is perhaps more commonly used in marketing research, but it could be useful in other areas of social research. With this technique, you the researcher decide on categories of people needed for your research and on the numbers desirable. Then you find a way of meeting such people until your numbers or quotas are met. For example, you may stand at the school gate, knock on doors after 5 p.m., or even stand in a bus terminal! In fact you can go anywhere that you are likely to encounter the categories of persons needed. You can see the potential for sample bias here! The persons that you choose to approach or who actually stop to talk with you may be different in important ways from those who you allow to go by or from those who do not stop. Like convenience sampling, this technique is perhaps most useful when you want to get a feel for the types of opinions people hold and not to get a representative set of views.

In this section, different approaches to selecting a sample were discussed. As a researcher, you must make decisions about which approach is most appropriate for your study, and you must be able to defend your choices. Remember that the sample you select will be the source of the data that will inform your research. To this end, it is a good idea to use multiple sources, that is, to include people who may have different perspectives that can help to shed greater light on the problem being investigated. This is in keeping with the notion of triangulation. Thus, for example, you may collect data from a sample of jurors to get their perspective on some aspect of the judicial system, but you may also collect data from a sample of lawyers and witnesses who might present another perspective that can provide additional insight into the research problem. By drawing on these different sources, you can present a more comprehensive picture of the problem and can come to more meaningful conclusions. Hence, we recommend that, wherever possible, your research sample should include people with different characteristics and possibly, different perspectives.

THE IMPORTANCE OF SAMPLING

As you must realise by now, sampling is more than just grabbing people to fill out your questionnaires or to answer your interview questions. It is a critical task that calls for thought and planning. Before selecting a sample, you must have a clear vision of the purpose of your research, the target population and the extent to which it is accessible, how you are going to analyse your data as well as the time frame for your research. The persons that you include in your study contribute significantly to the credibility of your findings. For instance, if you administer a questionnaire to 12 voters in one neighbourhood in one district in one corner of your country, the extent to which your findings could apply to other types of voters is limited. If you then make sweeping generalisations about voters' opinions in the country, then your finding would be viewed with scepticism or even derision! So always try to ensure that your sample is adequate for the study you are doing.

The truth is though, that no matter how well you plan or how careful you are, in the real world, foul ups can occur. In such cases what can you do? Consider this scenario: for your survey research, you selected your sample with care, using an appropriate random sampling technique and making it large enough to make generalisations credible! You even added a small percentage extra to account for attrition! In fact, you did all the right things! But then only 37 per cent of the sample returned the questionnaire. You send out follow up letters but only a few more trickled in, leaving you with 38 per cent response rate. This is somewhat low and you have no way of knowing exactly who the non-respondents were because the instrument was completed anonymously. What do you do? Should you withdraw from your certificate or degree programme? Should you plan another study?

While you could do either of those things, they may not be sensible or practical. However there are other measures that can be taken that would still allow you to continue with your research. As an example, if you are using statistical procedures, you may decide to use those that do not assume random sampling. You could also make only tentative generalisations, acknowledging in your reporting that this is the best that can be done based on the number of instruments returned. If it is possible to identify a population of which the returned questionnaires could be representative, then aim your conclusions at that population. The thing is to demonstrate that you understand the limitations imposed on your research because of the inadequate sample. That in itself is a sign that you understand the research process and that you are competent enough to deal with the challenges that researchers face in the real world.

This brings us to the final point that we want to make in connection with the issue of sampling. In the report of your research, you must provide the readers with all the relevant information about your sample. You must describe how it was selected and why. You must also explain any circumstances that changed the make up of the group whose data informed your conclusions and justify why you might have chosen to persist with the research even though the sample had dwindled. You must provide enough information so that the readers can judge for themselves how much credibility they are going to ascribe to your findings. Therefore, in the methodology chapter of your research, you should provide a thorough discussion about your sampling!

As you can see, sampling is a very important aspect of your research project. If you do it well, you can produce a piece of research that is informative and worthwhile, even if everything does not go as planned. However, if you use poor sampling, even if things go as planned, your research could still be questionable.

8

DATA COLLECTION TECHNIQUES

TIP

To ensure that your research is valid, critical attention should be paid to collecting and analysing data. In this chapter, we will explore some common data collection techniques and data collection instruments.

The purpose of the data collection activity is to gather information that you can use to get answers for your investigation. Common techniques for doing this include surveying, interviewing, observing and analysing documents. Let us consider some major details about each of these techniques.

Surveying

Surveying as a data collection technique involves selecting a sample of participants, preferably using a probability sampling technique, and administering an instrument. Appropriate instruments include questionnaires, attitude and rating scales, and tests.

As a data collection procedure, surveying has certain characteristics that make it advantageous to you, the researcher. These include the fact that you can collect data related to many variables from a relatively large sample in relatively short time in order to describe the current status of a phenomenon. The sample is often selected to include a wide cross section of a given population and allows you to get a good picture of how the target population feels about the matter you are investigating. But there are also limitations. The disadvantages associated with surveying as a data collection technique include those that are common to techniques that involve self-report. Self-report is when the participants are asked to report on their activities, views, attitudes, and achievements. Most of these will be considered when we deal with questionnaires as data collection tools, since this is the most widely used tool used for surveying. Suffice to say that collecting data by surveying may be hindered by factors such as low response rate, and superficial or useless data. Furthermore, if your sample is not properly selected, you may be restricted in the strength of the conclusions that you can draw from the data collected.

If you decide to collect data by survey, you would have to decide how to administer the instrument to the respondents. Some common methods are by mail; by telephone; individually or group administration by the researcher (where the administrator delivers the instrument to the respondents and allows them to complete it while he/she waits or asks the respondents to drop it off in some central location such as in a box); individually administered in a face-to-face interview-like manner; and electronically. Each of these methods has strengths and challenges. Some of them are given below in Figure 8a. You should weigh the pros and cons of each method when selecting, and choose the method that is most efficient and productive for you.

Interviewing

Put simply, interviewing may be considered as a question and answer session. Normally, the researcher asks the questions and the research participant supplies the answers. Some texts refer to it as a face-to-face conversation between the researcher and the participant. But this over simplification may be misleading because interviewing as a data collection technique calls for great skill. There are some pitfalls that you must avoid if the data that you obtain is to be useful to you. So, let us consider some dos and don'ts for conducting interviews.

The first thing that you must do is to be prepared. Based on your research problem and your research questions, you need to formulate questions that would elicit from the interviewee the relevant information. You may want to practise before the actual interview to get a 'feel' for how things might go. You should pay attention to how you are going to record the responses. Are you going to do so manually or will you use some sort of recording device, be it audio or video? Whatever you decide, make sure that you have access to the equipment that you want, and that it is in good working order. Obtain extra audio or video tapes and batteries, and, if need be, learn how to use this equipment properly. Of course, even if you are planning to use some recording device, make sure that you have plenty of paper and writing tools. Your respondent may have a change of heart about recording the interview and you may have to write down the responses. Remember, you should have the interviewee's permission to use electronic recording devices, and you should give them some control, allowing them the option of turning off these devices if they do not want some sensitive information on record.

Figure 8a
Some Advantages and Disadvantages of Different Approaches to Administering Survey Instruments

	ADVANTAGES	DISADVANTAGES
By Mail	1. Instruments can be distributed to a relatively large number of participants in a short time. 2. Respondents tend to find the anonymity of the mailing system reassuring and tend to be more open with their responses. 3. For the most part, can be relatively inexpensive.	1. Instruments may be lost or discarded by the respondent. 2. Response rate may be small. 3. The researcher cannot follow up on responses nor seek clarification. 4. Is inadequate for respondents who cannot read.
By Telephone	4. It is relatively inexpensive and fast. 5. A large percentage of the respondents over a wide area can be reached. 6. Tends to yield a high response rate.	5. Some sectors of the population would not be included, e.g. those with unlisted numbers or those without a telephone. 6. It is easy for the respondent to opt out by simply hanging up the telephone.
Administered by the researcher to individuals or groups	7. Works well when the respondents are located in one central area	7. Can be time consuming 8. May require several trained administrators
By Face-to-face Interviewing	8. Allows both researcher and respondent to seek clarification if necessary.	9. Can be time-consuming to conduct. 10. Inexperienced administrators may influence respondents. 11. Time is needed to properly train the administrators.
Electronically (e.g. by e-mail)	9. Instruments can be distributed to a relatively large number of participants in a short time. 10. A large percentage of the respondents over a wide area can be reached. 11. For the most part, can be relatively inexpensive.	12. May be discarded by recipients contributing to a low response rate. 13. Can only be used with respondents with access to the Internet. 14. Possibility of multiple responses from a single respondent.

During the actual interview, there are some things that you can do to increase the chances of gathering useful data. Gay and Airasian (2003) give some advice on this matter. They suggest that you listen more and talk less. This allows you to hear what the respondent is saying and allows you to identify points that you want to follow up or that you want the respondent to clarify for you. Be careful with the types of questions that you ask, as you do not want to 'put words in the respondent's mouth.' The aim is to allow the respondent to answer as accurately as possible without being biased by you and your own views and opinions. Another thing is that you should make a conscious effort to avoid interrupting the respondent. If something is said that you want to follow up on, make a note and return to it after the respondent stops speaking. That way, you do not break the respondent's line of thought. If you do, you may distract them from making valuable points.

Interviewing should not be considered an easy way of collecting data. It is more than just asking a few questions. You must have a purpose for the questions and must also display some level of skill in asking them and following up important points. Therefore, preparation is vital. However the crucial work to be done after the interview is sometimes neglected or seen as less important. For instance, if tapes are not used, as soon as possible after the interview, you should find a quiet place and write down everything that you can remember about the interview. Even if you were taking notes during the interview, you may not have written it all down at that time. You may want to record impressions that you had from the interviewee's body language, any events that may have occurred during the interview and so on. You should do this soon after the interview because the human memory is notoriously fickle and you would not want to lose anything that could contribute to a rigorous piece of work.

If you use recording devices, remember that tapes have to be transcribed. This is not as easy as it sounds. It may take up to eight hours to transcribe an hour-long interview, depending on the quality of the tape, perhaps longer if you want a verbatim transcription that includes notation of all the pauses, speech patterns, intonation, pronunciation, the ahs, ums and so on. A faster way might be to listen to the tape and summarise the points made, only doing verbatim transcription for comments that you may want to quote in your report. Your choice here depends on how you want to use your interview data. There are times when verbatim transcription is a must; other times merely capturing ideas will suffice. For more in depth information on interviewing and transcribing, you may want to read Kvale (1996) or Berg (2006).

There are different approaches to interviewing that you may choose. You may do structured interviews, semi-structured interviews or unstructured (open) interviews. Structured interviews can be thought of as administering a questionnaire orally. You, the interviewer read the questions and record the responses in a very uniform way. So, for example, you may read options from which the respondents choose. Such highly structured interviews tend to be suitable for survey research. The advantage of this approach is that you obtain highly standardised data that is easy to code and compile in a database. The disadvantage is that you can miss extremely valuable and rich information by restricting the respondent too much. Perhaps at the other extreme is the unstructured interview approach. With this approach, you would have a general topic of interest that you want to hear about from the respondent. You may raise this initially, and then let the conversation develop on its own. This calls for great skill because you must be in control of the conversation without hampering the respondents' flow of thoughts. You must be subtle about bringing the respondents back to the topic of interest if they go too far off track, and you must also be skilled at following up comments or information that can enhance your work. Open interviews can yield rich, in depth information.

The approach to interviewing that you may however find yourself using most often is the semi-structured approach. With this approach, you use a prepared guide that contains examples of questions that you want to ask. However, you do not use these questions in the same restrictive way that you would with a structured interview, nor do you give the respondent the same leeway that you would with an unstructured approach. The interview guide helps you to make sure all the relevant issues are covered, but allows some freedom as to how they are covered.

Interviewing is quite unlike surveying in one fundamental way. With surveying, you are often interested in investigating a phenomenon on a wide scale, but with interviewing, you are interested in getting in depth information. Indeed, this is one of the advantages of conducting interviews: you get to collect rich, in depth data. Other advantages include being on hand to clarify questions for the respondent and being able yourself to ask the respondent to clarify any answers for you. You can also follow up any thing that is of interest right at the time at which it is raised. This is not possible with surveying. Of course you may realise by now that interviewing can be a very time-consuming activity. It does take time to speak to your respondents face to face, and often, individually, that in itself takes time. Then also think of the time needed to transcribe the interview notes or recordings. It is perhaps for that reason that samples for interviewing are often somewhat small, but the quality of data collected tends to make up for this. Sometimes though, the number of participants you interview can be increased. This is the case if you interview them in groups. This is called focus group interviewing.

FOCUS GROUP INTERVIEWING

This type of interview, also a focus group discussion, is a group discussion led by an interviewer or moderator. Focus group interviews serve several purposes. For example, you may want to carry out an investigation, but you may not quite know the extent of the problem. Conducting a focus group discussion can help you to focus your investigation. You may also use focus groups to help you to identify and clarify relevant issues that you should address in a larger study. For example, the discussion can help you to formulate questions that can be included on a questionnaire to be sent to a wider sample. Another purpose of focus group interviewing is to facilitate the exploration of controversial topics. For example, you may want to understand young people's beliefs, attitudes and concerns in relation to sexual practices and the spread of HIV. These are some instances when you could use focus group interviewing.

Planning and conducting focus group discussions call for lots of skill, but you can do it if you prepare well. You do not want your focus group discussion to collapse into a mere question and answer session. The key term is perhaps discussion. You want the members of the group to discuss the topic among themselves. Your task is to keep things moving, to keep the discussion on track and to ensure that all invited get the opportunity to air their views. The wonderful thing about focus group discussions is that if your participants are well selected, you can gain in depth information from the group about the phenomena that you are studying. Of course as with everything else, there are some cautions. For example, you need to be able to control the discussion without influencing it. You also need to be able to draw out shy participants and curb exuberant ones. This calls for a measure of skills and you may have to undergo some training before you embark on this method of interviewing to collect data for your research.

TIPS FOR PLANNING AND CONDUCTING FOCUS GROUP INTERVIEWS

Planning a Focus Group Interview

- **Identify participants**: six to ten people is a desirable number, enough to allow diversity among them but not too many as to make the activity unmanageable;
- **Choose the place**: somewhere that is comfortable and that will put the participants at ease; should allow for circular seating; should facilitate electronic recording, either audio or video;
- **Prepare your questions**: A set of open-ended questions relevant to the discussion should be prepared for the moderator; avoid questions that can be answered with 'yes' or 'no'; choose questions that keep the discussion going; prepare probes; start with general questions and move to the more specific ones; prepare closing questions for winding things down;
- **Prepare yourself**: Hone your skills at controlling group discussion, you may want to read up on what skills are needed and practise before the actual interview; ensure that you are knowledgeable in the area of the discussion; study the questions to be asked;
- **Choose an assistant if possible**: This person should be prepared to provide assistance in the background; for example, the assistant should be prepared to arrange the room, set up and monitor equipment, take careful notes, handle refreshments and other incentives you may be offering;

Conducting a Focus Group Interview

- **Before the interview**: Greet participants and put them at ease; establish the general tone of the discussion; try to create a relaxed, fun but purposeful atmosphere; give out name tags (participants can choose what name they want to use); have participants sign any consent forms that you may have; collect any other demographic information that you may need; check the recording equipment;
- **At the start of the interview**: Welcome participants; inform about the purpose of the interview and the proposed length; establish ground rules; you may have an ice breaking activity if you desire; point out the system of recording (you may want to check the equipment again, technology can be very fickle!)

- **During the interview**: Ensure that each participant gets a chance to speak (you may have to subtly encourage shy ones and curb overly eager ones); keep the discussion moving and on track; ask the questions, prompt, probe and ask for clarifications but do not answer the questions yourself; monitor your own body language and reactions (looking shocked and declaring 'lord have mercy!' should be avoided at all costs!); monitor the time; you or your assistant should also keep an eye on the recording equipment (is the red recording light still on?); your assistant should be taking note of the proceedings;
- **At the end**: If you have an assistant, have a debriefing session; write up any additional information that might not be caught on the tape or video that is important to the interview, for example any thoughts or impression you may have about events that occurred; check the quality of the recording; if the quality is poor it is easier to reconstruct the discussion immediately after it has occurred than to have to do so three days later; make arrangements for transcription of the interview.

Observation

Observation involves looking and listening, but whether or not you collect useful data for your research depends on how you look and listen and what you look and listen for. Both quantitative and qualitative research can involve observation, but each methodology uses different ways of recording and using observation data. Let us explore this further.

Observation from a quantitative perspective can be a highly structured activity. Here, the observer can have an instrument made up of a list of behaviours, and can record each time one of the behaviours is observed in the research setting. That way, by the end of the observation period, the research knows how many times each behaviour occurred. Another approach is for the researcher to have a checklist of behaviours and to indicate which of the behaviours were observed, the number of times is not recorded. The problem with these approaches is that the researcher may fail to notice some occurrences of the listed behaviours, or some behaviour not listed may occur and be overlooked, but may be vital to explaining the interactions in the research setting. Another quantitative approach to observation is called systematic observation. With this approach, the researcher has a set of categories of behaviour and for say ten minutes, makes five-second observations. That means that every five seconds, the researcher records the category of behaviour that is occurring, using a coding scheme. There are several existing instruments for this purpose, but perhaps the most widely used one is the Flanders Interaction Analysis System (Flanders, 1970), used for analysing teacher and student interaction in the classroom. Using these instruments calls for training and practice, so if you decide to use them, allow enough time for you and anyone who may be assisting you to develop competence.

Observation from a qualitative perspective tends not to be linked with any structured instrument. The researcher collects data in the form of field notes. So, for instance, you may sit in a classroom to observe what goes on there. You would record in a notebook everything that is going on around you. This could include not only what you see and hear, but also impressions and thoughts that you have as you observe. As with interviewing, you may find it necessary to locate a quiet spot soon after the period of observation to write down other thoughts, impression or comments that might be useful later when you analyse your data. In today's technological age, you might seek permission to use video recording, which would allow you to view the activities on multiple occasions.

In keeping with the positivist inclinations linked with quantitative research, the structured observation activities are underpinned by the notion of the objective observer, who does not interact with or influence the setting being observed. These notions typify non-participant observation. As a non-participant observer, you try to be a 'fly on the wall,' taking no part in the activities in the observed setting. This is sometimes very difficult to accomplish, especially if you are observing small children, who, when in need of assistance while the teacher is busy doing something else, have the tendency to approach the 'other adult' in the room. These little ones can be exceptionally persistent, and you may find it extremely hard to ignore them. Indeed, you might find it necessary to intervene to save them from harm.

The other form of observation is participant observation. As a participant observer, you become a member of the group or part of the setting that you wish to observe. Let us say that you wanted to study the life of exotic dancers for a sociology project. You may get yourself hired as a nightclub bouncer (if you are of the correct size!), or a bartender or even a server. Some 'conscientious' researcher may even get hired as one of the dancers or some other position that would allow you to observe the dancers. Doing participant observation could give rise to ethical issues, some may even be tempted to go into the situation without revealing the true purpose of their presence (covert observation). However, research ethics call for informed participation, which suggests that those being observed as part of a study should be aware of this fact. But even if you do inform the participants that they are being observed (overt observation), there is the question of what you will tell them. You might be faced with several questions, to which there may be no correct answers, only the application of personal ethics. Such questions might include: How much information do you give? Is it lying if you withhold some information? Is there any information that you should not use because it was entrusted to you as a colleague and not as a researcher? When faced with these situations, you must remember that, as a researcher, you are to do no harm to the participants in your research.

As with all forms of data collection, observation has advantages and disadvantages. Let us start with the positive. The greatest advantage of observation as a data collection technique is its directness. You do not have to rely on reports; you can see for yourself what people do and hear what they say. Observation is considered more appropriate than questionnaires or interviews because participants may, deliberately or otherwise, give distorted accounts of their actions and feelings, but with observation, you are able to obtain more accurate information. However, your being there can in fact be a disadvantage of observation. How? Well, the ones being observed may behave differently from what is normal because they are aware of being observed. Hence, to ascertain whether observed behaviour is 'stable', these ones would have to be observed long enough to establish that these are true representations of how these ones would normally behave. Herein lies another disadvantage of observation: it can be time consuming. If you are doing systematic observation, it can also be time-consuming. Time is needed to develop a suitable observation schedule for this purpose, and even if you can use some existing schedule, you must take time to become proficient at using it. So, as said before, if you are going to collect data by observation, give yourself enough time to adequately prepare for and carry out the task.

In this section, we have discussed the three major approaches to collecting research data. You need not feel that you are restricted to using only one approach for any given piece of research. Indeed it is a good habit to practise using multiple data collection approaches. This is in keeping with the notion of triangulation, discussed earlier in the chapter on sampling. Here, triangulation would involve the use of more that one data collection approach in order to obtain a wider perspective of the problem being investigated. Thus, a survey approach may be bolstered by interview data from a small portion of the sample, and/or by observation data. So, whenever possible, use as many data collection approaches as are appropriate.

We have explored approaches for collecting data for your research. Now, we will examine some typical instruments that you can use.

VALIDITY AND RELIABILITY OF DATA COLLECTION INSTRUMENTS

There are several different instruments that you can use to collect data for your research. These include tests, questionnaires, rating scales, attitude scales, checklists, observation schedules and interview schedules. Whichever type of instrument you decide is best for your purpose, you need to check two things: (1) that it is valid and (2) that it is reliable. Let us briefly consider these two concepts as they relate to data collection tools.

Validity

An instrument is valid to the extent that it measures what it is expected to measure or that it collects the data you need to answer your research questions. There are different types of validity for which instruments may be checked. Of course, you do not have to apply all of them to every instrument you are planning to administer. The purpose of the instrument and how it is to be used, will determine which type of validity is appropriate. The thing to remember is that if your instrument is invalid, then so will be your data, your findings and any conclusions that you may draw.

Types of Validity

Face validity refers to the extent to which the instrument looks like those commonly used for the particular purpose for which you are using it. As an example, if you are collecting data by means of a mathematics achievement test, face validity answers the question 'To what extent does this test look like a mathematics test based on this particular content?' Face validity is establish by expert review, that is, you allow someone who has expert knowledge of the area (for example your supervisor) to have a look at the instrument and make a judgement.

Content validity is the degree to which the instrument measures the intended area. For example, if your mathematics test mentioned earlier is supposed to assess students' knowledge of fractions, content validity answers the question 'Do the items included here test fractions or something else?' Content validity can be established by matching the items on the instrument to the intended objectives of the items. Before constructing your mathematics test, you should draw up a table of specifications. A table of specifications is a plan that details the areas to be tested, the level at which they will be tested and the number of items to be included for each area. After you have written the items, you can again have an expert make a judgment as to how well the content of the test matches its purpose.

Construct validity refers to the degree to which the instrument measures the intended theoretical construct. A construct is an intangible characteristic that cannot be observed or measured directly. Constructs must be inferred through verbal or non-verbal behaviour. Therefore you must ensure that your instrument is indeed measuring the desired construct. Construct validity can be established using multiple approaches, namely be investigating convergent validity and discriminant validity. Convergent validity determines how well the instrument measures the desired construct, and is established by ascertaining how well the instrument correlates with other instruments known to measure the desired construct. Discriminant validity verifies that the instrument is not measuring some other construct. It is ascertained by establishing that the instrument has no correlation with instruments that measure different constructs.

Criterion-related validity can take two forms: concurrent validity and predictive validity. The same method is used to determine both forms, with timing being the fundamental difference. Concurrent validity answers the question 'How does the instrument match up with some other (often well-known and well-respected) instrument that measures the same variable?' To determine concurrent validity, the two instruments are administered to some defined group either at the same time or within a short period. The correlation between scores from the two instruments is found. If the correlation coefficient is high, then the test is said to have good concurrent validity.

Predictive validity answers the question of how well the particular instrument can predict performance on some other instrument in the future. For example, most Caribbean territories have an examination, the results of which are used for transferring students from primary to secondary school. You may want to find out how well this examination can predict these students' performance on examinations taken at the end of their course of secondary education (such as on the certification examinations set by the Caribbean Examinations Council). To determine predictive validity, the instrument for which the predictive validity is being established (called the predictor) is administered to a group. There is then a waiting period until the time when the behaviour to be predicted (called the criterion) occurs, and this is measured as well. A correlation is run between the two sets of data. Again a high correlation coefficient is desirable and is an indication that the predictor instrument can indeed predict performance in the future. In case you are wondering how high the correlation coefficient should be, the answer is the higher the better!

Consequential validity determines the extent to which the instrument creates negative consequences for the respondent. This form of validity is perhaps more relevant to tests, which are becoming more and more prevalent, and which may induce negative reactions, such as test anxiety, in the test takers. Hence, consequential validity answers the question 'How does the test affect those involved in its administration?' Consequential validity can be determined through observation, and can help identify instruments that can have a harmful effect on the respondents. It is conceivable that any such effects can influence the quality of the data collected.

Validity is a very important characteristic of any instrument that you will use to collect data. If your instrument is weak in validity, then your data, findings and conclusions will lack credibility. And that would be a shame after all your hard work, wouldn't it. So, save yourself from such horror and ensure that you have a valid instrument.

Reliability

Apart from validity, you also need to ensure that your instrument is reliable. That means that you must verify that the instrument will consistently measure what you intend it to measure, and that similar results will be found if it is administered each time it is administered to a group or similar groups. As with validity, there are different types of reliability, and the type that you apply to your instrument will depend on the purpose of the instrument and how it is to be used. Let us consider some different types of reliability.

Types of Reliability

Stability reliability or test – re-test reliability checks to ascertain if the instrument is stable over time, that is, will similar results be found if the instrument is administered on different occasions? You would apply this reliability test to an instrument that you want to administer on different occasions. To establish stability reliability, you would first administer the instrument to an appropriate sample. Then, a short time later (perhaps a week later), it can be re-administered to the same sample. After scoring the instrument, you would match the participants' scores and run a correlation procedure. If the resulting coefficient is high and positive, then the instrument can be said to have good stability reliability.

Alternate forms reliability or test of equivalence is used to ascertain whether two or more instruments are equivalent, that is, that they are both measuring the same characteristics, even though the actual items may be different. Perhaps the most familiar situation in which alternate forms reliability is appropriate is when you are creating two tests to be used for a pre-test post-test activity. Under these circumstances, you would want to be sure that tests are equivalent, that is, that they are testing the same concepts at the same level. To establish alternate forms reliability, you should first ensure that your tests are constructed according to a planned table of specifications. When this is done satisfactorily, you would then administer both tests to an appropriate sample either at the same time or over a short period of time. The participants' scores are matched and correlated. Again, a high positive correlation coefficient is an indication of good alternate forms reliability.

Internal consistency reliability is a measure of how well the items 'hang' together, that is, whether they are assessing the same characteristic or concept. Two ways of ascertaining this are the split half approach and the Cronbach coefficient alpha. With the split half approach, you divide the items on the instrument into two smaller tests and run a correlation procedure. If the two halves are highly correlated, then you can assume that they are assessing a similar characteristic. In order to work out the reliability for the single test, an adjustment has to be done using the Spearman-Brown formula. The Cronbach coefficient alpha is a measure of how well each item correlates with the other items on the instrument. It is somewhat more complicated to work out, but fortunately, with the advent of computers and data analysis software, it can be easily computed with a few key strokes (of course it helps to know which keys to stroke, but that is not too overwhelming a skill to acquire!). As with the other types of reliability, the degree of internal consistency reliability is given as a coefficient between 0 and 1, the higher the coefficient, the more reliable the instrument. A rule of thumb is that a coefficient between 0.7 and 0.9 is desirable.

Inter-rater reliability is commonly applied to instruments that are to be used in observation, where more than one observer is involved. It provides a measure of how consistently different observers rate the observed entity. This is an indication of the clarity of the instrument itself and the ease with which its intent can be interpreted by its users. To establish inter-rater reliability here, different observers can be asked to use the instrument to rate an entity. The extent to which there is agreement among the ratings assigned is an indication of the inter-rater reliability of the instrument.

Intra-rater reliability answers the question of how consistent the results are if a single observer uses the instrument on multiple occasions. Let us say that you were going to use the instrument in commercial banks over a one month period. The idea is that similar behaviours or events should receive similar ratings each time they occur. You do not want to give a rating of '1' on one occasion and a rating of '4' on another day. This might occur if you are not sure what you are looking for, that is, if the instrument is vague about what you are looking for. To establish intra-rater reliability, the user can be asked to do observations on different occasions (perhaps using a videotaped scene) and the extent to which there is agreement of ratings over time is an indication of the intra-rater reliability of the instrument. It should be evident that using observation tools calls for a period of training to ensure that the data collectors know what they are looking for and understand the criteria for judging observed events.

By now, we hope you are getting the idea that the instrument that you use for collecting data for your research is very important. The quality of the data you collect, and by extension, the quality of your research is dependent on it. So, to ensure that you have high quality instruments, we will offer some guidance and tips about selecting or constructing different kinds of research instruments.

TYPES OF DATA COLLECTION INSTRUMENTS

As mentioned earlier, there are several different kinds of tools that can be used to collect data for your research. We will focus on some that are commonly used, namely questionnaires, rating scales, attitudes scales, interview schedules and observation checklists.

Questionnaires

A questionnaire is a collection of items designed to collect data about a phenomenon from a group of respondents. This is not to be any haphazard group of items, but there must be a common thread: the items should be related to your research topic. Remember the purpose of the questionnaire is to collect data to help you to find answers related to the problem under investigation. Each item on the questionnaire should be linked to your research questions or hypotheses. Constructing a questionnaire then is a purposeful and sometimes difficult task. Here are a few tips to help you to produce an instrument of good quality.

TIPS FOR CONSTRUCTING A QUESTIONNAIRE

1. THE CONTENT

Your questionnaire should deal with a single issue at a time. Once you have identified your research topic, and formulated your research questions, then you have to decide what data you will need in order to answer them. In effect, what you do is to formulate objectives for items on the questionnaire.

You can identify relevant objectives for your questionnaire items from literature read, from casually observing activities related to the phenomenon that you are investigating, and having casual conversations with people who are likely to have information about the phenomenon. This exercise helps you to identify options that are reasonable to include for items where the respondents are required to select a response from a list of possible responses.

It is very useful when constructing a questionnaire to make a list of objectives for the items to ensure that whatever you include has a purpose. These objectives should come out of your research questions. Thus, you should ask yourself, what reasons do I have for constructing this questionnaire? What do I need to find out from the respondents in order to answer my research questions? If you end up with items that will not inform any of your research questions, dump them!!!! Include only relevant items on your questionnaire.

2. THE FORMAT

Generally, items on your questionnaire will be of two broad forms: Open-ended or closed.

Open-ended items, also called supply-type items, are those for which a question is asked and the respondents write their own answers, usually in spaces that you provide. An example of an open-ended item is:

How do you feel about having co-workers with disabilities in your workplace?

Open-ended items are preferable when:
- The researcher does not know all the possible answers to the question;
- There are so many possible answers that to list them all in a select-type item would be cumbersome;
- The researcher wants to avoid suggesting answers to the respondents;
- The researcher wants the respondents to use their words.

There are some advantages of using open items. For instance, they do not restrict the respondent to options that may be, for some of them, superficial. Indeed, they allow the respondents to freely express themselves on the issue that the item addresses. Another advantage of open items is that they can help you to collect rich, in depth data if they are well asked. On the other hand, there are some challenges associated with these item types. Open items for example, are not always easy to code and/or collate, and in fact can be time consuming to compile. You may also find it challenging if you want to categorise the responses because they may turn out to be extremely diverse. Finally, respondents tend to be put off by open items, so it is advisable to use them sparingly, only when the pros of using them far outweigh the cons.

Closed items, also called select-type or multiple-choice items, are those for which the question is asked and the respondents choose their answers from a number of options that are provided. Here are some examples of closed items.

Examples of Closed Items

1. Gender   ☐ Male   ☐ Female

2. Into which age group do you fall?
   - ☐ Under 20
   - ☐ 20–29
   - ☐ 30–39
   - ☐ 40 and over

   [Note that there are no overlapping categories (e.g. 20–30, 30–40). Each number appears in ONLY ONE category.]

3. Does your school have a policy on sexual harassment?
   - ☐ Yes
   - ☐ No
   - ☐ Don't Know

   [Including the 'don't know' option is useful. It takes the pressure to 'say anything' off those respondents who actually do not know.]

4. How often have you done the following activities in the past six (6) months?

Activities	Not at all	Seldom (1-2 times a week)	Sometimes (3 – 5 times a week)	Often (More than 5 times a week)
Left home without eating breakfast	☐	☐	☐	☐
Missed lunch	☐	☐	☐	☐
Had fast food for dinner	☐	☐	☐	☐
Nibbled cookies in bed at night	☐	☐	☐	☐

[Note that the terms 'seldom', 'sometimes', 'often' are defined. This is good practice so that all respondents have the same understanding of these terms.]

5. What types of programmes do you enjoy viewing on television? (Select ALL that apply)

☐ Police dramas
☐ Sitcoms
☐ Documentaries
☐ Science fiction
☐ Sports
☐ Cartoons
☐ Religious programmes
☐ Other: _____

[Such items may be awkward to collate in a database since each option must be dealt with separately. To reduce the awkwardness, you may want to ask the respondents to rank their three favourites types: 1 = most enjoyed; 2 = next best; 3 = third preference. The inclusion of the 'Other' option is useful for those respondents who enjoy none of the types of programmes listed.]

Closed items are preferable when:

- There are large numbers of respondents and questions;
- The responses are to be scored by machine;
- Responses from several groups are to be compared.

Closed items, like the open kind, also have strengths and challenges. Features in their favour include the fact that they tend to be relatively easy to code and collate. In addition, they allow for uniform measurement and hence greater reliability. On the other hand, closed items, if not properly constructed, can collect merely superficial data that contributes to poor quality findings. Further, it is possible that the options provided may not be relevant to some respondents. This possibility can be lessened though by including the 'Other' option which allows the respondents to include an option that is more suitable to them. Closed items may also prove irritating to those respondents who are dissatisfied with the questions asked and who want to express views on the issue, but have nowhere to do so. This risk can be reduced by providing space at the end of the questionnaire for the respondent to make any additional comments that would shed greater light on their feelings, views or beliefs.

Now a word of advice about how you layout your questionnaire. If there are parts of the questionnaire that may not be applicable to some respondents, use routing or filtering instructions. What does that mean? Perhaps this can best be explained with an example.

Question 1: Have you ever used computers as a teaching tool in your classroom?

☐ Yes ☐ No

If YES, go to Question 2   If NO, go to Question 5

Question 2: How many times have you used computers in the classroom this term?

OPTIONS FOR *Question 2 go here*

Question 3: What software did you use?

OPTIONS FOR *Question 3 go here*

Question 4: How satisfied were you with these lessons?

OPTIONS FOR *Question 4 go here*

Question 5: Have you had any training for using computers as teaching tools?

OPTIONS FOR *Question 5 go here*

In the example above, question 1 has routing instructions. These instructions route the respondents who answer NO around questions 2 to 4, which are only relevant to those answering YES on that item. This saves respondents from wasting time on items that are not applicable to them.

Figure 8b, below, offers some advice about construction a questionnaire.

Figure 8b
Pitfalls to Avoid When Constructing Questionnaires (Adapted from Bell, 1993)

- Avoid ambiguity, imprecision and assumptions.
- Avoid items that require the respondent to think far back in case memory fails or can be distorted .
- Avoid items that may ask for information the respondents do not have.
- Avoid double questions. (E.g. Do you smoke or drink? Yes   No)
- Avoid leading questions, often identified by emotive language. (E.g. Do you not agree that women who harass young men in the workplace should be fired?)
- Avoid presuming questions. (E.g. Why do you think children are not doing well in mathematics?)
- Avoid hypothetical questions. (E.g. If you were to inherit 1 million dollars, would you still continue to work?)
- Avoid offensive questions and questions covering sensitive issues. If it is offensive, remove it! If sensitive issues must be addressed, be extra careful with wording.
- Pay attention to the layout of the items. Make sure that they are not cluttered; that the font is readable. Aesthetics count!

Whatever care you might have taken when constructing your questionnaire, do not neglect to PILOT it. Piloting means identifying a sample of respondents who are similar to the ones you intend to include in your research (but who will not be involved in your research) and administering the questionnaire to them. Along with the questionnaire, you should include a cover letter and what we call an evaluation sheet. The cover letter explains the purpose of the questionnaire and how the data will be used, and asks the recipient to participate. The evaluation sheet asks the respondents to comment on the instrument. So, you might ask how long it took them to complete the instrument; whether the instructions and items were clear; if anything was offensive; if options were reasonable; if they felt important issues were adequately covered in the questionnaire or any other question that would help you to refine your instrument. This often neglected task goes a good way to raise the quality of your questionnaire, helping you to produce an instrument that is both valid and reliable. As you can see, constructing a questionnaire takes time. You cannot (or should not) just throw a few questions together the night before you plan to administer it. The data you collect might be absolutely worthless. Our advice, save yourself some grief by taking the time to plan and construct your questionnaire well ahead of the date that you propose to administer it to the research participants.

3. ADMINISTERING THE QUESTIONNAIRE

If you are using a questionnaire to collect data from your research, you have to decide how you are going to get it to the participants. There are several modes: by mail; by telephone; administered by the researcher; by face-to-face interview; and electronically. These have already been discussed earlier in the section dealing with surveying, and you can review them there in Figure 8A. Perhaps this is a good time to mention that questionnaires are most commonly used when the data collection technique is a survey and no doubt you can see why: these instruments provide a quick and relatively inexpensive way of collecting data from a large number of participants.

Sometimes, administering a questionnaire by mail can incur extra costs of which you must be aware. This happens if your return rate is low and you must send reminders to the participants. The cost of sending these reminders (sometimes two or three may be necessary to get the response rate to an adequate level) can put a considerable dent in your funds. Perhaps the trick is to find ways of encouraging the participants to complete and return the questionnaire the first time it is sent!

Besides questionnaires, there are other data collection tools that you should consider. Let us explore some of these.

Rating Scales

A rating scale is made up of the item(s) to be rated and a scale (on a continuum) on which the rating is to be done. The respondents place a mark on the continuum to indicate their rating of the items.

Examples of Rating Scales

How would you rate the training that you received during the workshop?

Very Unsatisfactory								*Very Satisfactory*
1	2	3	4	5	6	7	8	9

If there are many items to be rated similarly, these may be arranged in a matrix form.

Example 2

How would you rate your team leader on the following characteristics?

	Very Unsatisfactory					Very Satisfactory			
Ability to arbitrate	1	2	3	4	5	6	7	8	9
Ability to communicate	1	2	3	4	5	6	7	8	9
Ability to motivate	1	2	3	4	5	6	7	8	9
Ability to lead from the front	1	2	3	4	5	6	7	8	9

Rating scales should be accompanied by clear instructions about how to complete them. Sometimes it may be necessary to define terms and expressions so that respondents can understand what they are rating and the nature of the ratings. Often, rating scales are included on questionnaires and you may decide to do this if it is appropriate.

Attitude Scales

Attitude scales are designed to produce scores that are taken as an indication of the respondents' feelings about an object or event (called the attitude object). There are different types of attitudes scales, the most common of which is the Likert-type scale.

The Likert-type Scale

This type of scale, created by Rensis Likert (1932) is made up of a number of statements about the attitude object, accompanied by a range of responses that reflect different degrees of agreement, the most common being Strongly Agree, Agree, Neutral, Disagree, Strongly Disgree. This represents a 5-point Likert-type scale (some scales may have 7 points).

Construction a Likert-type Scale

Constructing a Likert-type scale can take some time. First you must collect statements about the attitude object from people with a wide range of attitudes towards the object. Then, the statements are assessed by 'judges' to identify those that are clearly positive or clearly negative. Statements that are neutral, ambiguous or borderline are discarded. If the judges cannot agree on whether an item is positive or negative, then it is also discarded. The remaining statements are put together with the selected scale and can then be piloted to find out how well it can discriminate between people with favourable and unfavourable attitudes towards that attitude object.

To score such a scale, positive items may be scored 5 for SA to 1 for SD. Negative items would be scored in reverse order. The respondents' attitude is assessed by summing the scores on the individual items. Thus, the higher the score obtained, the more favourable the attitude ascribed to the respondent.

Example of a Likert-type Scale

CODES:	SA = Strongly Agree; A = Agree, 'Sort of'; U = Not Sure; D = Disagree, 'Sort of'; SD = Strongly Disagree					
1.	I am sure that I can learn math.	SA	A	U	D	SD
2.	My teachers have been interested in my progress in math.	SA	A	U	D	SD
3.	Knowing mathematics will help me earn a living.	SA	A	U	D	SD
4.	I don't think I could do advanced math.	SA	A	U	D	SD
5.	Math will not be important to me in my life's work.	SA	A	U	D	SD
6.	Males are not naturally better than females in	SA	A	U	D	SD
7.	Getting a teacher to take me seriously in math is a problem.	SA	A	U	D	SD
8.	Math is hard for me.	SA	A	U	D	SD

(Excerpt from Modified Fennema-Sherman Attitude Scale for Mathematics http://www.woodrow.org/teachers/math/gender/08scale.html Retrieved: March 17, 2004)

The Semantic Differential Scale

The semantic differential scale, developed by Charles Osgood and his associates, is concerned with 'measurement of meaning.' It consists of a list of bipolar adjectives (e.g. smart – stupid; fast – slow; exciting – dull) about an attitude object. Osgood and his colleagues identified three major categories of meaning when considering an object: value dimension (good – bad), the potency/strength dimension (weak – strong) and the activity dimension (fast – slow). These pairs of adjectives are arranged at the extreme ends of a continuum (usually a 7-point scale). The respondents are required to indicate how they feel about the object by marking an X on the continuum.

(**Example** Smart __: x_:__:__:__:__:__ Stupid)

To construct a semantic differential scale, you could ask people with a range of feelings about the attitude object to generate adjectives that they would use to describe the object. Then you would arrange these in opposing pairs, ensuring that sometimes the positive adjective is given first and sometimes the negative one is. These are then randomly listed with accompanying scales. As with any good measuring instrument, you should pilot the scale to ascertain the extent to which it does the job for which it was designed. It may be necessary to discard any items that are not working on the scale.

A 7-point semantic differential scale may be scored from 1 to 7, going from the negative adjective to the positive adjective. The respondents' total scores are calculated by adding up the scores on the individual items, again with the higher scores indicating more positive attitudes.

Example of scoring items on a semantic differential scale

Smart __:__:__:__:__:__:__ Stupid
    7 6 5 4 3 2 1

Ugly __:__:__:__:__:__:__ Beautiful
    1 2 3 4 5 6 7

To try to identify different dimensions of attitude towards the attitude object, you would have to carry out a factor analysis to assess the relationship between the different adjective pairs.

Example of a Semantic Differential Scale

Instructions: For each pair of adjectives, place a cross (X) at the point between them which reflects the extent to which you believe the adjectives describe your BOSS.

Rude:	____ :	____ :	____ :	____ :	____ :	____ :	Polite
Honest:	____ :	____ :	____ :	____ :	____ :	____ :	Dishonest
Kind:	____ :	____ :	____ :	____ :	____ :	____ :	Cruel
Fair:	____ :	____ :	____ :	____ :	____ :	____ :	Biased
Strong:	____ :	____ :	____ :	____ :	____ :	____ :	Weak
Supportive	____ :	____ :	____ :	____ :	____ :	____ :	Unsupportive
Unreliable:	____ :	____ :	____ :	____ :	____ :	____ :	Reliable
Passive:	____ :	____ :	____ :	____ :	____ :	____ :	Active
Effective:	____ :	____ :	____ :	____ :	____ :	____ :	Ineffective

[Adapted from Robson, C.(1993), p. 265]

There are other less frequently used attitude scales, for example the Thurstone and Guttman scales. If you are interested in using any of these, you can read about them elsewhere. Here we only featured the most commonly used attitude scales. Just remember that whatever attitude scale you decide to use, pay attention to establishing its validity and reliability. The most appropriate form of validity to apply to attitude scales is construct validity, though others may also apply. In addition, internal consistency reliability is usually applicable to such scales.

Thus far, the data collection tools explored are generally associated with surveying. Let us now consider an instrument that you would need for collecting data by interviewing. Earlier, we discussed three different approaches to interviewing: structured, semi-structured and open interviews. For structured interviewing, your instrument would largely be a questionnaire administered face-to-face. For an open interview, your instrument may consist of a list of areas that you would want your respondent to touch on. As was mentioned earlier, you are most likely to use a semi-structured interviewing approach, and so, we are going to explore how to prepare an instrument for such an event.

Interview Schedules

If you are going to collect data by semi-structured interview, then you need to prepare an interview schedule. This consists of a list of areas/issues that you wish to address during the interview, with some key questions related to each area or issue. To construct a schedule, you must first have objectives for addressing the identified areas or issues. These can be taken from your problem and research questions. Before you formulate questions, the important task is to have a sound understanding of what data you need in order to properly investigate your research problem. As an inexperienced researcher, you may want to start by writing down as many questions as you can think of and then discard the ones that are irrelevant or inappropriate. You could then refine or modify the ones you decide to keep.

You should also include on your schedule some prompts. These are notes to yourself that would assist you in gathering rich interview data. Prompts are notes about issues that you want the respondent to address in the interview and that, should they not emerge naturally during the course of the interview, you are going to raise with the respondent. For example, let us say that you were going to interview social workers about their views on factors that contribute to abuse in homes. There are perhaps many factors that these professionals might identify, but you specifically want them to talk about alcohol consumption. You might make a note to yourself to prompt the respondents to give their views on the notion that alcohol consumption is responsible for much of the abuse experienced in homes. During the interview, when you ask that question and the respondent says nothing about alcohol consumption, the prompt would alert you to say something like 'Some of the other social workers interviewed spoke of alcohol consumption as a contributor to the abuse experienced in the home. What is your view on this?'

When you have constructed your interview schedule, it is a good idea to have it reviewed. To do this, have someone knowledgeable in the field (for example your supervisor) examine your research problem, research questions, the objectives of the interview and the interview schedule and make a judgment about the appropriateness of the questions to be asked. Based on the advice you receive, you may decide to discard, modify or retain the questions on the schedule. You may also decide to add other areas or questions to your instrument. Then, as suggested earlier, you should pilot the instrument, that is, practise using it with a small sample. This gives you an idea of how the questions will work. You may discover for example, that the language for some items is ambiguous to respondents. Piloting also gives you an opportunity to practise your interviewing skills, which as was mentioned before, might not come naturally to an inexperienced researcher.

Figure 8c below presents an example of an interview schedule before it was piloted. It was designed to collect data from users of community resource centres about their knowledge of, access to, use of and feelings about computers.

Figure 8c
An Example of an Interview Schedule

INTERVIEW SCHEDULE

A. KNOWLEDGE OF COMPUTERS

Tell me what you know about computers.

What are some places where computers are used?

B. ACCESS AND USE

1. Do you own a computer? (Or have access to one that belongs to someone else?)

2. What do you use the computer for?

3. How often do you use a computer?

C. FEELINGS ABOUT COMPUTERS

1. How do you feel about computers?

2. What do you like to do (best/least) on the computer?

3. What do you like about the computer?

4. What do you dislike about the computer?

D. FEELINGS ABOUT COMPUTERS IN COMMUNITY RESOURCE CENTRES

1. What do you think computers could be used for in resource centres?

2. Would you like to spend more time on the computer in resource centres? (Why/why not?)

3. Many say computers can help people to learn. What do you think?

4. Do you think community members should be asked to pay a fee to use the computers in the resource centres?

Focus group or 'focused interviews' as they were originally called are also a good way of collecting valuable data. A focus group can be defined as a group of interacting individuals having some common interest or characteristics, brought together by a moderator who uses the group and participant's interaction as a way of gaining information. Many social scientists have found focus groups to be useful in understanding people's interests, beliefs and attitudes towards a particular topic or programme. Below we have prepared some tips for planning and conducting focus group interviews.

TIPS FOR PLANNING AND CONDUCTING FOCUS GROUP INTERVIEWS

Planning a Focus Group Interview

- **Identify participants**: six to ten people is a desirable number, enough to allow diversity among them but not too many as to make the activity unmanageable;
- **Choose the place**: somewhere that is comfortable and that will put the participants at ease; should allow for circular seating; should facilitate electronic recording, either audio or video;
- **Prepare your questions**: A set of open-ended questions relevant to the discussion should be prepared for the moderator; avoid questions that can be answered with 'yes' or 'no'; choose questions that keep the discussion going; prepare probes; start with general questions and move to the more specific ones; prepare closing questions for winding things down;
- **Prepare yourself**: Hone your skills at controlling group discussion, you may want to read up on what skills are needed and practise before the actual interview; ensure that you are knowledgeable in the area of the discussion; study the questions to be asked;
- **Choose an assistant if possible**: This person should be prepared to provide assistance in the background; for example the assistant should be prepared to arrange the room, set up and monitor equipment, take careful notes, handle refreshments and other incentives you may be offering;

Conducting a Focus Group Interview

- **Before the interview**: Greet participants and put them at ease; establish the general tone of the discussion; try to create a relaxed, fun but purposeful atmosphere; give out name tags (participants can choose what name they want to use); have participants sign any consent forms that you may have; collect any other demographic information that you may need; check the recording equipment;
- **At the start of the interview**: Welcome participants; inform about the purpose of the interview and the proposed length; Establish ground rules; you may have an ice breaking activity if you desire; point out the system of recording (you may want to check the equipment again, technology can be very fickle!)

- **During the interview**: Ensure that each participant gets a chance to speak (you may have to subtly encourage shy ones and curb overly eager ones); keep the discussion moving and on track; ask the questions, prompt, probe and ask for clarifications but do not answer the questions yourself; monitor your own body language and reactions (looking shocked and declaring 'lord have mercy!' should be avoided at all costs!); monitor the time; you or your assistant should also keep an eye on the recording equipment (is the red 'recording' light still on?); your assistant should be taking note of the proceedings;
- **At the end**: If you have an assistant, have a debriefing session; write up any additional information that might not be caught on the tape or video that is important to the interview, for example any thoughts or impression you may have about events that occurred; check the quality of the recording; if the quality is poor it is easier to reconstruct the discussion immediately after it has occurred than to have to do so three days later; make arrangements for transcription of the interview;

However as with all other techniques there are advantages and disadvantages to using this method. The list below highlights a few of each.

Advantages of Using Focus Groups

- May be one of the few research tools available for obtaining data from children or from individuals who are not particularly literate
- Provide data more quickly and at lower cost than if individuals interviewed separately; groups can be assembled on shorter notice than for a more systematic survey
- Researcher can interact directly with respondents (allows clarification, follow-up questions, probing). Can gain information from non-verbal responses to supplement (or even contradict) verbal responses
- Data uses respondents' own words; can obtain deeper levels of meaning, make important connections, identify subtle nuances
- Results are easy to understand and more accessible to lay audiences or decision-makers than complex statistical analyses of survey data

Disadvantages of Using Focus Groups

- Have less control over group; less able to control what information will be produced.
- Produces relatively chaotic data making data analysis more difficult
- Small numbers and convenience sampling severely limit ability to generalize to larger populations
- Requires carefully trained interviewer who is knowledgeable about group dynamics. Moderator may knowingly or unknowingly bias results by providing cues about what types of responses are desirable

- Uncertainty about accuracy of what participants say. Results may be biased by presence of a very dominant or opinionated member; more reserved members may be hesitant to talk

Thus far, we have talked about instruments that can be used when data are being collected by surveying and interviewing. Let us now consider an instrument that is commonly used during observation: the checklist.

Checklists

A checklist is, as the name suggests, a list of events, behaviours or other characteristics that are of interest to you, the researcher. Again, in order to decide what goes on your checklist, you should have a comprehensive understanding of what is needed to answer your research questions or test your hypotheses, which as before, calls for specified objectives for doing the observation. Here is where the literature related to the area can be useful. It helps you to identify characteristics that are essential to the phenomena in which you are interested. Once you have made up the list, you need to have it validated. As with the interview schedule, you should do this by subjecting it to expert review, that is, having it reviewed by someone knowledgeable in the area. In addition, you should check reliability by applying inter-rater or intra-rater reliability, depending on how it is to be used.

When you are using a checklist to collect data, you have to decide how that should be done. Consider these two common ways. You may decide to check the characteristic on the list if it is observed at anytime during the observation period. Here, the concern is simply to acknowledge that the characteristic was present. There is no interest in the number of times it is observed. The second way is to acknowledge the characteristics every time that it is observed during the observation period. Here you would be noting not only the presence of the characteristic, but also the number of times it was observed. Sometimes, this is important to your research. This notion of the number of times the characteristic is observed can be taken to an even more sophisticated level if you use the systematic observation approach that was discussed earlier. As mentioned before, gaining competence at systematic observation requires high levels of training to properly use the instruments that are involved.

Figure 8d provides an example of an observation checklist. It was designed for observation of mathematics lessons.

There are other data collection tools that can be used along with checklists in order to collect a greater wealth of information. Diaries and journals can be useful. As the researcher making observations, you may want to keep a diary in which you record observations and events that are not on your checklist, but that can help to paint a clearer picture of the events that occurred during the observation period. You may also want to reflect on your observations, noting impressions, things that you may want to pursue further, questions that you may want to ask in another forum, and the like. It is always a good idea to write in your diary or journal as soon as possible after the observation period so that you can capture things as they are fresh in your mind. However you can also use diaries and journals in another way.

Figure 8d
An Example of an Observation Checklist

Class: _____   Teacher:_____
Date:_____   Time:_____
Observer:_____
Topic:_____

Instructions

Observe the teacher and students in the class. When the behaviours on the checklist occur, make a check mark (✔) in the box on the right of the behaviour. This is to be done at each occurrence of the behaviour.

	BEHAVIOURS	OCCURENCES
1.	Teacher uses language appropriate to the ability level of the students.	
2.	Teacher uses inappropriate language.	
3.	Teacher uses questioning to elicit responses from the students.	
4.	Teacher demonstrates new procedures for students where appropriate.	
5.	Teacher uses examples to illustrate points to the students.	
6.	Teacher uses teaching aids appropriate to the topic.	
7.	Teacher provides opportunities for students to ask questions.	
8.	Teacher clarifies points students find difficult.	
9.	Teacher allows time for students to practice skills being taught.	
10.	Teacher demonstrates a sound grasp of the content being taught.	
11.	Teacher involves a wide range of students in the lesson.	
12.	Teacher moves smoothly from one activity to another.	
13.	Teacher provides appropriate practice activities for the students.	
14.	Students ask the teacher questions.	
15.	Students question each other about the material.	
16.	Students work together to solve problems.	
17.	Students volunteer solutions to problems.	
18.	Students are respectful of each other.	

Sometimes you may want data from those you observe relating to their behaviours at the time when you are not observing. For this purpose, you may ask them to keep a diary or journal in which they record the relevant information. Let us say that you wanted to find out about adolescents' reading habits. You may do some observations, but clearly though necessary, that would not be sufficient. These young people would also be reading at times that you cannot observe and in a way that could inform your research. For example, they read at home, on the bus, at the beach, at the library and so on. In order to learn about this activity, you may ask them to keep a record of what they read, the length of time they read and where they read. You may also ask teachers or parents to keep a written record of their reactions to some phenomenon of interest to your research after you have interviewed them on the matter or observed their reactions for a period.

It is worth noting here that the diaries or journals do not have to be commercially made. These can be simple loose leaves, exercise books or anything things else that is appropriate and available at little or no cost. Just ensure that the entries are well documented in terms of date, writer, topic of the entry and the like. It is a good idea to remind the diary/journal writers to make their entries. It is also an excellent idea when dealing with children to collect their records regularly, perhaps once a week. This allows you to get the data before they misplace it and also gives you an opportunity to remind them to continue to make their entries.

TESTS

Testing is a significant approach to collecting data in social research, especially in education, but it is sometimes not given enough prominence as a data collection approach. Indeed there are different kinds of tests that you may use as a researcher. These include personality tests, aptitude tests and of course, achievement tests. Some of these may be pre-existing standardised tests, or you may choose to construct your own. If you decide to use a pre-existing test, remember that you must establish its validity and reliability for the purpose for which you intend to use it, which means that you ought to pilot it before using it for your study. If you are constructing your own test, then you must ensure that it is of a high quality. Guidelines for constructing and validating tests can be found in most introductory testing and measurement textbooks, and it would be worth your while to consult one of these when constructing a test as a data collection instrument for your research. As with all data collection tools, you must make every effort to produce a highly valid and reliable test. If you do not, your findings and conclusions would be questionable. And that is to be avoided at all costs!

SOME FINAL WORDS

Collecting data for research purposes can be a very demanding task. As a researcher, you are constantly making decisions about the best ways of obtaining quality information. Just remember that quality information is tied up with the validity and reliability of the instruments that you use. So always make every effort to establish their characteristics for any data collection tool that you use, and, when reporting your research, always include information about the instruments that you used. When reporting your research methodology, explain your data collection approach, discuss how your instruments were constructed and validated, as well as how their reliability was ascertained. This type of information helps the reader to have confidence in your research findings and conclusions. Finally, as mentioned earlier in this chapter, and in keeping with the notion of triangulation, whenever possible, collect data using multiple methods. This adds rigour to your research.

9

COMPILING AND ANALYSING DATA

INTRODUCTION

The purpose for conducting research is to investigate some phenomenon or problem. Having collected data, your next task is to organise them in a way that allows you to examine them carefully in order to find answers to the questions that you formulated earlier: that is, the data must be compiled. After that, you can apply data analysis techniques. Let us make it clear right here that the positioning of this chapter in the book is not an indication that thoughts about data compilation and analysis should come at the end of the data collection process. On the contrary! You should be thinking about this from the very beginning when you are planning your research. As you decide what data you will need and how you are going to collect them, you should also address the question of how they will be compiled and analysed. Far too often, new and inexperienced researchers spend time planning and administering research instruments, and then, faced with piles of data, ask in desperation 'what do I do with this now?'

Discussing data compilation and analysis is done at this point for teaching purposes. As you learn about the research process and put it into practice, you will find that it is not a linear process, but rather one in which you work on different aspects simultaneously. Now that we have cleared that up, let us offer some guidance and suggestions for compiling and analysing your research data.

COMPILING RESEARCH DATA

The manner in which you compile the data you collect for your research depends of course on the nature of the data. You are fortunate to be doing research in the computer age since there are several pieces of software that you can use for managing and analysing your data, whether they are interview data, field notes, survey data or test scores. So let us talk about compiling your data.

Compiling Interview Data

When we dealt with data collection in chapter 8, we discussed collecting data by means of interviewing. We mentioned that you would have to make decisions about how the interviews would be recorded, whether electronically or manually. Whatever your decision, the data have to be organised in a useful form.

If you recorded your interviews electronically, then transcription should be done. For this purpose, you may use a word processor such as Microsoft® WORD®. Transcription can be done in different ways, depending on how you intend to use the data. You may decide to do verbatim transcription or you may just listen to the audio tape or view the video tape and capture the essence of the interviewee's responses. If you made notes about body language or other factors relating to the interview, you may insert these afterwards in the appropriate places. Each interview should be kept in a separate document, with notes on the interviewee, the time and place at which the interview was conducted, who conducted the interview and any other relevant information. Remember, transcribing interviews can be time consuming, so you should start the transcribing as soon after doing the interview as possible. It can be a daunting task to have several interviews to transcribe at one time. Of course, if you can afford it, you can pay someone to do this job for you. If you recorded the interview manually, you should also transcribe your notes as soon after the interview as possible. This may be even more crucial than if you use electronic recording devices because the fresher the interview is in your mind, the more likely you are to recall other things that you may not have written down at the time.

Remember, when you are compiling interview data, make note of the context of the interview or of any event that occurred during the interview that might have an influence on what was said or done. This could prove extremely useful when you are analysing the data.

Compiling Field Notes

Field notes may be collected when you are collecting data by observation. This is where you write down events, activities and descriptions associated with the phenomenon being observed. As soon as possible after the observation session, you should type up your notes. When doing so, always note any background information that will help to contextualise the notes. You should note where the observation was done, who was present, what time of day it was, where you were in relation to the phenomenon being observed and so on. As said before, this background information is often very helpful once you start to analyse the data.

When compiling field notes, you should try not only to capture what occurred, but also your impressions of what occurred. Sometimes, when you observe something, you have thoughts about it that can take your investigation into other relevant areas. Making note of these thoughts would help you later, perhaps to ask questions or seek other information that can add richness to your research. Also, observation can become subjective, in that each individual may 'see' some things and not others. Recording your impressions could help you later to pinpoint why you zeroed in on some activities and not others.

Compiling Questionnaire Data

When some people think of questionnaire data, they may immediately think of sophisticated procedures for analysis and this can be a turn-off for many. But remember when we were discussing the construction of a questionnaire we mentioned that such an instrument may have different types of items. How you compile the data from a questionnaire often depends on the types of items and the manner in which you intend to use them.

For example, you may have open items where the research participants wrote in their responses. You may want to record these responses 'as is,' that is, exactly as the participant wrote them. You could do this in a word processing programme such as WORD®. However, we have found that using a spreadsheet (such as Microsoft® EXCEL®) can be very helpful. This way, you can set up columns to record relevant data about the participant (such as gender, age, employment status, and so on) that you would have collected on the questionnaire, to be matched with whatever responses were made. This will help later on when you do the analysis, since you could for instance, look at all the responses made by male participants or by participants in a certain age group.

Using a spreadsheet also allows you to go back to the data and perhaps do some categorising (e.g. labelling the responses as positive or negative). This would allow you to ascertain how many of the responses fell into whatever categories you decide to use. Also by having open responses compiled in this way, it makes it easier for you to locate specific responses that you may want to quote later when you report the findings of your research. Again, this adds richness to your research report.

When you are dealing with closed or select items on a questionnaire, it is highly recommended that you compile them in a spreadsheet-like database that would allow you to do your analysis as well. There are several pieces of computer software that are available to you, such as Microsoft® EXCEL®, StatView®, Minitab® and SAS® to name a few. However, we prefer the Statistical Package for the Social Sciences (SPSS®) software. This software allows you to set up a database into which you enter the raw data from your questionnaire. It can then perform several procedures that can help with the analysis of your data. We find this software easy to use and we believe that it is able to run the types of analysis procedures that beginner researchers (and even seasoned ones!) are likely to need.

You should decide how you are going to compile your questionnaire data at the time of designing the instrument. Then you can make preparations by assigning codes to the options of the items presented to the participants. These codes can then be applied in the electronic database. For instance, for the variable 'SEX' you may decide to enter '1' in the database if the respondent is female and '2' if male. These codes can be built into your questionnaire at the design stage. (Yes, we did say that you should be thinking about analysis even when designing your research instrument!). Then, when you prepare your database to accept the data from the questionnaires, you can indicate what the '1' and '2' mean in the column in which you enter the 'SEX' responses.

We recommend that you construct a data dictionary or codebook before you start to set up your database. This is a record of the codes you are going to use for the various items on your instrument. For example, Figure 9a(i) presents the questionnaire items that we met in chapter 8. Let us imagine that we administered this instrument to a sample of individuals and that we want to prepare a database into which we will compile the collected data. Before going to our computer, we can sit down and work out how the data will be coded and entered in SPSS®. Figure 9a (ii) is a data dictionary (or codebook) for the items on our questionnaire. You may recall that in chapter 8 we mentioned that items that required the respondent to 'select all that apply' could prove cumbersome. If you look at the data dictionary, you would see why. Notice that each of the options is coded as a separate variable, thus adding eight variables to the database. You can well imagine that if you include say five of these items each with about six options, that would add 30 variables to your database! This is not to discourage you from using items where the respondent can select multiple options. It is just to make you aware of the impact it will have on the size of your database, thus allowing you to make informed decisions when deciding on the format of your questionnaire items.

Figure 9a
Example of Questionnaire Items and the Corresponding SPSS® Data Dictionary or Codebook

(i) Questionnaire items

1. Sex ☐ Male ☐ Female

2. Into which age group do you fall?

☐ Under 20
☐ 20 – 29
☐ 30 – 39
☐ 40 and over

3. How often have you done the following activities in the past six (6) months?

Activities	Not at all	Seldom (1-2 times a week)	Sometimes (3 – 5 times a week)	Often (More than 5 times a week)
(a) Left home without eating breakfast	☐	☐	☐	☐
(b) Missed lunch	☐	☐	☐	☐
(c) Had fast food for dinner	☐	☐	☐	☐
(d) Nibbled cookies in bed at night	☐	☐	☐	☐

4. What types of programmes do you enjoy viewing on television? (**Select ALL that apply**)

☐ Police dramas
☐ Sitcoms
☐ Documentaries
☐ Science fiction
☐ Sports
☐ Cartoons
☐ Religious programmes
☐ Other: _____

5. Does your company have a policy on sexual harassment?

☐ No
☐ Yes
☐ Don't Know

6. How many siblings do you have? _____

(ii) Data Dictionary (Codebook)

Item No.	Variable Name	Type	Width: Decimal Place	Variable Label	Values / Labels	Missing	Measure
1	sex	Numeric	8 : 0	Sex of the respondent	1 – Male 2 – Female	9999	Nominal
2	age	Numeric	8 : 0	Age group of the respondent	1 – Under 20 2 – 20 – 29 3 – 30 – 39 4 – 40 & over	9999	Ordinal
3a	no_bfast	Numeric	8 : 0	Left home without eating breakfast in past 6 months	1 – Never 2 – Seldom 3 – Sometimes 4 – Often	9999	Ordinal
3b	no_lunch	Numeric	8 : 0	Missed lunch in the past 6 months	1 – Never 2 – Seldom 3 – Sometimes 4 – Often	9999	Ordinal
3c	fastfood	Numeric	8 : 0	Had fast food for dinner in the past 6 months	1 – Never 2 – Seldom 3 – Sometimes 4 – Often	9999	Ordinal
3d	cookies	Numeric	8 : 0	Nibbled cookies in bed at night in the past 6 months	1 – Never 2 – Seldom 3 – Sometimes 4 – Often	9999	Ordinal
4a	p_dramas	Numeric	8 : 0	Enjoys viewing police dramas on TV	0 – No 1 – Yes	9999	Nominal
4b	sitcoms	Numeric	8 : 0	Enjoys viewing situation comedies on TV	0 – No 1 – Yes	9999	Nominal
4c	document	Numeric	8 : 0	Enjoys viewing documentaries on TV	0 – No 1 – Yes	9999	Nominal
4d	sci_fi	Numeric	8 : 0	Enjoys viewing science fiction on TV	0 – No 1 – Yes	9999	Nominal
4e	sports	Numeric	8 : 0	Enjoys viewing sports on TV	0 – No 1 – Yes	9999	Nominal
4f	cartoons	Numeric	8 : 0	Enjoys viewing cartoons on TV	0 – No 1 – Yes	9999	Nominal
4g	religion	Numeric	8 : 0	Enjoys viewing religious programmes on TV	0 – No 1 – Yes	9999	Nominal
4h	tv_other	Numeric	8 : 0	Enjoy viewing other programmes on TV	0 – No 1 – Yes	9999	Nominal
5	harass	Numeric	8 : 0	Company has a policy on sexual harassment	0 – No 1 – Yes 2 – Don't know	9999	Nominal
6	siblings	Numeric	8:0	No. of Siblings	---	9999	Scale

Hence you can see that one item on the questionnaire can yield several variables in your database, and for each variable in your SPSS® database there is certain information you will need for setting up the database. The main ones are shown in the data dictionary above. Here is a brief explanation of each of these.

Variable name: this is the code name that you are going to use for the variable name. It may be restricted to eight characters. Though it can include a number, it must begin with a letter of the alphabet. It should have no special characters (e.g. *, /, -, ') and no spaces. Only the underscore character (_) can be used (e.g. no_bfast). You should try to choose a variable name that is descriptive of the data.

Type: In SPSS® you can enter different types of data (different formats). These include numeric (numbers), string (alphanumeric), dates and currency. You need to indicate the nature of the data you are going to be entering for each variable. The default type is numeric, that is, it is automatically set up to receive numbers.

Decimal places: The default value for Width is 8. There is usually no need to change this unless the variable has very large values. SPSS® also allows you to indicate the number of decimal places you want to be displayed. We recommend '0' unless you specifically want to use decimals. These are shown in two separate areas when you are setting up your SPSS® database.

Variable Label: This allows you to write a longer description for your variable. With only eight characters for the variable name you may have to use some odd-looking names. Writing a longer description ensures that anyone looking at your database (or even you looking at it some time later) will know what the variable is.

Values: These are the codes that you will use to represent the options presented on the questionnaire; that is, indicating what the numbers used for each variable mean. Not all variables will have value labels as there are instances where the numbers are not used as labels. Values indicate the actual amount of the thing being measured by the variable. For example Item 6 on the questionnaire has no value. The number entered in the database will be the actual number of siblings that the respondents indicate.

Missing: SPSS® allows you to specify a code that you will use to indicate that the data are missing. Data may be missing for several reasons, the most common being non-response from the individual who completed the instrument. If you do not specify a code, SPSS® will still interpret a blank space as missing data. It is not absolutely necessary for you to do anything in this column in the SPSS® database.

Measure: This refers to the level of measurement of the particular variable. This is an important concept because it has bearing on the types of analysis procedures that you can perform on the data. SPSS® allows you three choices:

Nominal – The numbers are just labels for grouping purposes; no order is indicated. E.g. 1 = Female, 2 = Male.

Ordinal – The numbers are labels for grouping purposes; there is inherent order, but the intervals between consecutive numbers are not equal. E.g. 1 =10–19 years; 2 = 20–29 years;   3 = 30–39 years

Scale – This includes two levels of measurement, interval and ratio. The differences between these two are explained later when we introduce quantitative data analysis. The numbers here represent actual quantities of the variable measured rather than labels. e.g. actual age in years; scores on a test; time (in minutes) taken to perform a task.

In SPSS®, setting up the database by applying the data dictionary is done on a page called 'variable view.' Figure 9b(i) shows what that page looks like. After setting up your database, you can then compile the responses given on the questionnaire. In SPSS®, this

Figure 9b (i)

SPSS Data Editor — Variable View (Example for RM Book)

	Name	Type	Width	Decimals	Label	Values	Missing	Columns	Align	Measure
1	idno	Numeric	8	0	Questionnaire ID No.	None	None	8	Right	Nominal
2	sex	Numeric	8	0	Sex of the respondent	{1, Female}	9999	8	Right	Nominal
3	age	Numeric	8	0	Age group of the respondent	{1, Under 20}	9999	8	Right	Ordinal
4	no_bfast	Numeric	8	0	Left home without eating breakfast in the past 6 months	{1, Never}	9999	8	Right	Ordinal
5	no_lunch	Numeric	8	0	Missed lunch in the past 6 months	{1, Never}	9999	8	Right	Ordinal
6	fastfood	Numeric	8	0	Had fast food for dinner in the past 6 months	{1, Never}	9999	8	Right	Ordinal
7	cookies	Numeric	8	0	Nibbled cookies in bed at night in the past 6 months	{1, Never}	9999	8	Right	Ordinal
8	p_dramas	Numeric	8	0	Enjoys viewing police dramas on TV	{0, No}	9999	8	Right	Nominal
9	sitcoms	Numeric	8	0	Enjoys viewing situation comedies on TV	{0, No}	9999	8	Right	Nominal
10	document	Numeric	8	0	Enjoys viewing documentaries on TV	{0, No}	9999	8	Right	Nominal
11	sci_fi	Numeric	8	0	Enjoys viewing science fiction on TV	{0, No}	9999	8	Right	Nominal
12	sports	Numeric	8	0	Enjoys viewing sports on TV	{0, No}	9999	8	Right	Nominal
13	cartoons	Numeric	8	0	Enjoys viewing cartoons on TV	{0, No}	9999	8	Right	Nominal
14	religion	Numeric	8	0	Enjoys viewing religious programmes on TV	{0, No}	9999	8	Right	Nominal
15	tv_other	Numeric	8	0	Enjoys viewing other programmes on TV	{0, No}	9999	8	Right	Nominal
16	harrass	Numeric	8	0	Company has a policy on sexual harassment	{0, No}	9999	8	Right	Nominal
17	siblings	Numeric	8	0	Number of siblings	None	9999	8	Right	Scale

Figure 9b (ii)

SPSS Data Editor — Data View (Example for RM Book) with column headers: idno, sex, age, no_bfast, no_lunch, fastfood, cookies, p_dramas, sitcoms, document, sci_fi, sports, cartoons is done on a page called 'data view'. Figure 9b (ii) shows what that page looks like. There are several reference books which can help you with the setting up of an SPSS® database.

Any numerical data for which you want to run statistical analysis can be compiled in an electronic database such as SPSS®. Responses from attitude scales, rating scales, scores from tests and such like can be compiled in an SPSS® database. From such a database, you can run simple descriptive analysis or more sophisticated procedures. However before that, you must ensure that your data are carefully compiled and that you check them for errors. Errors can include inappropriate responses from participants and/or data entry errors. There are some data cleaning procedures that you can apply. You can read about these in books that teach you to use the software.

After compiling your data, whether from interviews, observation or questionnaires, and having checked to eliminate errors, the next step is to do your analysis. In the next section, we will make some suggestions for analysing your data.

ANALYSING RESEARCH DATA

Many an inexperienced researcher has fallen into depression or become extremely manic when faced with the task of analysing data collected. There is no need for this. Just remember that the purpose of data analysis is to find answers to the research questions that you formulated when you conceptualised the study. The type of analysis that you use will depend on several factors. These include:

- The paradigm that informed your research approach (is qualitative or quantitative analysis appropriate?)
- The nature of your research questions
- The nature of the data collected (some forms of data cannot be appropriately subjected to certain kinds of analysis)
- The manner in which the data were collected
- Your own skills and/or those to which you have access.

You should bear these factors in mind when deciding how to analyse your data. Too often, inexperienced researchers are tempted to run all kinds of data analysis procedures just to impress others. Do not allow this to happen to you. Do not waste time and energy running analyses because you (or your supervisor) think that they look fancy. If it is not the best way or an appropriate way of interrogating your data then do not do it. This is especially true for quantitative data analysis procedures.

Another misconception that some inexperienced researchers have relates to both quantitative and qualitative analysis. Some believe that whenever numbers are present, then it is quantitative analysis, that is, that there should be no numbers in qualitative analysis. This is not necessarily the case. It is not the presence of numbers that make analysis quantitative, but how the numbers are being used. Consider this illustration:

An inexperienced researcher doing a study for a Bachelor of Science degree in the social sciences interviewed 25 individuals. When she analysed the data, she found that a number of the interviewees expressed similar views on some of the issues that she explored. In reporting this, she used expressions such as 'a few of the respondents...' and 'many of the respondents....' When asked why she did not say how many since the number of interviewees was so small, she indicated reluctance to use numbers because her analysis was supposed to be qualitative, and she felt that including numbers would make it less so. Thus rather than writing for example 'six of the respondents...' or '24 per cent of the respondents...,' she chose to use the vague terms indicated above.

What you need to remember is that numbers are not taboo in qualitative analysis. Rather, it is drawing conclusions based on statistical analysis that renders analysis quantitative. So, next time you hear someone say 'I hate maths and numbers so I am going to do qualitative research,' do set them straight. You would be doing them a great favour and helping to negate a misconception.

So, the question is then, what are some common, useful approaches to analysing data? Let us look at a few. First we will consider some qualitative techniques by exploring the analysis of narrative data. Then we will examine some quantitative techniques.

Analysing Narrative Data

As with most things in research, there are several ways of analysing narrative data. We shall mention a couple of them here. However, you must choose the approach that best serves your purpose. A key part of analysing narrative data is to read and re-read several times. This helps you to acquire a thorough knowledge of the data and for you to get insights into the kinds of issues and features that may be highlighted. Doing this also gives you a feel for what might be the best way to analyse your data and present your findings. Here, narrative data would include responses to interviews (semi-structured or open) and those supplied by participants on open-ended questionnaire items.

A relatively simple approach to analysing such narrative data is by question asked. This means that you examine all the responses to a particular question to find patterns, trends, commonalities and differences among the various responses. Next to each response you may have a column in which you write comments or codes as you analyse the data. Figure 9c below gives an example of data compiled from a questionnaire. Some secondary students were asked whether they thought computers would be helpful for learning mathematics, and to give reasons for their responses.

Figure 9c

An Example of How Narrative Data May be Analysed for Patterns, Trends, Commonalities and Differences

ID	SCH	FORM	SEX	RESPONSE	Codes
1	SCH 1	4	f	Yes. I think it would help me because the computer is more modern and knows more, because you can see how every other country does their maths.	Positive
2	SCH 1	4	f	Yes. I strongly agree it would help me. I guess it would set down the problems and go through the steps one at a time.	Positive
6	SCH 1	4	f	I do not think it can help me in mathematics because when I am doing mathematics I have to use paper. And I am not familiar with the keys.	Negative
62	SCH 1	4	m	I think that computers are good for helping with school work and I like computers because I can talk to other people on the internet which is fun to do. I would not really use it (at) school all the time because sometimes I like to study my school work.	Positive
64	SCH 1	4	m	I could put a software programme in the computer and be able to go at my own pace and it wouldn't make you feel bad and you wouldn't get fed up and mad and when I have done with the disk I would take it home with and work with it.	Positive
65	SCH 1	4	m	I would like to work with a computer in a math class because it would help me with my work that I can't figure out.	Positive
148	SCH 1	1	m	I don't believe that because I want to learn myself.	Negative
154	SCH 1	1	m	I do not have to use a computer to do mathematics because my mind is very good for mathematics.	Negative
159	SCH 1	1	m	I think that using computers in maths classes would be very good because when there are problems in maths the computer would be there to help you find the answer. A computer is very helpful.	Positive
163	SCH 1	1	m	I think computers will help us in mathematics. It would be easy to count and add and subtract.	Positive
165	SCH 1	1	m	We should not use computers for maths because you would not have a brain for yourself. No it could never agree because you need to think for yourself.	Negative
167	SCH 1	1	m	I think that it is a good idea to put computers in school because it would help you to learn how to use computers and it will help you with your mathematics.	Positive
170	SCH 1	1	m	The computer will be good in a maths class and it would help me out in my work all the time.	Positive
173	SCH 2	4	f	I have no problem using a computer in mathematics because it would only be like a tool like a calculator, and I understand that it cannot think for you, it is only there to guide you and help you.	Positive

Figure 9c (cont.)

ID	SCH	FORM	SEX	RESPONSE	Codes
175	SCH 2	4	f	I don't think that computers should be used to aid math because mathematics is a subject which challenges the mind and computers would not give the person the opportunity to do so.	Negative
183	SCH 2	4	f	I think that it is an okay idea but there are limitations. I agree that they would get the work done faster and accurately but you can't have the computers doing all the work. You have to think sometimes on your own and if this is introduced I know that it might lead to people depending on the computer to do simple math work for them.	Ambivalent
184	SCH 2	4	f	Yes, I agree that the computer should be used in mathematics because the graph work is readily done for you. Most computers have a scientific calculator set in it, and it would cut down the cost for parents.	Positive
185	SCH 2	4	f	I do not think computers should be used in mathematics because it will be confusing and a difficult task. Actually to tell you the honest truth I do not know why it should not be used it just don't seem right.	Negative
264	SCH 2	4	m	I do not think a computer should be used in mathematics. Reasons for this are when children get accustomed to using computers in this subject when the time come for them to work without the assistance of a computer they would find it very hard to get the work done. Also I doubt you would be able to use computers in the CXC mathematics exam so it would make no sense training children to use a computer when they can't use it at CXC.	Negative
268	SCH 2	1	f	No. I think it may not be a good idea because if it was supposed to help and give you the answers it would not help me to learn. Yes. If you were doing it yourself without answers and (it) might help you with a problem that you don't understand (like give you an example and then you would follow it). It would be alright.	Ambivalent
283	SCH 2	1	f	Yes, I think computers should be used in maths because using the computer itself, will make the lesson very exciting.	Positive
285	SCH 2	1	f	Yes because it would be easier on our brains to remember the times table from one to 16.	Positive
286	SCH 2	1	f	Yes I think computers should be used in maths because there are some children who can't get through with some of the problems and there are certain things people can't always understand in maths.	Positive

After compiling the data in perhaps an EXCEL® database, these responses should be read several times and codes added. The codes indicate whether the response is a positive one or negative. The reasons given can also be coded, since students gave different reasons for their responses. In the end, the researcher could identify the percentage of the sample who felt that computers would be useful for learning and the percentage who felt otherwise. In addition, by taking all the positive responses, the researcher could then explore the kinds of reasons given. A similar thing could likewise be done with the negative responses. This exploration could give insight into the students' knowledge about computers as tools for learning, as well as their feelings about having to use computers in mathematics classrooms. The researcher could also learn if the students have misconceptions about what computers can and cannot do.

In order to make your analysis more useful, you could decide to explore differences of opinion among students with different characteristics. You may try to ascertain whether girls and boys differ in the views, or whether older and younger students differ. The sample includes students from two different schools. If these schools serve students with different characteristics, then you may also want to explore the responses by school. This kind of exploration can sometimes bring wholly unexpected and startling revelations to light. Finding out these things can help the researcher to come to conclusions and make appropriate recommendations based on evidence.

Apart from analysing narrative data by focusing on responses to specific questions, you could also analyse by broad themes or issues. Using this approach, you would identify a theme or issue and then search the data for instances in which references were made to that theme or issue. This approach is suitable when the data were collected by interview, where the questions may not have been asked in exactly the same way, but the same issues were explored. This allows you to find out the views of the different respondents by identifying places where they addressed the theme or issue under consideration.

For this type of analysis, you may identify the themes of issues beforehand, and then as you read and re-read the interview data, use a coding system to indicate where the respondent touched on each of them. We have used colour coding as well as notes in the margins of the transcribed interviews. If you are coding on the computer, highlighting text in different colours is helpful. If you are reading from a hard copy, then coloured pens will do just as well. As you may well imagine, this can become very complex at times. You may therefore want to explore using computer software to help you. Yes, there are pieces of computer software that can help with the coding and analysis of narrative data. These include NVIVO and ATLAS. Before you get beside yourself thinking that the software will do the analysis for you, be warned, it will not! Generally, this software helps you with the coding and organising of your data, but you still have to read and re-read the data and decide what codes to apply to which data. Yes, you have to do the thinking! With the software you can retrieve data and move them around with greater ease. Some of this software is expensive and you would have to take some time to learn how to use it, but if you can convince your institution to invest in it, then go for it!

Of course with data from focus groups, you must not only identify trends and themes and patterns, you must also consider the context in which the comments were made. In other words, you should not isolate the statements of an individual. These statements were made in light of a discussion and the flow of conversation that led to them is important.

There may be times when you do not have any themes or issues identified beforehand. In these instances, you may want to read and re-read the data and as you do so, themes and issues emerge. As they do, you can code them in much the same way as described above. This is an interesting and sometimes complex way of analysing narrative data. It is often used by students pursuing higher degrees, whose research is designed to develop theory based on evidence. This is referred to as grounded theory. Looking at this approach in depth is outside of the scope of this book, but if you are interested in pursuing it, we recommend that you read Glaser and Strauss (1967).

We described in detail a couple of relatively simple approaches to analysing your narrative data. These would definitely be useful to inexperienced researchers at any level. However, depending on the level of the qualification you are seeking to acquire, you may need to carry out more sophisticated analysis of your narrative data. For example, you may consider applying discourse analysis.

Discourse analysis involves the study of how humans use language to communicate (sometimes implicitly), with special attention to how the senders (e.g. speakers, writers) of messages construct messages for the receiver (e.g. hearers, readers). It also involves analysing how the receivers of the messages process the messages in order to interpret them. With discourse analysis, your task is to examine the language used for clues that could shed light on the situations of the one communicating. The way a person answers a question can be influenced by their relationship with others, can reveal something about their level of education, the community from which they originate, and other characteristics that can help to explain why they behave the way they do, or why they say the things that they say.

Discourse analysis can be used on several types of materials. For instance, transcripts of audio or video taped talk (e.g. interviews, conversations, and other verbal interactions), written documents (e.g. diaries, journals, letters), text transmitted by oral traditions (e.g. proverbs, folktales and folk songs) and printouts of online communication (e.g. email and chat). If you decide to carry out discourse analysis, Johnstone (2002) suggests that there are three basic questions that you should consider, namely:

- Why is this text the way it is?
- Why is it no other way?
- Why these particular words in this particular order?

To answer these questions, you need to think about issues such as:

- What is the text about.
- Who said it, or who wrote it or signed it.

- Who the intended audience was.
- Who the actual hearers and readers are.
- What motivated the text?
- Is the language used consistent with what is common in the setting or context of the community?

For discourse analysis, these considerations are important since clearly what a person is talking about as well as who is present and who is the intended audience, influences what is said and how it is said.

Discourse analysis can be fascinating and very revealing, but somewhat complex. However you should not be intimidated by it. If you are seriously interested in pursuing it, you should read on it extensively. We recommend Johnstone (2002) as a good starting point.

ANALYSING NUMERICAL DATA

Earlier we talked about compiling your data in a database. We recommended using SPSS® software. Once this is done, you are almost ready to run your analyses. However, before we introduce you to data analysis techniques, there are some basic concepts with which you need to come to grips. The first of these is the concept of levels of measurement.

There are four levels of measurement. This just means four different scales on which variables can be measured. The four levels are nominal, ordinal, interval and ratio.

Nominal scale – Numbers on this scale are used like names or labels in the same way that a number on a cricketer's shirt is used. These can be used for labelling categories.

> Hence, if we wanted to classify persons by gender, females could be designated '1' and males '2.' Arithmetic calculations with these numbers would be meaningless. As said earlier, they are used for categorisation or grouping purposes.

Ordinal scale – Numbers on this scale tend to indicate order. However, as pointed out earlier, the intervals between consecutive ranks are not necessarily equal.

> For example, on our questionnaire (page 126), for the variable age, '1' indicates that the respondent is in the Under 20 age group, '2' indicates that the respondent is in the 20–29 age group, '3' indicates that the respondent is in the 30–39 age group and '4' indicates that the respondent is in the 40–49 age group. A 16-year-old would be designated a '1,' a 27-year-old a '2' and a 31-year-old a '3.' From this we know that the respondent with the '1' is younger than the person with a '2' and the one with a '3' is older then the others. Hence the inherent order. However, there is an 11-year difference between the person with the '1' and the one with a '2,' but only a four year difference

between the individuals with the '2' and the '3.' Thus, measurement on the ordinal scale indicates rankings, where there is no fixed interval between the ranks. As with numbers on the nominal scale, arithmetic computations with numbers on the ordinal scale would be meaningless.

Interval scale –   Numbers of the interval scale indicate the actual amount of the thing that the variable is measuring. For measures on this scale, the intervals between consecutive numbers are equal, so that the interval between 1 and 2 is the same as the interval between 2 and 3. (As you can see, this is different from the example we looked at for numbers on the ordinal scale!) Thus, the numerals used are real numbers, not category codes, and as such, we can perform arithmetic operations on the data – add, subtract, multiply and divide. However, on the interval scale, there are arbitrary zero points rather than a true or absolute zero. In other words, a score of zero on the interval scale does not mean a total absence of the characteristic being measured. To illustrate: a sample of individuals may be asked to indicate for a number of items their feelings towards an object on a scale from 0 to 4. Their attitudes towards the object may then be measured by summing their score on each item. Let us say Respondent A selected all zeros, giving an overall attitude score of 0. Does this mean that Respondent A has no attitude towards the object? Not at all! Perhaps if different items were used there may have been a score! Thus the score 0 does not mean an absence of attitude. Because there is no absolute zero, there are some restrictions on how we can interpret the scores. For example, we can say that a score of 15 is ten points more than a score of 5, but we cannot say that a person who scores 15 has three times the attitude of someone scoring 5. To make the latter statement, there must be an absolute zero.

Ratio scale –   Measurement on the ratio scale is similar to that on the interval scale, except that there is an absolute zero. Thus on our questionnaire above, the variable 'siblings' is measured on the ratio scale. If a respondent answers 0, this indicates a total absence of siblings, that is, the respondent is an only child. Also, a person reporting 4 siblings has two times as many siblings as someone reporting 2. Thus we can describe the relationship between the number of siblings in ratio form: 2 to 1.

Variables measured on the nominal and ordinal scales are also called categorical or discrete. They are often used to group members of the research sample according to the characteristics the variables are measuring. For instance, if the variable is measuring sex, then the data collected can be used to group the sample as either males or females. Being able to do this allows us to explore characteristics of male participants and female participants and if it is appropriate, to determine if these two groups differ. Variables that are measured on the interval and ratio scales are said to be continuous. Such variables can take on values on a continuum between two extremes. This means that they can take on fractional values, unlike discrete variables which can only take on whole numbers. SPSS® software treats measurements on the interval and ratio scale in the same way. This is because the difference between these two levels of measurement (the presence or absence of an absolute zero) is not important in the analysis of data in the social sciences. In fact, as indicated earlier, these two levels are combined and labelled as 'Scale' measurement for that software and some textbooks simply group them under the heading 'interval.' These measurement scales are very important in statistical analysis of data because some statistical tests have minimum level of measure requirements. This is linked to concepts of parametric and non-parametric procedures which will be dealt with in chapter 11.

Now that you have been introduced to these levels of measurement, we can move on to the quantitative data analysis procedures. We will explore two types of statistical procedures, descriptive and inferential. The former will be introduced in the next chapter and the latter will be presented chapter 11.

10

DESCRIPTIVE STATISTICS

INTRODUCTION

As the name suggests, descriptive statistics are used to describe the characteristics of a data set or to describe relationships between variables. They tend to be used to summarise the data set. This makes presenting and interpreting your data much more manageable. As you work your way through this chapter, remember that you should be aiming for conceptual understanding. Do not become too bogged down with any mathematics that is included. With the introduction of data analysis software, the mathematics are taken care of behind the scenes (you will develop great respect for software writers!), done at your request by clicking on buttons. Your task is to understand what procedures are to be done under which circumstances so that you can click on the appropriate button. So relax, deep breath, let's go!

SUMMARISING DATA

Descriptive statistics involving only one variable are said to be univariate; those involving two variables are called bivariate, while those involving more than two variables are called multivariate. Why use descriptive statistics? Perhaps an illustration will provide an answer. Let us say that you asked 50 people to select the colour that they like best from Red (R), Blue (B) and Green (G).

Let us assume that the responses you recorded are shown in Figure 10a.

Figure 10a

```
R B B B G R B G R B
R B G G B R G B B G
G R R B B B R G R R
B G G B R R B G B B
G B R R B R G G B R
```

Now suppose you want to answer questions such as which colour is most popular, or least popular, or how many more people select one colour over another colour. Looking at the data set you can see that you could answer these questions, but you would have to count in the set very often. Now these are only three colours and a sample of 50. What if there were 12 colours and a sample of 500? It becomes difficult. However, by summarising the data first, you can answer these and other questions with very little difficulty.

Consider this other illustration: Suppose you measured the pulse rate of 20 men and 20 women for a study of fitness levels. Let us say your results are as shown in Figure 10b.

Figure 10b

Sex	F	F	F	M	M	F	M	F	M	F
Beats/min	76	70	78	74	82	90	76	78	69	71
Sex	F	F	M	F	M	M	F	F	M	M
Beats/min	75	80	84	82	76	98	96	78	88	74
Sex	M	M	F	F	M	M	M	F	F	M
Beats/min	70	72	88	79	69	94	78	78	76	92
Sex	F	M	F	F	M	M	F	F	M	M
Beats/min	76	86	88	76	72	74	78	70	88	70

In comparing the levels of fitness of the males and females in the sample it is difficult to just use the above raw data. To make the data more useful, you would have to find appropriate ways of summarising them.

These two illustrations provide examples of the usefulness of descriptive statistics. So, let us look at some descriptive procedures.

Frequency Distributions

This univariate procedure involves summarising a single data set by using counts or percentages. Let us say we conducted a study with a sample of 250 students at the University of the West Indies Cave Hill Campus, and one item asked the students to indicate the faculty in which they were registered.

In order to make greater sense of the data collected, it may be summarised in a frequency distribution such as the one shown in Figure 10c.

Figure 10c
Example of a Frequency Distribution

Faculty	No. of Students	Per cent
Humanities & Ed	62	25%
Law	41	16%
Science & Tech	69	28%
Social Sciences	78	31%
Total	**250**	**100%**

With the data presented in this summarised form, it is much easier to use it to learn about the characteristic of faculty as it relates to the sample of students. Thus we can easily see that the largest proportion of the students was registered in the Faculty of Social Sciences, and the smallest proportion in the Faculty of Law.

The procedure for constructing a frequency distribution can be found in any elementary statistics text, but if you are using SPSS®, you can generate one with a few simple clicks of your mouse. Click on <Analyse>, <Descriptive Statistics> and select <Frequencies…> and follow the directions on your screen. You need not memorise this if you intend to purchase any of the recommended SPSS® texts.

Graphical Summaries

Sometimes presenting your data in numerical form does not have the impact that you would wish, and it may be better to use a picture to do so. For this purpose, you may want to use a graphical representation. There are several different types of graphs from which you may choose. These include line graphs, bar graphs, and pie graphs. You would have met these before in your mathematics classes (and probably felt that you would never need them outside of maths!). Again, SPSS® can generate a variety of graphs. These can be found by selecting <Graphs> from the main menu. If you know how, you can generate a frequency table in SPSS®, transfer it to EXCEL® and create your graph in EXCEL®. This is what we do because we prefer the appearance of the EXCEL® graphs over the SPSS ones. Figure 10d presents illustration of graphs generated from the frequency distribution above.

Figure 10d
Examples of Graphical Summaries of Data

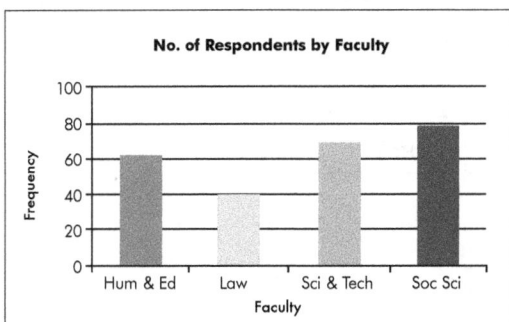

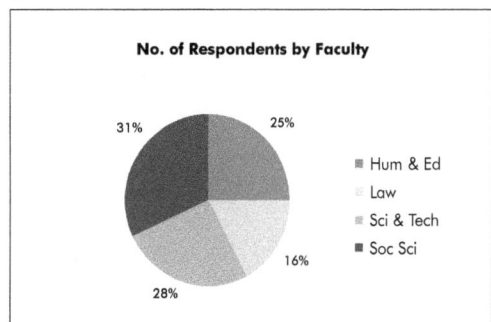

Frequency distributions and graphical representations are used primarily for categorical data (from variables measured on the nominal and ordinal scales). These forms of data summarisation can also be used for interval (remember this also includes ratio) data. However, you may have to group the data first to create categories. For example, if you asked respondents to write their ages in years, to display this variable (age) in a frequency distribution or graphically, you may have to group the data as follows: 20 years & under; 21–40 years; 41–60 years; 61–80 years. You can imagine why this is so, since the range of ages could be so wide and the frequency for the individual ages may be so small that the distribution may be unwieldy. Hence, grouping may be necessary. This changes the variable from a continuous one to a discrete (categorical) one. Let us now explore some of the univariate descriptive analysis that can be done with continuous data.

Measures of Central Tendency

Think back to our example about the study in which the pulse rate of a sample was taken. If you look back at that data you will remember that it was difficult to really say much about them as they were presented. In order to glean information from the data set we need to find a way to summarise it. In this case, the thing to do is to find a single value to represent the entire data set. It is common to seek a central value, and these approaches are called measures of central tendency. There are three measures that are commonly used. These are the mode, the median and the mean. Yes, these are the same ones that you would have met in your mathematics classes, so you are not learning any thing new here! Let us do a recap of them now.

The mode is the score or category with the largest frequency in the distribution. It is usually used with categorical data, though it can be used with continuous data as well. An example of this is a marketing survey that asked 1,000 children to identify their favourite beverage and obtained the results shown in the frequency distribution below (Figure 10e).

Figure 10e

Preferred Beverage	Frequency
Fizz Pop	164
Cherry Cooler	103
Tasty-Ade	99
Sugar Buzz	398
Tangy-Lemon-Lime	236
Total	**1,000**

Here the mode is Sugar Buzz. Can you see why? Yes, because that beverage was selected by the highest number of children. Note that the mode is the category and NOT the actual frequency.

The median is the score in the middle position of the data set after the scores have been organised in numerical order. Half of the scores lie below the median and half lie above it. The median is used for data that is at least at the ordinal level of measurement. It cannot be used for nominal data. You may remember from your mathematics classes that they are two scenarios for which you may be finding the median: when the data set has an odd number of scores and when the number of scores is even. Finding the median when the number of scores is odd is straightforward. When it is even, a little more effort is needed. We have included an example below as a reminder.

To identify the median for the data set (with an odd number of scores):
2, 5, 3, 4, 1, 6, 7, 4, 3, 2, 2, 1, 6, 5, 5
First, arrange the set in numerical order:
1, 1, 2, 2, 2, 3, 3, 4, 4, 5, 5, 5, 6, 6, 7
Then, find the middle position by dividing the number of scores by 2
$15 \div 2 = 7 \text{ r } 1$
The middle position is (7+1)th score, i.e. the 8th score
The median score is 4 (underlined above)

To identify the median for the data set (with an even number of scores):
2, 5, 3, 4, 1, 6, 7, 4, 3, 2, 2, 1, 6, 5
First, arrange the set in numerical order:
1, 1, 2, 2, 2, 3, 3, 4, 4, 5, 5, 6, 6, 7
Then, find the middle position by dividing the number of scores by 2
$14 \div 2 = 7$ (There is no single middle position)
The median is located between the 7th and 8th scores (underlined above). It is calculated by adding the scores in these two positions and dividing the result by 2.
$(3 + 4) \div 2 = 7 \div 2 = 3.5$
The median score is 3.5

The mean is the most commonly known measure of central tendency. The mean is found by adding all the individual scores in a data set and dividing by the number of scores in the set. The mean is only found for data at the interval or ratio levels of measurement.

The mean is denoted by the symbol $\frac{\Sigma X}{N}$, read as 'Sigma X divided by N,' where Σ (a Greek letter) means 'the sum of,' X refers to the scores in the data set and N is the number of scores in the set. Thus, for the data set 3, 4, 2, 7, 8, 1:

$$\begin{aligned} \text{Mean} \quad &= (3+4+2+7+8+1) \div 6 \\ &= 25 \div 6 \\ &= 4.2 \end{aligned}$$

Before you start to panic and run off to purchase a high powered calculator, you should know that if you use SPSS® software, these statistical procedures can be run in seconds, even if you have a data set with thousands of cases. So the important thing here is not how to calculate the mode, the median and the mean, but when it is appropriate to use each of them. The key is to be aware of the measurement scale on which the variable that you are trying to summarise is measured. The measure of central tendency that you select should be appropriate for the data that you have. You should be aware though that each one has shortcomings. Some of these are listed below in Figure 10f.

Figure 10f
Some Shortcomings of the Measures of Central Tendency

Mode:
• There may be two modes (bimodal) or more modes
• The mode may not represent a central mark. For example, in the data set 0, 0, 0, 4, 4, 5, 6, 7, 8, 8, the mode is 0, but majority of scores cluster around 6.
Median:
• The median does not use all the information given by the scores. For example, if a score below the median of 55 were changed, say from 9 to 39, the median in not affected.
Mean:
• The mean is affected by extreme scores. For example, the mean of 1, 2, 2, 5, 50 is 12. This is much higher than most of the scores in the data set. The extreme score 50 inflated the mean. Similarly, in a set of high scores, an extremely low score could lower the mean.

Continuous data can also be described graphically. For example you could display it on a histogram, and from that you can generate a frequency polygon. The data set can also be described in terms of the shape of the frequency polygon. Figure 10g shows the various shapes the polygon for a data set may assume. These may be symmetrical, positively skewed or negatively skewed. A symmetrical shape indicates that equal proportions of the scores fall above and below a central point. A positive skew indicates that the scores tend to be bunched near the lower end of the continuum, while a negative skew indicates that they bunch near the upper end.

Figure 10g
Possible Shapes of Distribution of Scores

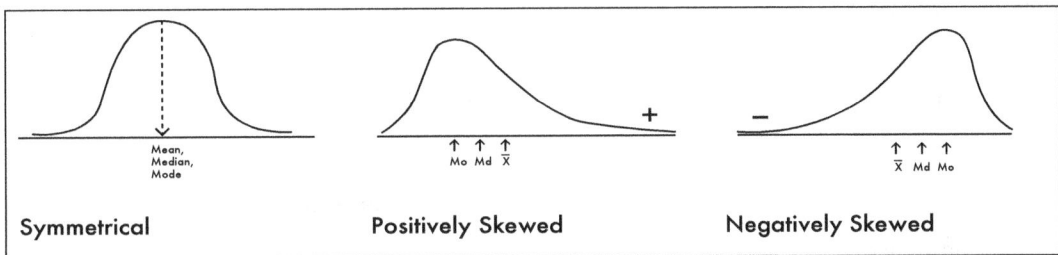

The shape of the distribution also gives information about the position of the three measures of central tendency in relation to each other. If you are seriously interested in this, again you can investigate it in a statistics text.

In order to introduce the next descriptive statistical concept, we can look at an illustration involving two data sets.

Set A: 3, 6, 4, 5, 4, 7, 3, 8   Set B: 5, 1, 1, 0, 4, 5, 3, 21

The mean of Set A is 5 (40 ÷ 8 = 5). The mean of Set B is also 5 (40 ÷ 8 = 5). So if we used the mean to represent these two data sets, you may get the impression that they were similar in composition. However, the reality is far different. The scores in Set A are tightly clustered together while those in Set B are more spread out. By just using the mean alone, valuable information about the spread of the scores is hidden. Thus in order to give a clearer description of the data sets, we need to provide further descriptive information; we need to present a measure of dispersion.

Measures of Dispersion

Measures of dispersion, also called measures of spread and measures of variability, indicate how clustered or spread out a data set is. In other words, measures of dispersion give an indication of the homogeneity of the data. There are different measures of dispersion. Commonly used ones are the range, the interquartile range, the standard deviation and the variance.

The range is the difference between the highest and lowest scores in the distribution. Hence for the data set 21, 4, 76, 43, 69, 58, the range is 72 (76 – 4). With all the scores under 100, a range of 72 indicates that the scores are widely spread out. A weakness of the range is that it only involves two scores, and does not tell about the variation of the scores between the maximum and minimum scores. As you can imagine, the range is affected by extreme scores.

The interquartile range addresses the weakness of the range. Instead of finding the difference between the lowest and highest scores, it finds the difference of two scores within the data set. You will recall that the median of a data set divides it into two parts, the half below the median and the half above it. Well, the middle score of the half below the median is called the lower quartile (Q1) and the middle score of the half above median is called the upper quartile (Q3). The interquartile range is the difference between Q1 and Q3. Now, before you panic again, have a look at an example.

Data set: 1 2 2 4 4 4 6 7 8 9 9 10 10 13 16

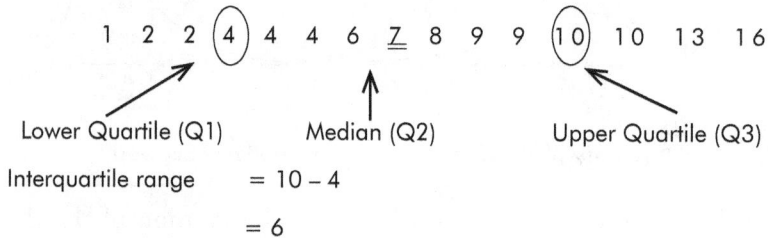

Lower Quartile (Q1)   Median (Q2)   Upper Quartile (Q3)

Interquartile range   = 10 – 4

                       = 6

Though this is an improvement on the range, it still does not take all the scores into account. The range or the interquartile range is reported if you use the median as your measure of central tendency.

The standard deviation (SD) is a measure of the variation of each score from the measure of central tendency, notably the mean. The SD increases or decreases depending on the extent to which the scores cluster around the mean. The smaller the SD, the closer the scores cluster around the mean. Like the mean, the SD takes into account each score in the data set.

The standard deviation is the square root of the sum of the squared deviations from the mean divided by the number of scores less one . Okay, calm down and let us illustrate. Say the scores of 10 respondents on an instrument are: 5, 4, 2, 6, 7, 3, 4, 4, 5, 4. We can work out that the mean is 4.4.

- First we work out by how much each score deviates from the mean by subtracting each of them from the mean.
- Next we square each of the deviations.
- Then, we sum the squares of the deviations. We get 18.4.
- Then we divide the sum of the squares of the deviations by N-1, where N is the number of scores in the data set. Thus we divide by 9. So 18.4 ÷ 9 = 2.04.
- Finally, we find the square root of that result, ($\sqrt{2.04}$) and voilà! a standard deviation of 1.43.
- This is worked out below for the given data set.

There! That wasn't so bad, was it?

Scores (X)	Deviation (Mean - X)	(Deviation)^2
5	-0.6	0.36
4	0.4	0.16
2	2.4	5.76
6	-1.6	2.56
7	-2.6	6.76
3	1.4	1.96
4	0.4	0.16
4	0.4	0.16
5	-0.6	0.36
4	0.4	0.16
SUM = 44		**18.4**

$$SD = \sqrt{\frac{18.4}{9}}$$

$$= \sqrt{2.04}$$

$$= 1.43$$

The variance is the square of the standard deviation. Thus, variance = SD^2. Thus, using our example above,

$$\text{Variance} = (1.43)^2$$
$$= 2.04$$

As you can see the standard deviation and the variance are worked out using the mean. The mean is only meaningful if the data are continuous. It follows then that the standard deviation and the variance are only appropriate if your data are continuous, that is, on the interval or ratio scale.

As with the measures of central tendency, you can obtain these measures of dispersion quite easily using the SPSS® software. Indeed, whenever you ask the software to run a measure of central tendency, it is advisable to request an appropriate measure of dispersion at the same time. Of course, these procedures may also be run using EXCEL® software.

So far we have only been looking at descriptive statistics using one variable. However there are those that involve two variables (bivariate). Let us explore two commonly used ones: cross-tabulation and correlation.

Cross-tabulation

When we had only one variable to consider (e.g. scores on an attitude scale), we could list the scores in a single column. When we have two variables, we would have two columns. This would make finding sense in the data even more complex, but a cross-tabulation can help. A cross-tabulation table is a two-dimensional grid with one variable represented on each dimension.

Variable 1

Variable 2

Each cell represents a pair of characteristics, one from each variable. Everyone in the sample would contribute a count to only ONE cell. That way we can see how many members of the sample possess the characteristics measured by the variables. Let us illustrate.

Suppose we had data from 20 people about their preference of political party. The group, consisting of both males and females indicated whether they preferred the Here and Now Democratic Set (HANDS) or the Followers of Old Tradition Set (FOOTS).

Sex	Party Preference
F	HANDS
M	FOOTS
M	HANDS
M	HANDS
M	FOOTS
F	HANDS
F	HANDS
M	FOOTS
M	HANDS
F	HANDS
F	FOOTS
M	FOOTS
M	HANDS
F	HANDS
M	FOOTS
F	FOOTS
F	HANDS
M	HANDS
F	FOOTS
F	HANDS

As you can see, each member of the sample contributed a measure to each of the two variables. As it is, it is not easy to answer questions such as which party is most popular or is one of the parties preferred by more females than males from this raw data. As before, we need to use a cross-tabulation to summarise them.

Notice that there are TWO variables, Sex and Party Preference. Each variable has two conditions. We can display these data in cross-tabulation form that could look like this:

		Party Preference		
		HANDS	FOOTS	Total
Sex	Female	*		
	Male			
Total				

From our raw data then, the first row would contribute a count to the cell with the asterisk (*), that is the cell for females who prefer the HANDS party. When all the data are entered in the table, our cross-tabulation would look like this:

		Party Preference		
		HANDS	FOOTS	Total
Sex	Female	7	3	10
	Male	5	5	10
Total		12	8	20

Now, with the data summarised in this form it is easy to see that HANDS is the more popular party and that is it is preferred by more females than males. Imagine what a big help such a table would be if you have a sample of 200 or 2,000 instead of just 20! This table is also called a two by two (2x2) contingency table; two by two because each variable has two conditions, thus giving two rows and two columns. Cross-tabulation is generally used with categorical data, though it can be used with interval data as well. You would use it to help to see if there is an association between two variables. In our example above we learned that the females in the sample tended to prefer the HANDS party! Therefore there seems to be an association between being female and having a preference for that party. There appears to be no such association for the males, since equal numbers of them selected both parties.

If you had these raw data compiled in an SPSS® database, the software could generate the cross-tabulation in no time at all with just a few clicks! SPSS® can also generate the table using percents instead of actual counts. You can decide the best way to display the information.

Simple Correlation

There are other ways of describing associations or relationships between two variables. We can do this by exploring the correlation between them. When we analyse data by running a correlation, we obtain a co-efficient that tells us about the relationship between the variables of interest. Two commonly used correlation procedures are the Pearson Product Moment correlation (r) and the Spearman Rank Difference correlation, also called Spearman Rho (ρ). The one you select will depend on the nature of your data. For example, in order to use the Pearson correlation, both of your variables must be measured on the interval scale, your sample should have been randomly selected and it is usually recommended that the sample size should be at least 30. If you violate any of these requirements, it is recommended that you use the Spearman correlation instead. The Spearman measure of relationship has fewer requirements, the most important one being that the data must be able to be ranked, that is, it should be at least on the ordinal scale.

Whether you use the Pearson or Spearman correlation procedure, you will obtain a coefficient that, when interpreted, provides a description of the relationship between the two variables of interest. This correlation coefficient has two attributes to which you need to pay attention; magnitude and direction. The magnitude (or size), which ranges from 0 to 1, describes the strength of the relationship between the two variables. A correlation coefficient of 0 indicates the absence of a relationship between the variables while a coefficient of 1 indicates a perfect relationship. Different guidelines for interpreting the size of the correlation coefficient are given. Figure 10h below is our suggestion.

Figure 10h
Guidelines for Interpreting Correlation Coefficients (Adapted from Burns, 2000)

Coefficient	Correlation	Relationship
0.90 – 1.00	Very High	Very Strong
0.70 – 0.89	High	Marked
0.40 – 0.69	Moderate	Substantial
0.20 – 0.39	Low	Weak
<0.20	Slight	Negligible

If you find other guidelines that you prefer, then go ahead and use them! But remember, you should always cite the source of the guidelines that you use.

Apart from its size, the coefficient may be positive (+) or negative (-), which describes the direction of the relationship. A positive coefficient indicates that a high (or low) score on one variable is matched by a high (or low) score on the other variable; that is, the variables vary in the same direction. This is also called a direct relationship. A negative coefficient indicates that a high (or low) score on one variable is matched by a low (or high) score on the other variable; that is, the variables vary in opposite directions. This is also called an inverse relationship. Some students make the mistake of interpreting a negative coefficient as a weak relationship. This is not the case. The negative sign is no indication of the size of the relationship, only the direction. Thus a coefficient of -0.90 would be a very strong inverse relationship, using Burn's classifications. Figure 10i below is to emphasise this point.

Figure 10i

Examples of Interpretations of Positive and Negative Correlation Coefficients

Correlation Coefficient	Description of Relationship
-0.85	Very strong direct relationship
+0.85	Very strong inverse relationship
-0.52	Substantial direct relationship
+0.52	Substantial inverse relationship
-0.15	Negligible direct relationship
+0.15	Negligible inverse relationship

Let us explore how simple correlation might be applied by considering an example. Let us say that you were interested in finding out if there was a relationship between the salaries earned by a randomly selected sample of 300 individuals in the banking industry and the number of years of formal education that they had. To do this, you administered a questionnaire on which the participants were asked to indicate to the nearest one hundred dollars their annual salary and to report in years the amount of time that they spent in formal education (primary, secondary, tertiary undergraduate and tertiary postgraduate, as well as professional education). Both of these variables are being measured on the interval scale (remember we are using this term to include the ratio scale), the sample was randomly selected and the size is relatively large.

Based on the data collected, let us assume that the Pearson correlation procedure would be appropriate, and that when you run it in SPSS® you obtain a coefficient of 0.63. Following the guidelines above, this can be described as a moderate correlation and it indicates a substantial relationship between salary earned by the participants and the number of years that they spent in formal education. There! That was not so difficult was it? Sometimes though, you are not particularly interested in obtaining a correlation coefficient right away, but you want to have an idea of any possible relationship between the two variables that you are studying. You may do this by examining a pictorial representation of the relationship using a scatterplot. Let us see how this can be done.

A scatter plot is a two-dimensional graph with the scores for one variable plotted on the horizontal axis and the scores for the other variable on the vertical axis. This graph helps us to explore the existence of a linear relationship between two variables. Each participant has one score on each variable, for example 10 for Variable 1 and 6 for Variable 2. A point is plotted on the graph to indicate each participant's position with respect to the two variables.

When all the pairs of scores are positioned, the shape of the plotted points is an indication of the strength and direction of the relationship between the variables. Figure 10j below shows some examples of scatterplots.

Figure 10j
Examples of Scatterplots

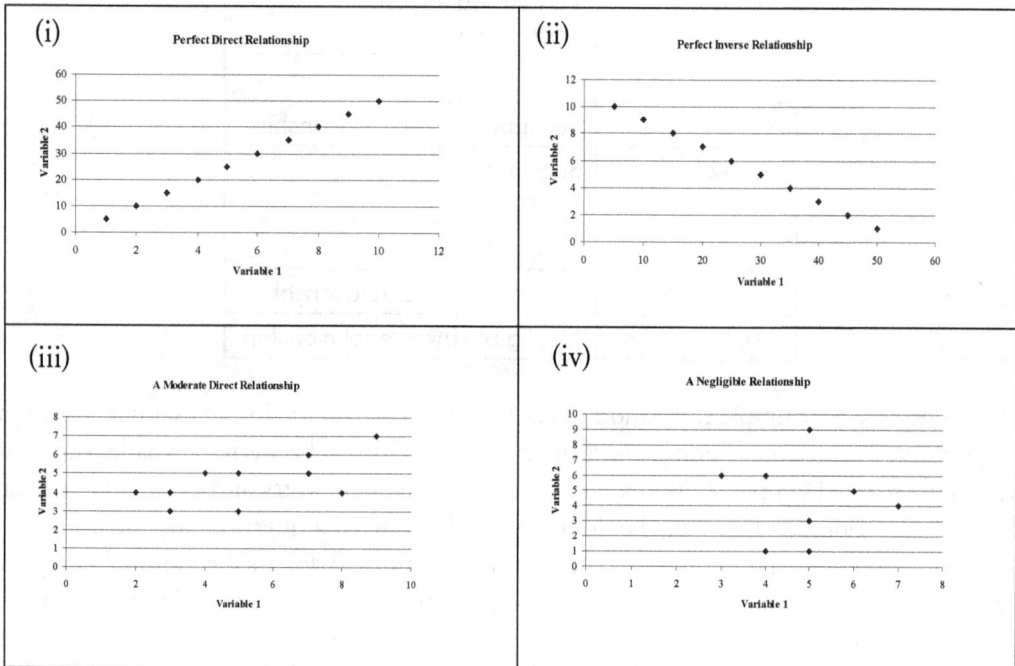

The graph in Figure 10j(i) represents a perfect direct correlation; the corresponding coefficient is (+1.00). Figure 10j(ii) represents a perfect inverse correlation, with a corresponding coefficient of (-1.00). For a perfect correlation the points form a straight line, inclining for direct relationship and declining for an inverse relationship. Now notice that in Figure 10j(iii) the plotted points are not tightly clustered, though the shape does suggest an inclining line. This indicates a correlation that is not as strong as the one shown in (a) or (b). In fact, this scatterplot represents a moderate correlation (0.64). In Figure 10j(iv) the plotted points appear to be randomly placed, with no indications of a straight line. This graph indicates a negligible relationship (-0.07). We can infer that there is no linear relationship between the two variables here.

Whether you run scatterplots or not may depend on what you hope to achieve in presenting your data to the reader. Sometimes a pictorial representation does the job very well in communicating your point. If so, then by all means use a scatterplot. But sometimes you may be required to produce one prior to some other procedure. Again, there is no need to fear. Both SPSS® and Microsoft® EXCEL® software can be used to generate these graphs.

SUMMING UP

In this chapter, we explored ways of compiling and analysing data that you collect for your research. We explained some ways that you can compile and organise numerical data, and mentioned some computer software that can help you with this task. If you compile your data using the computer, always make more than one copy of the files. We recommend that when you enter your data in a file, you should keep a copy of the original data set. This way, if you make mistakes or for some reason you lose the file you are working with, you can always go back to the original data. Keep data files in different places: on your hard drive, on a CD, on a flash drive. If we sound paranoid about it, that is because we know the absolute horror of losing data after spending many long hours compiling them. A word to the wise....

We also introduced you to ways of analysing the data after compiling them. We suggested how you may approach making sense of numerical data with the help of computer software. Remember though, the software will only perform the procedures that you instruct it to do. It cannot think for you! The value of the software is that it frees you from mundane routine activities so that you can devote more time to the intellectual ones such as making decisions about how to interrogate the data and interpreting the outcomes of your interrogations. So, for example, you should not be worrying about whether you remember the formula for finding the mean or the standard deviation for a data set. Your main concern should be deciding whether finding the mean and standard deviation would be appropriate for the data that you have collected. When you have come to a decision, you can make use of the computer software to do the calculations for you. You will find that as you become more confident in your research skills, you would be eager to apply more sophisticated procedures to analyse your data.

This thought can lead us nicely into the next chapter. Sometimes, you want to do more with your numerical data than description. There are times when you will want to use data collected from a sample to learn about the population from which the sample was selected, that is, you may want to make inferences. For this purpose, you would need to apply inferential statistical procedures which are the subject of the following chapter.

11

INFERENTIAL STATISTICS

INTRODUCTION

In this chapter, we will introduce some concepts related to the use of statistics for making inferences. As we mentioned in an earlier chapter, sometimes you may want to learn something about a particular population, but for practical reasons, you may not be able to collect data from all its members. For example, you may want to learn about attitudes that secondary school students have towards people who are HIV-positive. Now it would not be practical for you to ask all of the secondary school students in your territory questions to determine this. Your best bet is to select a sample of students that can represent the population, collect data from them, and then use those data to make inferences about the entire population.

But before we talk about anything new, let us remind you of an important concept that was discussed in an earlier chapter: the notion of a random sample. Remember that when you select a sample from a population for your research, it is only one of many possible samples and, if it is randomly selected, you have no control over who will be selected. It is therefore possible that even a random sample is not exactly representative of your intended population. For example, the variable that you are measuring can be present in varying degrees in members of the population. It is possible that when you select your sample, by chance, you may select only members of the population with high levels of the variable. Here is a simple illustration of that fact.

Let us imagine that a population of 20 people, indicated by the letters A to T in the alphabet, had the measurements shown for some variable that was of interest to you.

A	B	C	D	E	F	G	H	I	J	K	L	M	N	O	P	Q	R	S	T
1	2	3	4	5	6	7	8	9	10	11	12	13	14	15	16	17	18	19	20

Now suppose that you selected a random sample of five people and chose N, P, R, S, and T. These people have scores of 14, 16, 18, 19 and 20 respectively. Now the population mean (the sum of the 20 scores divided by 20 or 210 ÷ 20) is 10.5, while the sample mean is 17.4 (87 ÷ 5). Thus, the sample mean deviates from the population mean by about 7 points.

Now if you remember about sampling, the idea is to obtain a group with a mean that reflects the population mean. If you take the sample mean in our example, you may want to say that this sample represents some other population because the sample mean is very different from the population mean. Indeed, you may even want to suggest that the sample was in fact taken from a population that differed from the one given above. And of course, you would be wrong! You would be making an error, but not one that you have any control over. This is merely a function of having selected one random sample! It is only by chance that this is the sample you ended up with. This illustration should drive home the point that when you select a sample from a population in order to learn something about that population, there is the chance that you can make errors in your conclusions. You may recall that this is called sampling error and it can be measured. SPSS® can report this measurement when you run statistical procedures.

The notions of chance and error are pretty much integral to inferential statistics. It can sometimes take a while for you to fully grasp it all, but that does not mean that you cannot apply inferential statistical procedures successfully. Hopefully, that is exactly what we are going to help you to do. To accomplish this, we must introduce some concepts that are basic to inferential statistics. These include standardised scores, the standard normal curve, and aspects of probability theory. Let us consider each one briefly.

STANDARDISED SCORES

This concept can perhaps best be explained in terms of test scores, since even if you are not an education student, you have been to school and can well relate to such scores. Let us imagine then that you are in a class that took two tests – a mathematics test and a Spanish test. And let us say that you scored 35 on a mathematics test and 60 on a Spanish test. On which test did you have the better performance? If you said Spanish, you are probably sharing your answer with many others. But the truth is, we probably cannot answer that question based solely on the two raw scores. That would be like comparing guavas and grapefruits. The two tests could have characteristics that make them as different as guavas and grapefruits, thus making it inappropriate to compare performance by simply comparing raw scores. For example, the degree of difficulty of the tests may have been different. Similarly, if you were asked 'which is longer? 3 metres or 5 feet,' you would not say 5 feet because 5 is more than 3, would you? You would recognise that the two scales of measurement are different and before you can compare them, you would match the two measurements to each other or at least try to convert them to the same scale. Thus, you may measure 3 metres and then 5 feet and physically compare them or you may convert the metres to feet (3m = approx. 10 feet).

This is the idea you have to have in mind when thinking of comparing a score of 35 on a mathematics test and 60 on a Spanish test. Before you can compare them, you need to make sure that the measurements are on the same scale or standardise them. In order to do this, you would need to know the group mean and standard deviation (remember these from the previous chapter?) for the set of scores since the formula for calculating standard scores (also called **z-scores**) is z = (x - 0) where x is the individual student's score; 0 is the mean for the set of all the scores in the group; and SD is the standard deviation for the set of scores

$z =$	$\dfrac{(x - \bar{x})}{SD}$	Where x is the individual student's score Is the mean for the set of all the scores in the group; and SD is the standard deviation for the set of scores

So for our example, you would need to find out the class mean and standard deviation for the mathematics and Spanish tests. Now let us say that we found out that for the Spanish test, the class mean was 75 and the standard deviation was 10, while the mean for the Mathematics test was 30 and the standard deviation was also 10. When the formula is applied, the resulting z-scores are -1.5 for Spanish and 0.5 for Mathematics (You can take our word for this. We are fairly handy with the calculator!). Now since the two scores are on the same scale (they are both z-scores), now we can compare them. Look at how they are positioned in relation to each other.

If you remember your number line from school, you will recall that as we move to the right, the numbers become larger. Thus, since the mathematics score is to the right of the Spanish score, then we can say that your performance in mathematics was better than that for Spanish in relation to the other members of your class. The idea to go away with here is that in order to compare two measures, they must be on the same scale. Let us now explore another concept that is handy for understanding and interpreting inferential statistics: the normal distribution.

THE NORMAL DISTRIBUTION

Experts tell us (and we take their word for it since we do not have the time or the inclination to try to prove it for ourselves!) that in the social world, many of the characteristics that we measure exist in a given population in certain proportions. What does that mean, you may ask. Let us explain with a couple of examples.

Have you ever noticed that ladies with really big feet or really small feet sometimes have a hard time finding shoes to fit them? This is probably because shoe manufacturers also listen to the experts. According to these experts, if we had the time and patience to obtain the shoe size of all the ladies in a large population, we could calculate the mean and standard deviation for ladies' shoe sizes for that population. They further tell us that if we plot a graph of shoe size against the number of ladies who wear each shoe size, then the graph would have a particular shape, and that the proportions of the population of ladies wearing each shoe size could be predicted before we even examine the distribution. What are these magic proportions?

Let us say that we knew that the mean shoe size for ladies in a particular population was 7 and the standard deviation was 1.5. Statisticians tell us that approximately 34.1 per cent of the population would wear a shoe size between the mean and one standard deviation (SD) above the mean, that is, between sizes 7 and 8.5; approximately another 13.6 per cent wear a size between 1SD and 2 SD above the mean, that is, between sizes 8.5 and 10; a further 2.2 per cent wear a size between 2SD and 3SD above the mean, that is, between sizes 10 and 11.5. These proportions are the same for sizes below the mean. Thus approximately 34.1 per cent of the population would wear a shoe size between the mean and one standard deviation (SD) below the mean, that is, between sizes 5.5 and 7; approximately another 13.6 per cent wear a size between 1SD and 2SD below the mean, that is, between sizes 4 and 5.5; a further 2.2 per cent wear a size between 2SD and 3SD below the mean, that is, between sizes 2.5 and 4.

We can draw a histogram (this looks like a bar chart but the bars are touching) to show the distribution of shoe sizes and then construct a smooth curved line that joins the midpoints of the bars of the histogram (this is called a frequency polygon). This curve is called the normal curve (See Figure 11a below).

Figure 11a
Shoe Sizes

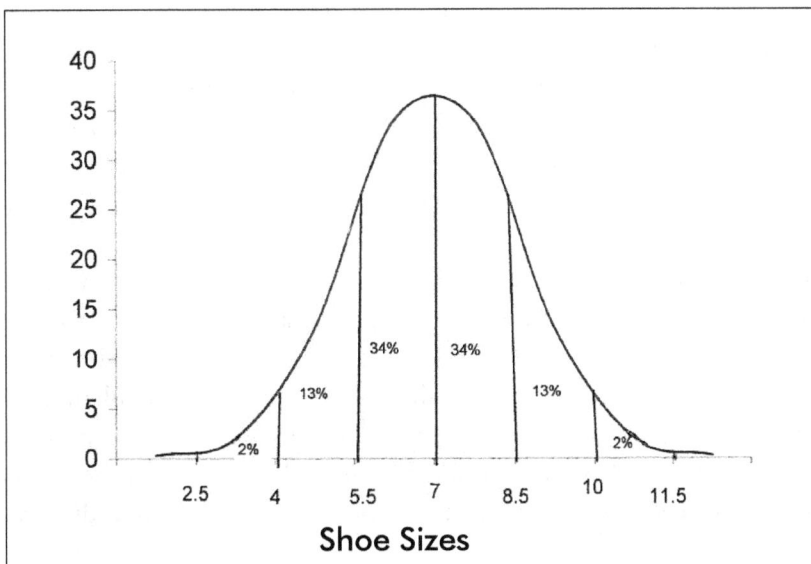

Shoe Sizes

If we consider the area between the curve and the horizontal axis (the line along which the shoe sizes are plotted), it indicates that almost the entire population (2.2% + 13.6% + 34.1% + 34.1% + 13.6% + 2.2% = 99.8%) wears shoe sizes between 2.5 and 11.5 or 3SD below the mean and 3SD above the mean. This is the magic that statisticians tell us is true for most (if not all!) of the attributes or characteristics that we measure in the social world! This 'truth' comes in rather handy for making inferences about a population based on measurements gathered from a sample. However before we can have fun with this fact, there is one more thing we need to do with the normal distribution.

Think about this: if we were to measure the shoe sizes of the men in the population, we would expect to get a similar looking distribution (because we believe the statisticians!). However there may be differences. For example, the mean shoe size for the men may be 8.5 and the standard deviation may be 2. The resulting proportions and ranges of shoe sizes are shown in Figure 11b below.

Figure 11b

	Shoe Sizes	Proportion of the Population
Between 2SD and 3SD Below the mean	2.5–4.5	2.2%
Between 1SD and 2SD below the mean	4.5–6.5	13.6%
1SD below the mean	6.5–8.5	34.1%
1SD above the mean	8.5–10.5	34.1%
Between 1SD and 2SD above the mean	10.5–12.5	13.6%
Between 2SD and 3SD above the mean	12.5–14.5	2.2%

Notice that although the proportions of the male population falling within the various distances from the mean are the same, the means and standard deviations are different – the mean is higher than that for the ladies and the standard deviation is greater too! Thus, if we had to plot the two curves, they might be similar, but the one for the men would be shifted to the right and would be more spread out (the SD is larger than that for the ladies). Now let us say we had a man and a lady both wearing a size 6 shoe. Can we compare them? For example, can we say that they both have small feet? The question is, with whom are we comparing them?

Think about it, a woman wearing a size 6 shoe is fairly normal. She is in the 34.1 per cent that is within 1SD of the mean for women. But a man wearing a size 6 shoe is less common: he is in the 13.6 per cent between 1SD and 2 SD below the mean. Hmmm! Are you seeing it? It is similar to the Spanish and Mathematics tests dilemma that we met earlier. We cannot really compare these two quantities because they are being assessed on two different scales. We had to know the mean and standard deviation for the two populations before we could make a judgement. In other words, we had to standardise the shoe sizes by seeing where they fell when compared to the mean for the population from which they were taken. Notice that when we did that, we referred to the mean as the reference point and then considered how far the measurement was from the mean in terms of standard deviations. And we could do this for both the ladies and the men! Aha! We have found a standard measurement that we can use for both sets of shoe sizes: we can measure them with reference to the mean and standard deviation. Indeed we are converting two normal distributions to one standard distribution which we call the standard normal distribution.

THE STANDARD NORMAL DISTRIBUTION

The standard normal distribution is a normally shaped distribution with a mean of 0 and a standard deviation of 1. This is a very important distribution because it allows us to compare scores or measurements from different samples, from the same sample and much more. In order to do this, we must convert the scores or measurements to standard scores. And yes, we have introduced you to standard scores before. Remember the z-scores? Well these z-scores are really standard deviation units. In other words, they are measures of how many standard deviations below or above the means a score is. A negative z-score tells you that the score is below the mean and a positive z-score tells you that the score is above the mean. Thus, a z-score of -1.7 tells you that the score is 1.7 standard deviations below the mean, while a z-score of 1.7 tells you that the score is 1.7 standard deviations above the mean.

The standard normal distribution can be understood by combining what we know about the normal distribution and standard scores. We have seen it already, but let us repeat it again. For the standard normal distribution,

2.2% of scores fall between 2SD and 3SD Below the mean

13.6% of scores fall between 1SD and 2SD below the mean

34.1% of scores fall 1SD below the mean

34.1% of scores fall 1SD above the mean

13.6% of scores fall between 1SD and 2SD above the mean

2.2% of scores fall between 2SD and 3SD above the mean

Put another way,

68.2% of scores fall within 1SD of the mean

95.4% of scores fall within 2SD of the mean

99.8% of scores fall within 3SD of the mean

This is illustrated graphically in Figure 11c below.

Figure 11c

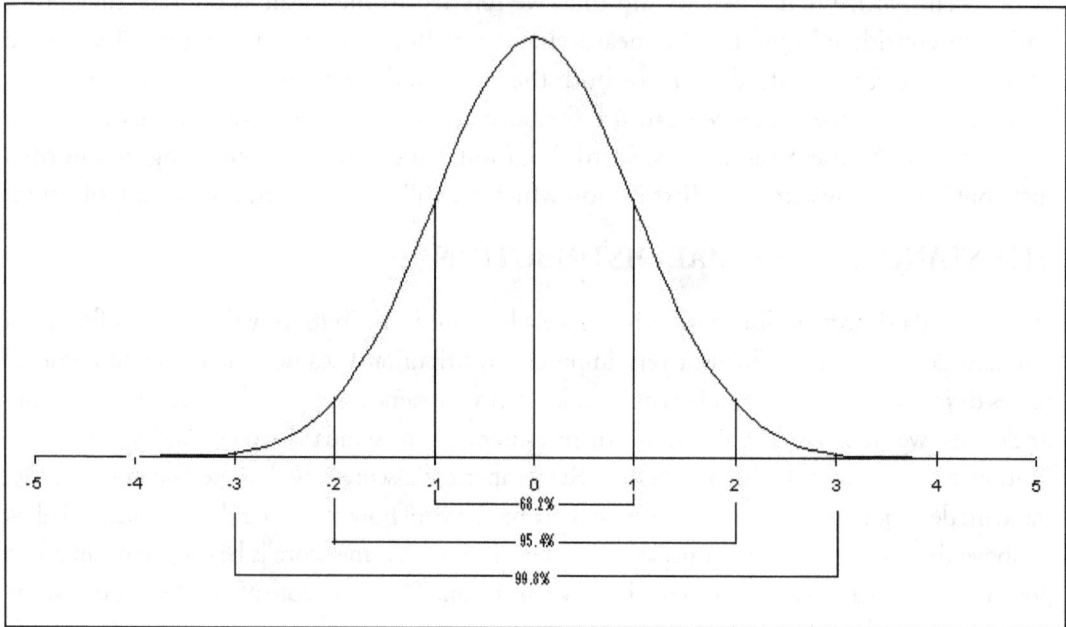

As was said before, this and other characteristics of the standard normal distribution make it a very useful tool when we want to make inferences about a population based on sample data or when we want to test hypotheses. We will soon explore how that works, but before we do, we need to have a look at another very important concept – the notion of chance and probability.

PROBABILITY THEORY: TAKING A CHANCE

If you would think back to what was discussed in the previous two sections of this chapter, you will recall that we found that for many of the attributes that we measure in the social world, known proportions of a population fall within given distances from the mean. Do you remember the example of the ladies' shoe sizes? We determined that if the mean shoe size for ladies were 7 and the standard deviation were 1.5, then we would expect approximately 34.1 per cent of the women in the population to wear a size between 7 and 8.5. So then, if you were to meet a lady from that particular population, what is the chance or probability that her shoe size falls in the 7–8.5 range? Well, we expect that 34.1 per cent of the entire population (100%) of ladies wear shoes in this size range. So the probability of meeting such a lady would be 34.1 per cent out of 100 per cent or 34.1/100. Since probability is usually expressed in decimal form, we can say the probability of meeting a lady whose shoe size falls in the 7 to 8.5 range is 0.341.

Let us try another one. What would be the probability of meeting a lady whose shoe size falls in the 2.5 to 7 range? No, this is not a trick. Let us reason it out together. Perhaps if we see the distribution graph (Figure 11d) as we think, this would help. Just remember that the area under the curve represents the population, and that the proportions shown represent proportions of the population.

Figure 11d

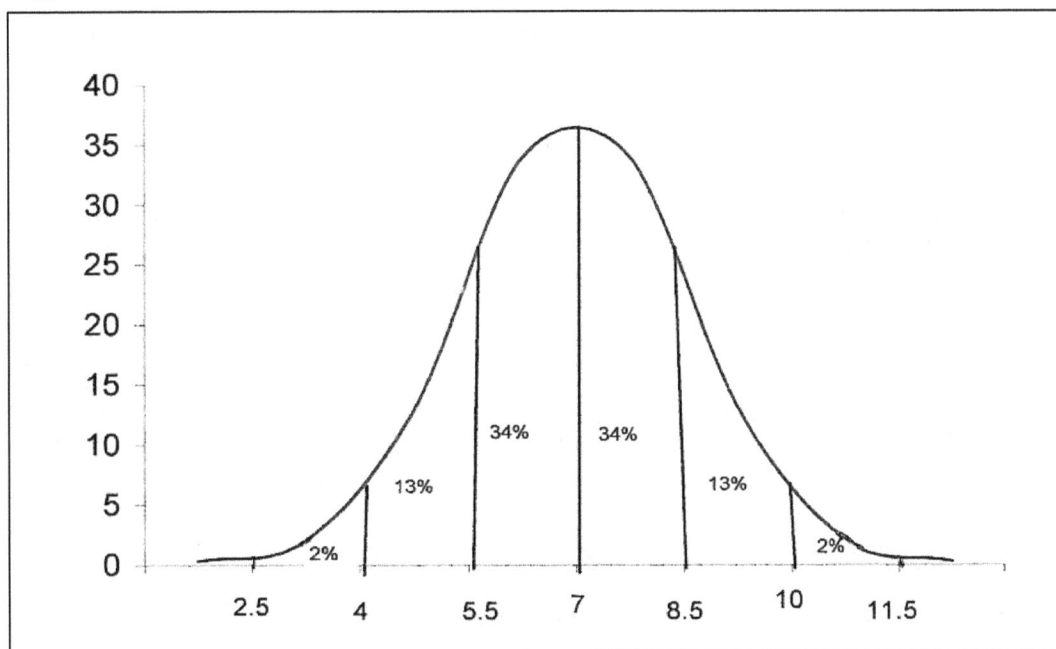

From the graph about 2.2 per cent of the area under the curve fall between 2.5 and 4; about 13.6 per cent fall between 4 and 5.5; and about 34.1 per cent fall between 5.5 and 7. So to find out what proportion falls between 2.5 and 7, we simply add those proportions (2.2+13.6+34.1) to obtain 49.9 per cent. This tells us that about 49.9 per cent of the ladies in that population wear shoes in the 2.5 to 7 size range. Now the original question was, what is the probability of meeting a woman whose shoe size falls between 2.5 and 7? We can now say that 49.9 per cent out of 100 per cent of the ladies fall in this category. So the probability of meeting such a lady would be 49.9/100 or 0.499.

By now you may notice that this is the proportion of ladies whose shoe sizes are up to 3 standard deviations below the mean. Because the curve is symmetrical, then you would expect the proportion of the ladies whose shoe sizes fall between 7 and 11.5 (3 standard deviations above the mean) to be similar. If you check the diagram above you will confirm this to be so. Thus the probability of meeting a lady whose shoe size falls between 7 and 11.5 would also be 0.499. By extension then, the probability of meeting a lady whose shoe size falls between 2.5 and 11.5 would be 0.998 (0.499 [3SD below the mean] + 0.499 [3SD above the mean]).

If you are asked the probability of meeting a lady whose shoe size is smaller than 2.5, what would you say? Again, let us reason on it! We know that the probability of meeting a lady from the population whose shoe size is any size at all is 1 (that is, a certainty, since all the women will have a shoe size!). We also know that 0.998 (99.8%) of the ladies wear a shoe size between 2.5 and 11.5. That means that 0.002 (0.2%) of them wear a shoe size smaller than 2.5 or larger than 11.5. Further, because the curve is symmetrical, we know that half of this 0.2 per cent will fall below 2.5 and the other half above 11.5. (Are you with us on this? If not, take your time and reason on it.) Thus, 0.1 per cent or 0.001 of the area under the curve falls to the left of 2.5 and the same proportion falls above 11.5. So then, the probability of meeting a lady whose shoe size is smaller than 2.5 is 0.1 per cent out of 100 per cent, or 0.1/100, or 0.001. This is a very small probability as it represents one out of every 1,000 ladies in the population.

What does all this mean? Well, you may have noticed that the farther away from the mean the shoe sizes are, the smaller the probability of meeting a lady who wears that size. This is a phenomenon that statisticians tell us is common for many of the characteristics that we measure in the social world – that the probability of finding these characteristics beyond a certain level in a given population is extremely small. So, when we observe these characteristics in certain quantities, we may assume that the individual with the characteristic does not belong to the particular population, but to some other population! This concept is very important when we are using inferential statistics. Remember, for inferential statistics, we are using data collected from a sample to make inferences about the population from which it was taken. Let us see how that works.

MAKING INFERENCES: STILL TAKING CHANCES

If you recall what we discussed in the chapter on sampling, you will remember that we pointed out that when you select a sample from a population, you are obtaining only ONE of many possible samples. You may also recall that we pointed out that the mean score for the characteristic that you are measuring may not be an exact reflection of the population mean, but that it may vary somewhat. In other words, we expect that if we select two samples from a population, their means on whatever characteristic that we are measuring may be different. The size of the difference between the means raises the question – can these two samples be from the same population, and the difference we see be just chance fluctuation or are the samples from two different populations? The answer to this question will help us to learn something (or make inferences) about the population(s) from which the samples were selected. In order to answer it, we need to select and run an appropriate statistical procedure called a test of significance.

Tests of Significance

Tests of significance are used to test the null hypothesis (H_0) that there is no difference or association or relationship between two or more variables. Put another way, tests of significance assess the conjecture that any differences or relationships observed are attributable to chance fluctuations that can occur when different samples are selected from the same population. Based on the results of the tests of significance, we make a decision to either reject this null hypothesis or retain it. These tests allow us to compare two or more measurements obtained from samples and make inferences about the populations from which the samples were taken by deciding whether to reject or retain the null hypothesis.

For instance, suppose we measured the attitudes of two groups towards some object and the measurements for the groups differed. We can use a test of significance to determine whether we should reject or retain the null hypothesis (H_0) The difference between the two measures is not statistically significant). In other words we test to determine whether the observed difference is just a chance fluctuation that we obtain by selecting two random samples from the same population, or whether the two groups appear to be from two difference populations. Let us consider an example.

A researcher used a random sampling technique to select two groups of individuals. The two groups were similar on several characteristics, such as age, gender, annual earnings, levels of education, and general health. One group however was made up of people raised in two-parent homes and the other group was raised in single-parent homes. The researcher then administered a scale to measure their attitude towards marriage. The scale yielded a single score (out of 50) that could be interpreted to indicate whether the participant had a positive or negative attitude towards marriage, with the higher the score, the more positive the attitude. The group raised by single parents had a mean score of 39.4 and the group raised by two parents had a mean score of 37.9. This gives a difference of 1.5. Now, even if the two groups are from the same population, we might still obtain a difference in means, but we would expect those means to fluctuate within a certain range. The question is then, is this difference between the two means within the range that we would accept as just a chance fluctuation or not?

To answer this question, you can run a test of significance called the t test for independent samples. This procedure converts the difference to a standard score called a t score. That t score would then be plotted on the standard normal curve and the probability of obtaining such a score can be ascertained. We can then use that probability to make a decision as to whether to reject or retain the null hypothesis. What null hypothesis, you may ask. In this case, the null hypothesis would state that the difference between the two means is not statistically significant; that is, that the difference observed is just a chance fluctuation that can be expected when different samples from the same population are selected. We will discuss how to make this decision a little later. Here we are just trying to explain how tests of significance work. Let us consider a second example.

Suppose the researcher had also measured the number of years the participants lived with their parents and wanted to determine if there was a significant relationship between this variable and attitude towards marriage. As you may recall from the previous chapter, the researcher can run a correlation procedure to obtain a correlation coefficient. That coefficient can be interpreted to shed light on the size and direction of the relationship. However, the question may be asked: is it a statistically significant relationship? In other words, is the relationship significantly different from no relationship at all? Again, in order to answer this, a test of significance can be performed. In this case, the null hypothesis being tested would state that there is no significant difference between the obtained correlation and a correlation of zero. In other words, that the relationship observed is no different from no relationship at all. The test of significance would help you to decide whether to reject or retain this null hypothesis.

Generally then, tests of significance allow us to examine differences between group data to determine whether these differences can be attributed to chance or something else. Tests of significance can also help us to decide whether relationships or associations observed between variables are significantly different from no relationship at all. There are however, many different tests of significance, each applicable under different circumstances. The key for you is to be able to select an appropriate one to apply to your data. It is also important for you to remember that tests of significance assess a null hypothesis, which is either rejected or retained based on the outcome of the tests.

Again, we are quite pleased to tell you that you are living in the days of data analysis heaven! In the past (the days of data analysis hell?), you would have had to whip out your trusty calculator and try to apply complicated (and sometimes downright scary-looking!) formulae for tests of significance. Today however, computer software such as SPSS® does all the 'donkey' work for you! Your task is to know which test to apply and how to interpret the output. And of course, we are happy to provide guidance on these tasks. Now if you use SPSS®, when you run a test of significance, the programme returns a value (e.g. t score), and the probability of obtaining such a value. Let us discuss how you use the probability information to make decisions about the associations/relationships and group mean differences that you may observe.

Interpreting Tests of Significance

You may recall that at the start of this chapter, we suggested that applying inferential statistical procedures involved taking risks or chances and the possibility of incurring error. Well, this is where that comes in! And, it draws on several concepts that we met earlier, so let us help you to make the connections here.

You will recall that when we explored the standard normal curve and its link to the probability of events occurring, we came to the conclusion that the probability of some events occurring by chance is very small. When we do inferential statistics, we select a probability that we decide is too small for us to assume chance occurrence. A common such point in social research is 0.05. What does that mean? Well, we are saying that if the probability of an event occurring is 0.05 or less, then we will assume that it is not a chance occurrence and something contributed to its occurrence. This is how we decide whether to reject or retain the null hypothesis. Let us see how that works.

Going back to our example above about attitudes towards marriage, we found a difference of 1.5 between the means for the group of participants raised in two-parent homes and those raised in single-parent homes. The question was, is this difference large enough for us to say that these two groups are so different as to be from different populations? The null hypothesis would state that the observed difference in means is not statistically significant (i.e. it is just a chance occurrence). Suppose we used SPSS® to run a test of significance (the t test as suggested earlier) and we learn that the probability of obtaining such a difference by chance is 0.473. Now this probability is high and indeed much higher than the 0.05 point that we selected. So, then, what is our conclusion? That the probability of obtaining such a difference by chance is so high, that we can assume that its occurrence here is in fact a chance occurrence. Thus, we retain the null hypothesis.

But what if SPSS® returned a probability of 0.039? Again, we have to refer to our selected point. Remember, we decided that if the probability of an event occurring is 0.05 or less, we are going to assume that it is too small to be a chance occurrence. Let us see then. Now 0.039 is smaller than 0.05 and therefore within the limit which we will assume is too small to be a chance occurrence. So then, what is our conclusion? That the difference between the means for the two groups is large enough as to suggest that it cannot be taken as chance fluctuation for samples from the same population, but that the two groups are from different populations. Hence we would reject the null hypothesis which states that statistically, there is no difference between the means observed for the two groups. What we would be saying in essence then, is that there is a statistically significant difference between the means of the two groups on the particular variable. Next, we would check to see which mean is higher. In our example, the mean for the group raised in a single-parent home is higher than that of the other group. We would therefore conclude that the group raised by single parents has a significantly more positive attitude towards marriage than does the other group. In a research study, we could then go on to examine the data and the literature to see if we could ascertain why this might be so, and how it relates to your research questions. Figure 11e summarises the use and interpretation of tests of significance.

Figure 11e
Summary of the Use and Interpretation of Tests of Significance

1. Tests of significance are used to help us to decide whether observed differences and relationships in group data may be attributed to chance (not statistically significant) or to 'real' differences or relationships (statistically significant).

2. Tests of significance are used to test the NULL hypothesis, which stated that any difference or relationship observed is not statistically significant.

3. Based on the results of the test of significance, the null hypothesis is either REJECTED or RETAINED.

4. When using SPSS software to execute tests of significance, the probability of obtaining the particular difference or relationship is given. (We call this $p_{observed}$.)

5. To make the decision, you must select a probability level that represents the point that is small enough that we are willing to attribute to something other than chance. (We call this p_{select}.) Commonly selected probability levels are 0.05, 0.01 and 0.001.

6. Rule for making the decision is:

If $p_{observed} \leq p_{select}$ | Reject H_0 [If observed probability is less than or equal to the selected probability, then **REJECT** the null hypothesis]

If $p_{observed} > p_{select}$ | Retain H_0 [If observed probability is greater than the selected probability, then **RETAIN** the null hypothesis]

As you can see, the decision to reject or retain the null hypothesis is not an arbitrary one, but based on probability theory and the notion of chance. And, as with anything involving chance, there is some risk involved. Let us explore the risks involved here and its significance to your findings.

Risking Error

The notion of rejecting or retaining the null hypothesis is based in the assumption that the probability of some events occurring by chance is so small, that when we observe those events, we attribute the occurrence to 'something' other than chance. The 'something' is usually assumed to be variations on the independent (or grouping) variable. Thus, for our example, when a significant difference was observed in their attitudes towards marriage, we linked those differences to the type of homes in which the members of sample were raised (single-parent vs. two-parent).

The thing to note here though is that because the probability of an event occurring by chance is small, it does not mean that it cannot actually occur by chance! Thus, when we observe the event, it may indeed be one of the rare occasions when it is a chance occurrence. What does that mean? Well, it means that when we make the decision to reject the null hypothesis using our decision rule above (that is, saying that the observed difference or relationship is not a chance occurrence), we may in fact be wrong. In other words, we may be committing an error! Now, do not panic! This error, called a Type I error, is not one over which you have control once you have establish a p_{select}, so it is not bad judgement on your part. This is in fact a statistical error that is associated with applying probability theory. The only control you have over the error comes when you decide on a value for p_{select}. How?

Consider this. When you establish p_{select}, let us say at 0.05, you are saying that if the probability of an event occurring by chance is 0.05 or less, you will attribute its occurrence to 'something' other than chance. But as mentioned before, it may in fact be one of the rare chance occurrences. What that means is that by establishing p_{select} at 0.05, you are saying that you are prepared to risk making an error 5 out of 100 times or 5% of the time. In essence then, the risk of making a Type I error is linked to the p_{select} you establish in that the smaller your p_{select}, the smaller the risk of committing such an error. This is why when students try to get us to tell them the probability level at which they should make their judgements, we usually reply 'it depends on how much risk you are willing to take!' Of course, the risk that you take would in turn depend on the severity of the consequences if you attribute observed results to 'something' when in fact they come about by chance.

Now before you go off deciding to set your probability level to as close to zero as you can, we must tell you briefly about Type II error. A Type II error is recorded when observed differences and relationships are NOT chance occurrences, but you have set your probability level so low, that they appear to be. Consider this. Suppose in order to reduce the risk of committing a Type I error, you set your probability level for making decisions about the null hypothesis at 0.0001 or 1 in every 10,000. Now let us say that when you run the test of significance using SPSS, it indicates that the probability of observing the particular difference or relationship is 0.001. Using the rule above, you would retain the null hypothesis that the observed difference or relationship is not statistically significant (it is a chance occurrence). The fact may be that conditions of the independent variable are linked to the observed results and that it is not a chance occurrence. But your probability level is so small, that you would fail to pick this up. This is your Type II error: failure to reject a null hypothesis that is not true. Type I and Type II errors are explained graphically in Figure 11f below.

Figure 11f
Type I and Type II Errors

		H_0 is:	
		TRUE	FALSE
Possible Decisions	Reject H_0	Type I Error	Correct Decision
	Retain H_0	Correct Decision	Type II Error

The point being made here is that if you try to avoid making a Type I error by selecting a very small probability level, you in fact increase the risk of making a Type II error. Again, your decision about committing any error is dependent on what is at stake or as mentioned before, the consequences of making a 'wrong' decision. This is all part of the excitement and uncertainty of dabbling in probability and chance. But if you are going to apply inferential statistics to your data, then these are the risks you have to take!

Now before we explore these exciting tests of significance, there is one more concept to meet.

Degrees of Freedom

There is one other measure that you need to be aware of when you are dealing with tests of significance: degrees of freedom. The technical definition for this term is 'the number of scores in a data set that are free to vary.' Yes, we can hear you saying 'Huh?' So let us explain with an example. We have found this to be best. Consider this:

Suppose you know that the mean of five scores (let's call them A, B, C, D and E) is 6. What else do you know about this data set? Well you can work out that the sum of the scores is 30 (mean times the number of scores or 6 x 5).

Thus you know that A +B +C + D + E = 30. Now, in order to work out what each score is, you need more information. You need to know some of the scores.

If we said that A = 5, can you say what the other scores are? Not really. But you would now have additional information. You now know that 5 + B + C + D + E = 30.

Therefore, B + C + D + E = 25. But you need more information to work out the other scores. If we told you that B = 7, would that help? Yes, because now you would know that 7 + C + D + E = 25.

Therefore, C + D + E = 18. You still cannot say what the other scores are. They can take on several different values (or vary). What if you found out that C = 6? Then you would know that 6 + D + E = 18.

Therefore D + E = 12. Again you do not know the value of these two scores. They can vary. Now if we tell you that D = 8, aha! If D + E = 12 and you know that D = 8, then E must be 4. It cannot vary if the data set is to meet the criterion of having a mean of 6.

So, for a set of five scores, if we know the mean, then 4 of the scores are free to vary, that is, there are 4 degrees of freedom. Once you know four of the scores, then the last one is also known, it cannot vary. Thus, if you start with the mean of 5 scores, only 4 (5 – 1) of them are free to vary. We can make the general statement that, for the mean, the degrees of freedom can be found using the formula (n – 1) where n is the number of scores in the data set.

Like the mean, each test of significance has an associated formula for calculating the number of scores in the set that are free to vary, that is, the degree of freedom. You need not memorise these formulae if you are using SPSS®. This statistic is routinely included in the output, and is often quoted when you report your findings. Explaining the importance of knowing the degrees of freedom is outside the scope of this book, but if you are interested in finding out, then you should consult one of the several elementary statistics books that are on the market.

Now that we have filled you in on the background information, let us explore some common tests of significance.

Selecting a Test of Significance

As with everything else in research, applying inferential statistical procedures requires choices and decisions. And, as with everything in research, you need to make informed choices and to be able to defend those choices with appropriate reasons. One important choice that you must make relates to the particular tests of significance that you will apply to your data. The test that you choose would depend on factors such as:

- The question(s) you are trying to answer;
- The size of your sample;
- The manner in which the sample was selected; and
- The nature of the data.

But before we explore individual tests, let us consider a broad classification of these tests. Tests of significance may be grouped under two broad headings: parametric and nonparametric. Parametric tests make certain general assumptions about the population from which the data are collected. These assumptions include the following:

- That sampling distribution approximates a normal distribution;
- That the variances in the populations from which the samples are drawn are approximately equal;
- That the scores are on the interval or ratio levels of measurement.

Parametric tests involve the mean and standard deviation or the variance of the data sets collected from the sample(s) involved in your study. Thus, you should make sure that your scores are interval or ratio measurements otherwise the results may not make much sense. Apart from these general assumptions, there may be other specific assumptions associated with individual parametric tests. Thus, before you apply a test of significance to your data, you should check the assumptions to ensure that your data meet the criteria for the test. Having said that, statistics texts will inform you that parametric tests are very robust and can still return valid results if some of the assumptions are violated; that is, if your data do not meet all the assumptions of the tests.

On the other hand are nonparametric tests. These tests make no assumptions about population from which the data are collected, and rather than being based on means and standard deviations like parametric tests, nonparametric tests involve frequencies and ranks. Though nonparametric tests are said to be less powerful than parametric tests, they provide valid means of data analysis if your data violate the assumptions of parametric tests. For example, parametric tests are recommended when your data are categorical (on the nominal or ordinal scales of measurement) or if your sample is small. Indeed, there are nonparametric tests that are equivalent to several of the well-known parametric tests.

In the next section, we will introduce some common parametric tests and where they exist, we will identify their nonparametric equivalents. It should be noted though that not all nonparametric tests can be matched to a parametric one. Additionally, for each parametric test, we will present a scenario to illustrate its use. We will record the steps to be followed to run the specific test using SPSS® software. The SPSS® output will be presented and we will offer guidance as to how it can be interpreted. Remember, this list of tests is not exhaustive. Its purpose is simply to make you aware of regularly used tests of significance and to offer some general guidance as to when each one is appropriate.

SOME COMMON TESTS OF SIGNIFICANCE

T test for Independent Samples

This test is used to determine whether the observed difference between means for TWO groups is statistically significant. In order to use this test, you should have:

- One independent variable with TWO conditions (e.g. Sex: Male / Female)
- One dependent variable measured on the interval scale (e.g. scores on an attitude scale)

    H_0 tested: There is no statistically significant difference between the mean for Group 1 and that for Group 2 on the dependent variable.

The *nonparametric equivalent* of the t test for independent samples is the **Mann Whitney U Test**. It is used if your dependent variable is measured on AT LEAST the ordinal scale. In other words, you should be able to rank your data.

Scenario for the T Test for Independent Samples

In this scenario, let us say that you are investigating the claim that female employees at a company were paid significantly less than their male counterparts for doing the same jobs. To test this hypothesis, you selected a division in the company and ascertained the sex of each employee and their weekly salary. The data were entered in an SPSS® database in two variables: Sex of Employee (1- Female/2 - Male) and Salary Earned (to nearest $). To investigate the claim, the t-test for independent samples is applicable. Remember, this test determines if the difference between the means for two samples is large enough as to suggest that they are from different populations. An appropriate null hypothesis (H_0) would be:

> There is no significant difference between the mean salary of the female employees and that of the male employees.

To run the t-test for independent samples in SPSS®, you would follow these steps:

1. With the database containing the data open, click on <Analyse>, <Compare Means>, <Independent-Samples T Test ...>
2. Place the variable 'Salary Earned' in the window labelled Test Variable(s)
3. Place the variable 'Sex of Employee' in the window labelled Grouping Variable:
4. Click on <Define Groups>
5. Enter '1' (for females) for Group 1 and '2' (for males) for Group 2 and click on Continue.
6. Click on <Ok>.

The programme returns output looking like this:

T-TEST

Group Statistics

	Sex of Employee	N	Mean	Std. Deviation	Std. Error Mean
Salary Earned	Female	65	215.4000	38.29279	4.74964
	Male	70	243.2000	38.88392	4.64752

Independent Samples Test

		Levene's Test for Equality of Variances		t-test for Equality of Means						
									95% Confidence Interval of the Difference	
		F	Sig.	t	df	Sig. (2-tailed)	Mean Difference	Std. Error Difference	Lower	Upper
Salary Earned	Equal variances assumed	.129	.720	-4.181	133	.000	-27.8000	6.64898	-40.95143	-14.64857
	Equal variances not assumed			-4.183	132.533	.000	-27.8000	6.64518	-40.94434	-14.65566

From the first table you can see that the mean salary for the female employees is $215.40 and $243.20 for males. This means that the mean salary for females is $27.80 less than that for the male employees. So, is this difference statistically significant? To answer this question, you must consult the table labelled 'Independent Samples Test.' From this table, we can find the probability of obtaining a difference of this size ($27.80) and, comparing it with our selected probability level at which the hypothesis is to be tested, you would decide whether to reject or retain the null hypothesis. From the table, along with the observed probability, you should also identify the t statistic and the degrees of freedom. Looking at the table, you will notice that each of these columns has two values: one set is on a row labelled 'Equal variances assumed' and the other set labelled 'Equal variances not assumed.' So, which set of values should you use?

To choose you must consult the information from the 'Levene Test for Equality of Variance'. This test assesses the null hypothesis: there is no significant difference between the variances of the salaries for the two groups. It returns the probability of obtaining the differences in variances that were obtained for the two sets of salaries. This is your $p_{observed}$ which you would compare with your p_{select}. So, from the Levene test, $p_{observed}$ is 0.720. If you are carrying out your statistical tests at the 0.05 probability level, then $p_{observed}$ is larger than p_{select} (0.720 > 0.05). Using the 'rule', you would retain the null hypothesis. This means that you would conclude, as did the null hypothesis, that there is no significant difference between the variances of the two sets of salaries (one for female employees and the other for male employees). Put another way, the variances are equal. This is the answer to the question about which set of values you should use. Here, you should use the row labelled 'Equal variances assumed'. Having decided that, you have no further use for the Levene Test.

The results of the t test when equal variances are assumed are given in the first row, that is a t statistic of -4.181, degrees of freedom (df) of 133 and an observed probability (Sig.[2-tailed]) of .000. This might look strange since a probability of 0 indicates that it is impossible for an event to occur. The fact is that the SPSS software approximates to three decimal places. Thus, in order to register a result of .000, it means that the digit after the third 0 must have been less than 5. Since you cannot report that the probablity of the event occurring is 0, you must indicate what you do know, which is that the digit in the fourth decimal place must have been less than 5. Therefore, you report the probability as less than 0.0005 (< 0.0005). Now you can make a decision about the null hypothesis 'There is no significant difference between the mean salary of the female employees and that of the male employees' using the 'rule.' In this case, $p_{observed}$ is less than 0.0005 and p_{select} is 0.05. Therefore, $p_{observed}$ is less than p_{select} (a value less than 0.0005 < 0.05). This means that you should reject the null hypothesis. The conclusion is that there is a significant difference between the salaries earned by the female employees and those earned by the males. Since the mean for the males is higher, then we can say that the females earn significantly less than the males. You may report this finding as follows:

> The mean salary for the female employees was $215.40 (SD = $38.29) while that for the male employees was $243.20 (SD = $38.88). When a t test for independent samples was run, it revealed that there was a significant difference between these two means in favour of the male employees (t=4.181, df=133, p<0.0005). It can therefore be concluded that the female employees earned significantly less than did the male employees.

T test for Paired Samples

This test is used to determine whether the difference between the means of two sets of scores taken from the same sample on two different occasions is statistically significant. In order to use this test, you should have:

- Two scores for each member of the sample on the variable of interest (e.g. attitude scores BEFORE attending a course and scores AFTER attending the course).
- Scores on the interval scale.

H_0 tested: There is no statistically significant difference between group mean measured on Occasion 1 and that measured on Occasion 2.

The nonparametric equivalent for the t test for paired samples is the ***Wilcoxon Signed-Ranks Test***. It is used if your variable of interest is measured on AT LEAST the ordinal scale. In other words, you should be able to rank your data.

Scenario for the T Test for Paired Samples

A school counsellor was concerned that the first form students in the school seemed to have very low self-esteem. She decided to organise a three-week programme designed to improve this characteristic among the student population. She invited you to collect data to gauge the impact of the programme. Before the programme was introduced, you administered to the first form students a scale that provided a score that represented a measure of self-esteem, where the higher the score, the more positive the esteem. After the students had followed the programme, you administered the scale to the students again. This means that for each student you have two self-esteem measures – one taken before the programme and one taken after. These data are compiled in an SPSS® database. Your task is to determine if there is a difference between the before and after scores. The reasoning is that if the programme was successful, the after scores should be significantly higher than the before scores. For this purpose, you should use the **paired samples t test**. This procedure is also called the t test for paired samples. A suitable null hypothesis could be:

> There is no significant difference between the mean of the self-esteem scores obtained by the students before the programme and the mean of the scores obtained after the programme.

To run this procedure in SPSS®, follow these steps.

1. With the database containing the data open, click on <Analyse>, <Compare Means>, <Paired-Samples T Test ...>
2. Click on the 'Before' variable and the 'After' variable. The variable names should appear in the area labelled Current Selections.
3. Place the variables in the window labelled Paired Variables
4. Click on <Ok>.

The SPSS® output for the paired samples t test looks like this:

T-TEST

Paired Samples Statistics

		Mean	N	Std. Deviation	Std. Error Mean
Pair 1	Students' Self Esteem Scores BEFORE the Programme	40.38	90	5.427	.572
	Students' Self Esteem Scores AFTER the Programme	41.86	90	5.592	.589

Paired Samples Correlations

		N	Correlation	Sig.
Pair 1	Students' Self Esteem Scores BEFORE the Programme & Students' Self Esteem Scores AFTER the Programme	90	.093	.384

Paired Samples Test

		Paired Differences							
					95% Confidence Interval of the Difference				
		Mean	Std. Deviation	Std. Error Mean	Lower	Upper	t	df	Sig. (2-tailed)
Pair 1	Students' Self Esteem Scores BEFORE the Programme - Students' Self Esteem Scores AFTER the Programme	-1.48	7.422	.782	-3.03	.08	-1.889	89	.062

To use these results, first you should read the means for the before and after the programme scores. These statistics can be found in the table labelled 'Paired Samples Statistics.' The before mean is 40.4 (SD = 5.43) and the after mean 41.9 (SD = 5.59). In order to determine whether the difference between these two means is statistically significant, you should consult the table labelled 'Paired Samples Test.' From that test, you would examine the t statistic, the degrees of freedom and the observed probability [(Sig. (2-tailed)]. To decide whether to reject or retain the null hypothesis, apply the 'rule.' Now $p_{observed}$ is 0.062. If p_{select} is 0.05, then $p_{observed}$ is greater than p_{select} (0.062 > 0.05). Therefore, you would retain the null hypothesis, that is, you would conclude that there is no significant difference between the self-esteem scores obtained by the students before the programme was introduced and those obtained after the programme. This suggests that the programme appeared not to have the desired effect. You may report this finding like this:

The mean self-esteem score obtained by the students before the programme was introduced was 40.4 (SD = 5.43) and the mean score obtained after was 41.9 (SD = 5.59). When the t test for paired samples was run, it revealed that there was no significant difference between these two means (t=1.889, df=89, p=0.062). This suggests that the programme did not have the desired effect of significantly improving the students' self-esteem.

Now you may be wondering about the table in the middle of the output. This table is part of the default information provided by SPSS® when this test is run. It simply reports the correlation between the two variables and the associated probability. You may ignore this information if it is not relevant to your analysis!

One-Way Analysis of Variance (ANOVA)

This test is used to determine whether differences in means obtained for three or more groups are statistically significant. For this test, you should have:

- One independent variable with three or more conditions (e.g. Marital Status: Never Married/Married/Divorced
- One dependent variable measured on the interval scale (e.g. scores on an attitude scale)

H_0 tested: There is no statistically significant difference among the means obtained for the various groups on the dependent variable.

The nonparametric equivalent for the one-way ANOVA is the **Kruskal-Wallis Test.** It is used if your dependent variable is measured on at least the ordinal scale. In other words, you should be able to rank your data.

Scenario for One-Way Between Groups ANOVA

The Tourist Board is concerned that the tourism product is not as appealing to visitors from the Caribbean as it is to those from Europe and the USA. You are asked to investigate this phenomenon. For this purpose, you go to the airport to collect data from visitors who are leaving the country. You select a sample of visitors from these three regions (Caribbean, Europe and USA) and ask them to rate the appeal of the country as a tourist destination on a scale from 1 (Not at all appealing) to 10 (Extremely appealing). Thus, for each member of the sample, you have two vital pieces of data: Region of Origin and an Appeal Rating. These data are compiled in an SPSS database to be analysed. For this purpose, the **one-way between groups analysis of variance (ANOVA)** procedure is appropriate. A suitable null hypothesis would be:

There is no significant difference in the ratings assigned by visitors from the Caribbean, Europe and the USA.

To run the one-way between groups ANOVA, follow these steps:
1. With the database containing the data open, click on <Analyse>, <Compare Means>, <One Way ANOVA ...>
2. Transfer the 'Ratings' variable to the window labelled 'Dependent List:'.
3. Place the 'Region of Origin' variable in the window labelled 'Factor:'
4. Click on the button <Options...> and under the area labelled 'Statistics', select 'Descriptive' and 'Homogeneity of variance test'. Click on Continue.
5. Click on the button <Post Hoc...>. Under the area labelled 'Equal Variances Assumed', select 'Tukey'. Under the area labelled 'Equal Variance Not Assumed', select 'Tamhane's T2'. Click on Continue.
6. Click on OK.

The SPSS® output returned looks like this:

Oneway

Descriptives

Rating Assigned to the Country for Appeal

	N	Mean	Std. Deviation	Std. Error	95% Confidence Interval for Mean		Minimum	Maximum
					Lower Bound	Upper Bound		
Caribbean	48	3.54	1.624	.234	3.07	4.01	1	7
Europe	53	7.92	1.357	.186	7.55	8.30	4	10
USA	43	5.98	1.752	.267	5.44	6.52	3	10
Total	144	5.88	2.414	.201	5.48	6.28	1	10

Test of Homogeneity of Variances

Rating Assigned to the Country for Appeal

Levene Statistic	df1	df2	Sig.
1.662	2	141	.193

ANOVA

Rating Assigned to the Country for Appeal

	Sum of Squares	df	Mean Square	F	Sig.
Between Groups	484.402	2	242.201	97.967	.000
Within Groups	348.592	141	2.472		
Total	832.993	143			

Post Hoc Tests

Multiple Comparisons

Dependent Variable: Rating Assigned to the Country for Appeal

	(I) Origin of the Visitors	(J) Origin of the Visitors	Mean Difference (I-J)	Std. Error	Sig.	95% Confidence Interval Lower Bound	Upper Bound
Tukey HSD	Caribbean	Europe	-4.38*	.313	.000	-5.12	-3.64
		USA	-2.44*	.330	.000	-3.22	-1.65
	Europe	Caribbean	4.38*	.313	.000	3.64	5.12
		USA	1.95*	.323	.000	1.18	2.71
	USA	Caribbean	2.44*	.330	.000	1.65	3.22
		Europe	-1.95*	.323	.000	-2.71	-1.18
Tamhane	Caribbean	Europe	-4.38*	.299	.000	-5.11	-3.65
		USA	-2.44*	.355	.000	-3.30	-1.57
	Europe	Caribbean	4.38*	.299	.000	3.65	5.11
		USA	1.95*	.326	.000	1.15	2.74
	USA	Caribbean	2.44*	.355	.000	1.57	3.30
		Europe	-1.95*	.326	.000	-2.74	-1.15

*. The mean difference is significant at the .05 level.

Homogeneous Subsets

Rating Assigned to the Country for Appeal

	Origin of the Visitors	N	Subset for alpha = .05 1	2	3
Tukey HSD[a,b]	Caribbean	48	3.54		
	USA	43		5.98	
	Europe	53			7.92
	Sig.		1.000	1.000	1.000

Means for groups in homogeneous subsets are displayed.

a. Uses Harmonic Mean Sample Size = 47.652.

b. The group sizes are unequal. The harmonic mean of the group sizes is used. Type I error levels are not guaranteed.

Calm down! Indeed, sit down! Before you start to panic, we will examine this output table by table as we explain how to interpret it.

First, you should get a sense of the mean rating assigned by the visitors from the three regions. This can be found in the first table. From that table, you will find the size of each of the three groups (N), the mean and standard deviation of ratings assigned by each group. These statistics should be reported in the findings. The question is: is there a significant difference among these three means? To answer this question, you must consult the output labelled ANOVA. From this table, pay attention to the F statistic, the degrees of freedom (df) and the observed probability (Sig.). Notice that there are two degrees of freedom: Between Groups and Within Groups. Both of these should be quoted when you report these results. But how do you use the output to make a decision about the null hypothesis? Well, as before, you apply the 'rule.' Now $p_{observed}$ is less than 0.0005 (remember this is what you report when SPSS® returns an observed probability of .000). If your p_{select} is 0.05, then $p_{observed}$ is less than p_{select}. Therefore you would reject the null hypothesis and conclude that there is a significant difference among the ratings.

Now that you know there is a difference among the three sets of ratings, the question is, where does the difference lie? To find out you need to consult a post hoc multiple comparisons test. Post hoc tests are only consulted when the ANOVA results indicate that there is a significant difference among the groups. This information is in the fourth table in the SPSS® output. But remember, we ran a post hoc test assuming equal variances and one where equal variances are not assumed, so first you must decide which to use in our interpretation. To do this, you should consult the second table which contains the results of the Test of Homogeneity of Variances. This test provides information about the variances of the ratings from the three groups. You will remember that one of the assumptions of parametric tests such as ANOVA is that the variances are equal for the groups involved. The Test of Homogeneity of Variances checks this assumption. It returns a Levene Statistic that is interpreted in the same way as it was for the t test for independent samples. Thus, it assesses the null hypothesis 'There is no significant difference in the variances among the ratings assigned by the three groups.' The test measures the variances and the differences among them. The probability of obtaining such differences by chance is returned. This is your observed probability and you would compare it with your selected probability level to decide whether to reject or retain the null hypothesis. So then, from the second table in the output you make a judgement about the variances of the ratings. From the table, $p_{observed}$ is 0.193. If your p_{select} is 0.05, then $p_{observed}$ is greater than p_{select} (0.193 > 0.05), so you would retain the null hypothesis, that is, you would conclude that there is no significant difference among the variances or that the variances are equal. (This is a good thing! It indicates that your data meet that assumption of parametric tests!) This means that you are going to be looking at the Tukey HSD results.

The multiple comparisons procedure compares the mean rating of each of the three groups with the other two. For example, it compares the mean rating assigned by the Caribbean visitors to that assigned by the European visitors and that of the USA visitors. If the difference is significant, the mean difference is marked with an asterisk (*). If you like, you can verify this by checking the observed probability and applying our 'rule.' Now when you consult the table, you can see that the ratings assigned by the Caribbean visitors differ significantly from those assigned by the European and USA visitors. Further, there is also a significant difference between the ratings assigned by the European and USA visitors. What does this mean? Well, you should check the mean ratings to see which was higher since the higher the rating the more appealing the group found the country. Thus, you will find that the Caribbean visitors assigned a lower rating (3.54) than did the USA visitors (5.98) and the European visitors (7.92). This suggests that the Caribbean visitors rated the visitor appeal of the country significantly lower than did the USA and European visitors. To report the finding here, you may write:

The means and standard deviations of the ratings assigned by the visitors from the three regions are shown below:

Visitors' Region of Origin	Mean Rating	S.D.
Caribbean	3.54	1.62
European	7.92	1.36
USA	5.98	1.75

The results of the one-way ANOVA procedure that was run indicated that there was a significant difference among these mean ratings ($F[2, 141] = 97.967$; $p < 0.005$). The results of a Tukey HSD multiple comparison procedure revealed that there was a significant difference between the ratings of the Caribbean visitors and the USA visitors, between the Caribbean visitors and the European visitors as well as between the USA visitors and the European visitors. Thus, it can be concluded that the Caribbean visitors rated the appeal of the country significantly lower than did the USA and European visitors.

So far, we have only listed tests of significance that assess whether observed differences in means are statistically significant. But sometimes, you may want to ascertain whether observed relationships between two variables are statistically significant. Let us consider two commonly used procedures for such occasions.

Pearson Product Moment Correlation Test (r)

This is the same procedure that we met in the previous chapter on descriptive statistics. Only here, we go a step further. When we just want to describe the strength and direction of the relationship between two variables, we can calculate the Pearson r coefficient (or we can get SPSS® to do it for us!). We can go a step further by determining if the observed relationship is significantly different from no relationship at all. If you do this using SPSS®, this information is provided by default. As mentioned before, to use this procedure, you should have two variables measured on the interval or ratio scales.

H_0 tested: The observed relationship is not significantly different from no relationship at all (i.e. $r = 0$).

A nonparametric equivalent for Pearson correlation is **Spearman Rank Difference Test**, also called Rho (ρ). This nonparametric equivalent is used if the sample is small or your data are at least on the ordinal scale.

Scenario for Pearson Correlation

For this scenario, let us return to an example given in a previous chapter. A psychologist argued that men tended to feel pressured to marry and will do so despite their own feelings about the institution. Over a two-year period, she collected data from men who applied for a marriage licence for the first time and analysed them to find out if there is a relationship between the age (in years) at which men marry and their attitudes towards marriage (measured by a score that can range from 20 to 100, where the higher the score, the more positive the attitude). You are presented with the data from 200 men and you are required to run the procedure in SPSS® and interpret the output.

Here, the Pearson Correlation procedure would be appropriate because you are testing for a relationship and the two variables are measured on the interval scale. An appropriate null hypothesis (H_0) would be:

> There is not a significant relationship between men's attitude to marriage and the age at which they get married.

To run the procedure in SPSS®, you would follow these steps:

1. With the database open, select the following on the menu bar: <Analyse>, <Correlate>, <Bivariate …>
2. Place the two variables in the window labelled Variables.
3. You should leave the other three selection at the default options:
   - Under Correlation Coefficients, 'Pearson' should be selected.
   - Under Test of Significance, 'Two-tailed' should be selected.
   - 'Flag significant correlations' should be selected
4. Click on <OK>.

The resulting SPSS® output would look like this:

Correlations

Correlations

		Age of Marriage Applicants	Attitude towards Marriage Score
Age of Marriage Applicants	Pearson Correlation	1	-.140*
	Sig. (2-tailed)	.	.047
	N	200	200
Attitude towards Marriage Score	Pearson Correlation	-.140*	1
	Sig. (2-tailed)	.047	.
	N	200	200

*. Correlation is significant at the 0.05 level (2-tailed).

To interpret this output, you need to pay attention to the cell in the top right corner or the one in the bottom left corner. These two cells contain the same values and present the measure of the relationship between the two variables [Pearson Correlation], the probability of obtaining such a relationship by chance [Sig. (2-tailed)], and the sample size [N].

The Pearson Correlation coefficient is -0.14. Using the figure 10h (p. 154), this represents a negative relationship that is negligible. From this, two conclusions can be drawn. First, because it is negative, we know that as one variable increases, the other decreases. Thus, the older the men were when they first married, the lower the score on the attitude scale (or the less favourable the attitude towards marriage). Second, because of the magnitude of the coefficient, we know that the relationship is so weak as to be negligible. We can therefore say that it has little practical significance, that is, the result has little real usefulness. But what about statistical significance? In order to check for statistical significance we need to apply our 'rule.' Now if we are carrying out our test at the 0.05 probability level (p_{select}), we can compare this with our $p_{observed}$ which is 0.047. Now $p_{observed}$ is smaller than p_{select} (0.047 < 0.05), therefore, the null hypothesis (H_0) is rejected. The conclusion then is that the relationship between the two variables is statistically significant. To report this finding, you may write:

> A Pearson Correlation procedure was run to investigate the relationship between the age at which the participants first married and their attitude towards marriage. A slight inverse relationship was found (r = –0.14). This relationship was statistically significant (p = 0.047).

In case you are wondering why a negligible relationship can be statistically significant (and even if you are not we will mention it anyway!), remember this: if your sample is large, a relatively small correlation coefficient is likely to be found to be statistically significant. It is possible that if the same coefficient were obtained from a smaller sample, the relationship might not be statistically significant. So then, be aware that the size of your sample can influence this test.

Correlations can be used in studies that explore relationships between variables or in prediction studies. Each of these types of studies has specific considerations when interpreting the coefficients. What we have dealt with here is the very basics of correlational analysis. For a more in depth look at issues related to the interpretation of correlation, you might want to have a look at Hinton (1995).

Chi Square Test

The Chi Square test is a bit different from the others we introduced above in that it is a non-parametric test that has no parametric equivalent. To use it, your data should be categorical, since this procedure is based on frequencies or counts. This test helps you to determine whether the frequency distribution that you obtain from your data (observed distribution) differs significantly from what you would expect to find if the variables are statistically independent (expected distribution). The Chi Square test works by comparing the observed distribution with the expected distribution and determining the probability of obtaining the difference between the two distributions by chance. Remember, as explained earlier, we always expect some chance fluctuation in our data, but we also expect it to be within a certain range. Anything outside of the acceptable range may be attributed to factors other than chance. There are two forms of the Chi Square test – the goodness-of-fit test and the test of independence.

Chi Square Goodness-of-Fit Test

This test is used to determine if observed frequencies are a good fit for a particular pattern of expected frequencies or whether they differ significantly. It is applicable when we have data from one categorical variable and we can hypothesise about an expected pattern of frequencies. Let us see how it works by considering something that we all know about: playing with dice.

Let us say that you had a die (say from your Ludo or Snakes and Ladders game) and you had some time on your hands, so you decided to toss it 600 times. If it is a fair die (all six faces have an equal chance of coming on the top when the die is tossed), then you might expect a pattern of equal numbers of ones, twos, threes, fours, fives and sixes. However, we might obtain the results shown in Figure 11g below.

Figure 11g
Expected and Observed Frequencies of the Scores when a Die is Tossed 600 Times

Face of Die	Expected Frequency	Observed Frequency
1	100	93
2	100	106
3	100	104
4	100	103
5	100	101
6	100	93
	600	600

Notice that we do not obtain exactly equal distribution of scores; some have frequencies above the expected and some below. The Chi Square goodness-of-fit test helps us to decide whether the observed frequencies fit the expected pattern, allowing for chance fluctuations. The Chi Square test run in SPSS® returns the probability of obtaining these frequencies by chance and depending on the risk we are willing to take, we can make our decision. (We discussed this earlier in this chapter.)

Scenario for Chi Square Goodness-of-Fit Test

A principal is arguing that his school board's hiring policy is leaving him with staff significantly different from other schools. He shows that for the other schools, the hiring policy tends to result in equal numbers of teachers in six categories. He shows a table that indicated the number of teachers in each category at his school.

You can use a Chi Square (X^2) goodness-of-fit test to ascertain if the composition of his staff is significantly different from what might be expected. What conclusion would you reach? The table below shows the number of teachers in the various categories at the school and the null hypothesis to be tested.

Professional Status	Frequency
Trained Graduate	4
Trained Non-Graduate	6
Untrained Graduate	15
Untrained Non-Graduate	20
Special Grade	9
Teaching Assistant	6

H_0: The pattern of frequencies observed is no different from the expected distribution.

The professional status of the members of the school's staff was compiled in the database under the variable name 'Status.' The steps for testing the null hypothesis using the Chi Square Goodness of Fit Test using SPSS® software are as follows:

1. With the database open, select the following on the menu bar:
    <Analyse>, <Nonparametric test>, <Chi Square...>
2. Place the variable 'Status' in the window labelled Test Variable List.
3. Make sure that 'All Categories Equal' is selected in the Expected Values window.
4. Click on <OK>.

The resulting output is shown below.

Chi-Square Test (Goodness of Fit)

Status of Teachers at a Certain School

	Observed N	Expected N	Residual
Trained Graduate	4	10.0	-6.0
Trained Nongraduate	6	10.0	-4.0
Untrained Graduate	15	10.0	5.0
Untrained Nongraduate	20	10.0	10.0
Special Grade	9	10.0	-1.0
Teaching Assistant	6	10.0	-4.0
Total	60		

Test Statistics

	Status of Teachers at a Certain School
Chi-Square[a]	19.400
df	5
Asymp. Sig.	.002

a. 0 cells (.0%) have expected frequencies less than 5. The minimum expected cell frequency is 10.0.

Notice that the output includes a table with the observed frequency for each status group and the expected frequency (equal numbers for each status group). In order to decide whether to reject or retain the null hypothesis, you must look at the Test Statistics table. This table reports the value of 19.4, degrees of freedom of 5 and an observed probability (Asymp. Sig.) of 0.002.

Working at the 0.05 probability level (i.e. any event with a probability of occurring at 0.05 or less is deemed as not occurring by chance), what do we decide about the null hypothesis? Well, applying our 'rule', p_{select} is 0.05 and $p_{observed}$ is 0.002.

Thus, $P_{observed} < p_{select}$. Therefore H_o is rejected.

This indicates that the null hypothesis that there is no significant difference between the observed pattern of frequencies and the hypothesised expected pattern of equal distribution is to be rejected. We would therefore conclude that the pattern is significantly different from the expected pattern. Then we would examine the observed pattern and comment on how it is different.

In your report, after presenting the contingency table with the expected and observed distributions, you could write:

> The results of a Chi square goodness of fit test indicated that there was a significant difference between the observed distribution of staff across qualification levels and the expected distribution (X^2 = 19.4, df = 5, p = 0.002). Thus, the school had significantly fewer trained teachers and more untrained teachers than what was expected.

Chi Square Test of Independence

This procedure is applicable when you want to explore associations (relationships) between two categorical variables. You may recall that in the previous chapter, we mentioned a cross-tabulation as a means of exploring the frequency distribution when two variables are involved (if you don't, why not go back there and refresh your memory!). Well, the Chi Square test of independence helps you to determine whether the observed frequencies in the individual cells match an expected pattern. Let us expand on the example that we met in the previous chapter. In that example, we had two variables: sex (female/male) and party preference (Here and Now Democratic Set [HANDS]/the Followers of Old Tradition Set [FOOTS]).

Let us say that we polled 120 people, recording their sex and their party preference. Let us say that there were 60 females and 60 males; 80 for HANDS and 40 for FOOTS. The associated cross-tabulation table for these data are shown in Figure 11h below.

Figure 11h
Cross-tabulation Showing Party Preference by Sex

		Party Preference		
		HANDS	FOOTS	Total
Sex	Female	45	15	60
	Male	35	25	60
Total		80	40	120

The table above shows the observed frequencies. The expected frequency for each cell can be calculated by multiplying the row total by the column total and dividing the result by the over all total. Thus, to work out the expected frequency for the cell that represents the females who prefer HANDS and for females who prefer FOOTS, you would do this:

Expected Frequency for Females who prefer HANDS	Expected Frequency for Females who prefer FOOTS
$\dfrac{60 \times 80}{120}$	$\dfrac{60 \times 40}{120}$
$= \dfrac{4800}{120}$	$= \dfrac{2400}{120}$
$= 40$	$= 20$

The completed table of observed and expected (in brackets) frequencies for each cell is shown below (Figure 11i).

Figure 11i
Cross-tabulation Showing Party Preference by Sex

		Party Preference		Total
		HANDS	FOOTS	
Sex	Female	45 (40)	15 (20)	60
	Male	35 (40)	25 (20)	60
Total		80	40	120

The Chi Square test run in SPSS® returns the probability of obtaining the observed pattern by chance. We can then decide, based on the risk we are willing to take, whether to retain or reject the null hypothesis.

Scenario for Chi Square Test of Independence

A polyclinic introduced a new policy for dealing with patients visiting the facility. You are interested in finding out how the staff and patients feel about the new policy. To do this, you carry out a survey involving 200 individuals: 128 patients and 72 staff members. The respondent could like the new policy (Like), dislike it (Dislike) or have no opinion or not know about it (Don't know). The contingency table with the data collected and the associated null hypothesis are presented below.

Status of respondent	Opinion about the New Policy			Row totals
	Like	Dislike	Don't Know	
Patients	89	27	12	128
Staff Members	7	50	15	72
Column Totals	96	77	27	200

H_0: There is no association between the status of polyclinic user and opinion about the new policy implemented.

In order to test this null hypothesis, a Chi Square test of independence can be run. Let us say that you had the data compiled in an SPSS® database with the variables 'Status' and 'Opinion' The steps for doing this using SPSS® software are:

1. With the database open, select the following on the menu bar:
   <Analyse>, <Descriptive Statistics>, <Cross tabs …>
2. Place one of the variables in the Row(s): window and the other variable in the

Column(s): window.

3. Click on the <Statistics> button at the bottom of the dialogue box and select the Chi Square option. Click on Continue.

4. Click on the <Cells> button next and select the Expected option. The Observed option is selected by default and should remain selected. Click on Continue.

5. Click on <OK>.

The resulting output is shown below.

Crosstabs

Case Processing Summary

	Cases					
	Valid		Missing		Total	
	N	Percent	N	Percent	N	Percent
Status of Respondent * Feeling about the New Policy	200	100.0%	0	.0%	200	100.0%

Status of Respondent * Feeling about the New Policy Crosstabulation

			Feeling about the New Policy			
			LIKE the new policy	DISLIKE the new policy	Don't know	Total
Status of Respondent	Patient	Count	89	27	12	128
		Expected Count	61.4	49.3	17.3	128.0
	Staff	Count	7	50	15	72
		Expected Count	34.6	27.7	9.7	72.0
Total		Count	96	77	27	200
		Expected Count	96.0	77.0	27.0	200.0

Chi-Square Tests

	Value	df	Asymp. Sig. (2-sided)
Pearson Chi-Square	66.802[a]	2	.000
Likelihood Ratio	74.368	2	.000
Linear-by-Linear Association	46.952	1	.000
N of Valid Cases	200		

a. 0 cells (.0%) have expected count less than 5. The minimum expected count is 9.72.

In the output, the Case Processing Summary tells you how many cases in the database were included in the analysis and how many were left out. Cases are left out if data are missing. Thus, for example, if a patient did not give a response to the item on opinion, then that patient would be left out of the analysis.

The next table in the output is the 2 x 3 (2 rows, 3 columns) cross-tabulation that shows the frequencies, that is, the number of respondents expressing the various opinions. You will notice that there are two sets of frequencies: Count and Expected Count. The Count tells you the actual or observed distribution from your data. The Expected Count shows the pattern of distribution that you could expect if the two variables are statistically independent. As was mentioned earlier, the Chi Square test compares the observed pattern of frequencies with the expected pattern and gives the probability of obtaining the difference by chance. Those results are shown in the third table labelled Chi Square Tests.

From the Chi Square Tests table, you must pay attention to the statistics relating to the Pearson Chi Square. Note that a Chi Square value of 66.802 is being reported along with a degree of freedom (df) of 2. A probability [Asymp. Sig. (2-sided)] of .000 is also reported. Therefore, you report the probability as less than 0.0005 (< 0.0005). So then, the statistics that you report are:

$$\chi^2 = 66.802; \ df = 2; \ p < 0.0005.$$

Now, what decision do you make about the null hypothesis (H_0)? Well, applying our 'rule', P_{select} is 0.05 and $p_{observed}$ is less than 0.0005. Since $p_{observed} < P_{select}$, H_0 is rejected. This means that there is a significant association between the status of the respondents and their opinions about the new policy at the clinic. The question is: What is the association? To determine this, you must go back to the contingency table (cross-tabulation) and examine the observed and expected frequencies. You will notice that about 61 patients were expected to be for the new policy, but in fact a frequency of 89 was recorded, while about 35 staff members were expected to be for it, but a frequency of 7 was recorded. On the other hand, 49 patients were expected to be against the new policy, but in fact a frequency of 27 was recorded while 27 staff members were expected to be against it, but a frequency of 50 was recorded. So then more patients than expected liked the policy and fewer staff members did, while fewer patients than expected disliked the policy and more staff than expected disliked it. This is interpreted to mean that patients were significantly more likely to like the policy than did staff members and staff members were significantly more likely to dislike the policy than did patients. To report this finding, after presenting the contingency table, you may write:

> The results of a Chi square test of independence indicated that there was a significant association between the status of the clinic users and their feelings about the new policy ($\chi^2 = 66.80$, df = 2, p < 0.0005), with patients being more likely to like the new policy than did the staff members.

SPECIAL NOTE

The Chi square test of significance is very useful, but there are some things that you need to watch out for. For example, at the bottom of the test statistic, you will see this message '0 cells (.0%) have expected count less than five. The minimum expected count is 9.72.' You should pay attention to this message. One of the assumptions of the Chi square test is that your sample is large enough to ensure that the expected frequency for each cell is five or more. The test is still considered valid if a few cells do not meet this requirement. However, if too many of the cells have expected count of less than five, then your results may be unreliable. How many are 'too many?' There are several answers to this question. For example, Howell (1999) advises that for contingency tables with nine or fewer cells, all expected frequencies should be five or more, a restriction that he relaxes for larger tables. On the other hand, Preacher (2001) warns that the Chi square is inappropriate if the expected frequency is less than five in more than 20 per cent of the cells. This is the position that we usually take. If your data violates this assumption, you may consider reducing the number of cells by combining categories. For example, categories such as 'strongly dislike' and 'dislike' can be collapsed in to a single category. Other methods may be explored but these are outside the scope of this book.

A second issue to which you must pay attention comes about when you have a 2 x 2 contingency table, that is, each of your variables has two categories. To explore this, let us go back to one of our previous examples: sex of respondents and their preference of political party. You may remember that we had two parties the Here and Now Democratic Set [HANDS] and the Followers of Old Tradition Set [FOOTS]. We asked 120 voters which party they preferred. Let us run a Chi square test of independence to determine if there is an association between the sex of the voters and party preference. The SPSS® output is shown below.

Crosstabs

Case Processing Summary

	Cases					
	Valid		Missing		Total	
	N	Percent	N	Percent	N	Percent
Sex of Voter * Party Preference of Voter	120	20.0%	480	80.0%	600	100.0%

Sex of Voter * Party Preference of Voter Crosstabulation

			HANDS	FOOTS	Total
			Party Preference of Voter		
Sex of Voter	Female	Count	15	45	60
		Expected Count	20.0	40.0	60.0
	Male	Count	25	35	60
		Expected Count	20.0	40.0	60.0
Total		Count	40	80	120
		Expected Count	40.0	80.0	120.0

Chi-Square Tests

	Value	df	Asymp. Sig. (2-sided)	Exact Sig. (2-sided)	Exact Sig. (1-sided)
Pearson Chi-Square	3.750[b]	1	.053		
Continuity Correction[a]	3.038	1	.081		
Likelihood Ratio	3.780	1	.052		
Fisher's Exact Test				.081	.040
Linear-by-Linear Association	3.719	1	.054		
N of Valid Cases	120				

a. Computed only for a 2x2 table

b. 0 cells (.0%) have expected count less than 5. The minimum expected count is 20.00.

What we want to draw to your attention is found in the table with the Chi square test results. If you compare it with the previous Chi square output, you will see that there is some extra information. There is a line of statistics labelled 'Continuity Correction' with an accompanying note that says it is 'computed only for a 2 x 2 table.' For those of you who have done the Chi square test manually and know about the Yates correction, then this is what the continuity correction is about. For those who do not know about it, do not despair. You can read about it in any elementary statistics book. What is important to say here is that whenever there is a 2 x 2 contingency table, SPSS® presents the continuity correction. Whenever the continuity correction is presented, you should use it instead of the Pearson Chi square statistics. Thus, the statistics you would report for this example are $X^2 = 3.04$; df = 1; p = 0.081, and you would make your decision about the null hypothesis in the usual way, using the 'rule.' In this case, the null hypothesis would be retained since $p_{observed}$ (0.081) is greater than p_{select} (0.05). Thus, you would report that there is no association between sex and party preference and quote the statistics ($X^2 = 3.04$; df = 1; p = 0.081).

Here is a list (Figure 11j) of the tests of significance that were introduced in this chapter.

Figure 11j
Summary of Tests of Significance

Purpose	Parametric Test	Nonparametric Equivalent
Explore the difference between means obtained by two groups on the same variable	T test for Independent Samples	Mann Whitney U
Explore the difference between the means of two sets of scores on the same variable obtained by the same sample on two different occasions	T test for Paired Samples	Wilcoxon Signed Test
Explore the difference between means obtained by three or more groups on the same variable	One-way Between Groups ANOVA	Kruskal-Wallis Test
Explore the relationship between two variables	Pearson r	Spearman Rho
Explore association between two (categorical) variables	No Parametric Equivalent	Chi Square

A WORD OF ENCOURAGEMENT

Over the years of teaching courses in research methods, we have found that many students are terrified at the thought of statistical procedures. The chief complaint is 'I am really bad at Maths!' Well take heart. With the advent of computers and computer software such as SPSS®, you no longer have to grapple with fear-inducing formulae. As long as you know which procedure to apply then it can all be done in a few relatively easy steps after you have compiled your data in the database. Your main concern, apart from applying an appropriate procedure, is knowing how to interpret the output from the procedures.

In chapter 2 where we discussed ethics, we mentioned that you should pay close attention to the manner in which you analyse your data. Remember, from your research you are hoping to add to the body of knowledge in your field. If you attempt to do so using inappropriate statistical procedures, your research and you could lose credibility. If you need help, find a source of reliable help, but remember, practice makes perfect! The more research you undertake and the more data analysis you do, the more familiar you will become with the procedures. Persevere. There is much social research to be done in this unique Caribbean. So hone your skills and let's get on with it.

12

NOW TELL THEM WHAT YOU'VE DONE

So far, we have taken you through the research process from identifying an area to investigate to analysing the data collected to complete your investigation. So at this point, you have research findings and you must communicate them to the rest of the world in a concise, coherent manner: you are ready to produce your research report. In this chapter, we offer some guideline on how you might do this as painlessly as possible. Remember though that this is just general advice. Each institution may have specific instructions that their students are to follow. Find out whether there are any such requirements for your institution or department, and where they differ from what we suggest, then you should follow those of your institution. So, now that we have cleared that up, let us go on.

GENERAL FORMAT OF A RESEARCH REPORT

Whether you are writing up you research project for publication or as a paper or thesis to be graded, there is a general format that it should take. This format includes five major chapters or sections: (i) an introduction, (ii) critical review of relevant literature, (iii) the methodology, (iv) the findings and (v) the conclusion. Depending on the purpose of the write up, each section may be a single chapter or a number of chapters. Let us consider what should be included in each section/chapter.

The Introduction

This chapter or section sets the tone for the paper. This is where you report the things we discussed in chapter 3. It is here that you report the background of the research and the rationale for doing it. The background should explain to the reader the context of the research — what sparked your interest in the particular area. For example, you may have selected that area because it is topical or because of something that you learned in your course of study or because of some personal experience. You should also articulate the reason for carrying out the research, what you hope to accomplish and who you believe would benefit from your findings. The introduction is usually the first in depth contact that readers have with your study (they might have read the abstract, but that is of necessity very abbreviated). Therefore, you must capture their attention, whet their appetite for what is to come, make them want to read on.

In this chapter or section, you should present your problem statement and research questions or hypotheses. Sometimes supervisors advise that these be written after the literature review, but we believe that if these are stated up front, the reader has a clear understanding of what you are going to do from the outset and can judge the appropriateness of your literature when they are reading the review. In any case, you can re-state the problem and research questions and/or hypotheses after the review. We also recommend that this introductory chapter or section of your research is a good place to define terms and variables that are important to the study. Remember, many terms have a variety of meanings and you should indicate as early as possible the meanings you are adopting for your research.

One thing that we feel is worth mentioning here is the use of literature in this chapter or section. Often, inexperienced researchers write the introduction without any citations, even when what they are writing is crying out for references. They tend to express the belief that the introduction is the place where they can say anything they like, make any claims they want to without backing them up with literature or some other reference (personal communication, informal discussion, and so on). This is not the case! For example, you may write in the introduction 'People believe that …'. The question is, what evidence do you have to support that claim? Is it that people actually hold this particular belief or you just think that they do? If your research is based on the premiss that people hold this belief when in fact they do not, then you can see that your study is starting out on rocky ground, and this tends to lead to disaster later on.

On the other hand, some inexperienced researchers go to the other extreme, drawing from and discussing related literature so extensively that by the time they write the literature review, they are merely repeating what was already said. Now while it is a legitimate thing to make references to literature that you will discuss in greater detail in the review, you should limit mention to only as much as it takes to set the stage for the study, so to speak. We are of course aware that for some theses or research papers, the literature review is subsumed under the introduction of the report. But there should still be markers such as headings and sub-headings to indicate when you are setting the stage for the report of the study and when you are discussing related literature.

The Literature Review

In chapter 4 we gave fairly comprehensive advice on reviewing the literature. We would like to reiterate some of those points here. Remember that your review should be critical, that is, it should be a well thought out consultation and discussion of literature relevant to your research area. Again, we must remind you to pay attention to citations to avoid being found guilty of plagiarism. Do not get sucked in by the idea that if something comes from a website with no author given, you are not obligated to cite the source. The Internet is such a common source of literature nowadays that the various referencing styles all have a protocol for citing literature obtained online, with or without an author identified. Consult with the referencing guide associated with the style you are using to make sure that you follow the correct protocol. Academic institutions and journals take a dim view of researchers who appear to be taking credit for work that is not theirs. Furthermore, the ethical issues associated with plagiarism have become so prominent in recent times that claiming ignorance is no longer an acceptable excuse!

Having reinforced these points, let us consider some others. This might seem obvious, but we have seen many students who were guilty of this: writing an entire review, sometimes with as many as ten pages, with no headings or subheadings. This can make reading the review difficult. These markers cue the reader when you are shifting thoughts and ideas. They help to bring coherence to your writing and aid comprehension. Indeed, they also help you when you are writing. We have found that it helps when you have been using a system of annotations as we suggested in chapter 4. Often, the themes that you used translate well into subheadings, and the annotations make it relatively easy to develop the particular idea. The themes also help you to link the literature reviewed to your topic. In many cases, we have seen students writing literature reviews that are excellent generic essays on a topic, but there is no connection made between the literature and the investigation. Remember, when you write up your report, there should be a clear link between the various chapters or sections. The readers should be able to follow the common thread from start to finish. From your reporting, they should see why you included certain pieces of literature and excluded others. They should be able to see how the literature you selected informed your research questions, your methodology, your data analysis and the manner in which you present and discuss your findings. The way in which you construct your literature review goes a long way to ensure that this is done effectively.

The Methodology

It is often said that the methodology chapter or section is the most important in a research report. It is the chapter or section that tells the reader what you did, and equally important, why. Unfortunately, for many inexperienced student researchers, it is often the weakest chapter or section in the report. We have found that sometimes the student/researcher is so eager to report findings that they find exciting, that they overlook the fact that these finding have little credibility if the reader has no faith or confidence in the way in which they were derived. Thus, a well-written methodology reassures the reader that your findings are based on reliable evidence collected according to sound theory and well-reasoned, ethical practices. So, what do you write in that chapter or section to persuade the reader?

The answer to this question is generally the same for reporting research at any level, however the amount of details may vary. For example, if you are writing a dissertation for a higher degree, you may be required to include a detailed theoretical framework than if you are writing an undergraduate thesis or a research paper for a course of study below undergraduate work. For example, a piece of research carried out for a master's of philosophy or doctor of philosophy degree should include a theoretical and philosophical defence of the research approach adopted. This may not be as vital for reports at lower levels of study! So then, what do you report in the methodology chapter or section?

Well, you might start by identifying your research design (in case you are wondering what this is, see chapter 5). It is a good idea to justify the design chosen, but as mentioned earlier, the extent to which this is done may vary when you are writing for different purposes. You should also explain as clearly as possible how you selected participants for your study, again with justification for your approach. Remember, one of the characteristics of good research is that it should be able to be replicated. Clear description of your sample and how it was selected facilitates this. Also of importance is a clear description of the tools or instruments that you used to collect the data. Again, the details you include will vary, but the reader should be able to identify these instruments so that a judgement can be made about their appropriateness. Thus, in some cases, you would clearly and succinctly explain how instruments were constructed and validated, as well as any appropriate reliability statistics. In addition, you should also report how the data were collected and when. All of this information allows the reader to judge the rigour of the research and hence make a decision about the validity and reliability of the findings. It must be borne in mind that the purpose of conducting research is to find out about some phenomenon. Thus, after you have collected the data, how it is processed has an impact on what findings emerge. Again, in order to inspire confidence in your findings, you should explain how the data that you collected were analysed, justifying your actions.

You will notice that we are advising that when you write the methodology for a research paper, thesis or dissertation, you try to justify your choices. This is good practice. You will remember that people with different philosophical beliefs about what is knowledge and how it is generated will have different views on what is acceptable methodology. Thus, if a reader's philosophy differs from the one underpinning your research, then the reader may criticise your work. This is all part of the process of generating knowledge and coming to know. But while the reader may criticise your research because of philosophical differences, the reader should never be able to dismiss your work as being methodologically unsound. By justifying your choices, you allow the reader to see that you made considered choices, guided by some theory and not just made on whimsy! Even if for some reason you had to make choices that may have weakened your methodology, acknowledge this in the chapter or section. Remember, often in social research, Murphy's Law reigns, and everything that can go wrong, usually does! So quite often, your intended research plan does not go to plan. But in spite of any hiccups to your plan, you must demonstrate to the reader that you understand the research process and can follow it, even if things do not go as you expected. If you write up your methodology well, then this is the message you convey to the reader!

Reporting Findings

This chapter or section can sometimes be the most difficult to construct. When you analyse your data, a story emerges: a story guided by your research questions and/or hypotheses. You want to relate that story in a clear, logical and interesting manner, in language that can be understood by the readers. This can sometimes be extremely challenging and a good reason for giving yourself lots of time if you have submission deadlines to meet. While there is no absolute formula for writing up your results, if you are inexperienced, we can offer some suggestions. For example, you could present the data under subheadings that match your research questions. Perhaps this is easier to do if you have mostly quantitative data. If you have narrative data collected by means of open items on questionnaires or by interview, you could consider presenting the findings under subheadings that match the items or interview questions. As you become more experienced and comfortable with research you may find that you have a preferred way of presenting your findings. However, you must bear in mind that it is not always left up to you as to how the findings are presented. Sometimes, this is governed by guidelines associated with the discipline under which your research falls, by your institution, by your supervisor or, if you are writing for publication, the journal to which you are submitting the paper.

Apart from deciding on how to organise your findings, you may also have to decide what to include. The thing is, in this chapter or section, you are not only telling the reader what you learned from the evidence you gathered, but you are also presenting that evidence. You should therefore find concise ways of presenting that evidence. This evidence may be presented in tables, figures, charts, or excerpts from textual data. Always select the method that best communicates to the readers what you want them to know. A word of warning though! Do not fall into the trap of presenting the same information in several different forms! For example, many first time researchers feel that it is a good idea to try to impress the readers by giving them the same data in a table, in a bar chart, and in a line graph. This is all unnecessary and it can also be confusing! Your aim is to find the best possible way without cluttering your findings with pictures and tables. The simpler your presentation, the better!

Apart from deciding how to present the findings, you may also have to decide whether or not to include some discussion. We believe that there are different ways of presenting your findings. One way is to simply set out the results of your analyses, with perhaps only brief descriptive comments but no other discussion. This approach is often preferred for quantitative research. The main discussion is done in the following chapter or section. The second approach is to present the results of the analyses and comment on them at the same time. These comments may include comparison of your findings with those of previous studies, or even possible explanation of your finding. Again, this would have implications for your next chapter or section. Sometimes, you may have a choice as to how to present your data, but your presentation approach may be dictated by conventions of your field of study, the journal to which you are submitting your research report for publication or even your supervisor. When you do have a choice, always remember to select the best possible way of communicating your results to the reader.

Discussion/Conclusion

After presenting your findings, in the next chapter or section your task is to pull everything together to present a coherent discussion of your work, your findings and your conclusions you reached. Remember the purpose of your study! It is in this final chapter or section that you will remind the readers of this purpose, how you went about your investigation and what were your main findings. What else follows will depend on how you presented your findings in the previous chapter or section. If you presented them with no discourse, then this is where the main consideration of your findings would be presented. This would include a discussion of these findings in light of the literature that you reviewed as well as your research questions and/or hypotheses. You would also present the conclusions that you have drawn based on the findings, and discuss the implication of these. If it is appropriate, you may offer recommendations for action or future research.

On the other hand, if you included some discourse related to the findings in the results chapter or section, then the discussion/conclusion chapter or section of your report would look slightly different. For example, since you would have written about your findings in light of the literature, you would not want to repeat this. This would be tantamount to wastage of words. Thus, after reminding the readers of your purpose, methodology and main findings, you would then go on to write about these findings in relation to your research questions and/or hypotheses, as well as summarise your conclusions, and present implications and recommendations. Of course, rather than merely repeating them, you may want to elaborate on points already made in the previous chapter or section. Just be aware of practical concerns such as the number of words you are allowed for your report.

Sometimes, especially if you are writing a thesis for a master of philosophy or doctoral degree, you may be required to include a section in which you reflect on your experiences and what you learned as a researcher. Here, you would discuss events or circumstances that might have had an impact on your research, especially if the impact was negative. You could reflect for example, on what might have been done differently and how flaws may be corrected in future research. You may also reflect on how you have grown as a researcher. This is appropriate since these higher degrees are research oriented; a training ground for a possible career in the research field. Such reflection gives an indication of skills that you have acquired as a researcher. How this reflection is structured may also be influenced by your field of study, the philosophical paradigm in which your research is grounded or the predominant nature of your methodology (quantitative or qualitative).

As you can see, in this chapter or section you are wrapping up your report. Use subheadings as much as necessary, since you may be focusing on different aspects. Remember, by the end of this chapter or section, the reader should have a sense of completion of the work: they should see what you set out to investigate, how you proceeded, what your findings were and how they relate back to the original purpose of the study. The readers should have a coherent, cohesive picture of your research. Your task is to write this chapter or section in such a way that they do!

References

Right after your concluding section you should have your bibliography or list of references, whichever is acceptable in your field. If you follow the advice on keeping track of literature consulted that we offered in chapter 4 then this task should not be too daunting. You will remember that we advised that you record full bibliographic information for any such literature. If you were doing this, then you would just have to retrieve from that database, all works that are to be included in your bibliography or reference list. For a bibliography, you would list all the works that informed your research. If you are providing references then make sure that all works cited within the body of your text are included. These should be presented according to the protocol of whichever style you are following. As was mentioned in chapter 4, you should consult the referencing guide that explains the specific protocol that is appropriate to your work.

When you compile your list, cross-check spelling of names and dates of publication on the list with what is written in the text. If possible, ask someone with a keen eye to check these for you. It is sometimes very easy to make mistakes when recording this information. You can never be too careful with this. Indeed, it is better to be overly careful than to have to remove citations from your text because you do not have the correct bibliographic information!

Appendices

Sometimes you have large bits of information to which you want the readers to have access, but it is not appropriate or convenient to include it in the text. You may, for example, want to include copies of data collection instruments, data that were used to generate tables, or samples of textual data. This information can be included in appendices. Appendices are usually the last part of your report, inserted after the list of references. They may be identified by letters of the alphabet or by numbers, using either Arabic or Roman numerals. However you are labelling them, be consistent. Sometimes the appearance and labelling of the appendices may be governed by the style to which your report is conforming. Again, consult the appropriate guide book for advice. Remember that if your have a word limit for your research report, in some cases, the appendices contribute to this limit. To be certain, check with your institution or department to find out if this is the case. If it is, you may want to restrict the number and size of the appendices included.

The Abstract

It may seem odd to some that the first thing the readers of your report will probably see is the last thing that you should actually write, the abstract. This is a synopsis of the research report designed to give the reader a preview of what is conveyed in the document. In your abstract, you should include:

- The purpose of the study
- A brief description of your research design, mentioning the research approach, the sources of data tapped, the method of data collections, and how the data were treated.
- Major findings and conclusions.

Note that abstracts tend to have a limit of between 150 to 200 words. Now before you start to think that it is impossible to write all those things in so few words, we want to tell you that it is possible! Indeed, the more you do it, the easier it becomes. It is just a matter of writing a very tight summary of the work.

In some cases you may be asked to provide keywords associated with your work. These are word or short phrases that are used as identifiers for your work so that it can be retrieved by others who are interested in research in particular topics. If you are to supply keywords, choose those that best describe your work. For example, if your research examined employees'

ANATOMY OF AN ABSTRACT

This study investigated adolescents' perceptions and practices relating to condom use following a safe sex campaign.

A sample of 538 (259 male and 279 female) adolescents (16–20 year-olds) completed a questionnaire about their views, perceptions and sexual practices in relation to condom use. Sixty members of that sample (29 male and 31 female) also participated in six focus group interviews.

The findings revealed that 75% of the adolescents felt that the campaign was factual, informative and dealt with the harsh realities of unprotected sex openly but sensitively; 10% felt that the campaign was offensive and unnecessarily crude; 52% seriously re-assessed their sexual behaviour and intended to use condoms whenever they are having sex. Thirty-four per cent (34%) of the adolescents reported that the campaign had no impact on their sexual practices. Of these, just under half (49%) reported that they were not having sex and that they did not intend to until they were married or at least in a stable relationship. These views were distributed equally across the sexes.

These findings suggest that frank-talking safe-sex campaigns can have variable effects on the intended group.

Keywords: safe-sex campaigns; adolescents' sexual behaviour; condom use

---

attitudes towards their colleagues with disabilities, possible keywords could be 'disabilities in workplace' or 'attitudes' or any word or expression that captures the essence of your report. Keywords are usually inserted beneath the abstract. You should take some time to read the abstracts from theses, journal article and the like. That is an excellent way to see how abstracts are written. Remember, this may be the first contact that readers have with your work. If it is poorly written or does not give adequate information, then it may be the only contact, and that would be an absolute shame! After all the time you spent conducting and reporting your study.

FINAL FINAL WORDS

In this chapter, we offer some guidance and advice on reporting your study. This is an extremely important aspect of the research process. Indeed, this act of sharing knowledge generated by your research may be seen as the overall goal of conducting research in the first place. It is through your report that you convince the examiners that you understand the research process and that you can plan and execute a rigorous piece of work. Bear in mind that there is a general format in which research is reported:

1. Introduction
2. Literature review
3. Methodology
4. Findings
5. Discussion/conclusions
6. References
7. Appendices

Each of the components above may be presented in a section of your report, in a single chapter or in several chapters. This would depend for example, on factors such as the nature and purpose of the research, and the size of the document you are expected to produce.

FINAL WORDS

You may recall that in the first chapter of this book, we advised you to select a research area in which you are interested. Well, when you are writing your report you will no doubt understand why! There will be times when you will be thoroughly frustrated with your report: words will refuse to flow or will flow clumsily; organisational problems will rear up; submission dates will be looming! If you are not particularly enthusiastic about the topic of your research, then you are more likely to throw up your hands and quit. May that never be the case!

We hope that by now you are excited about doing research and rearing to go out and investigate the social world. We hope that the guidance and advice that we have offered in this book is sufficient to get you started. As with any endeavour, experience comes over time and, though you may be somewhat apprehensive and unsure of your self now, you will persist. The Caribbean is overflowing with social phenomena that, if systematically investigated over time, could add valuable knowledge to the existing body in many social fields. There are many lessons that the rest of the world can learn from our social interactions and experiences in the region, and it would be a shame if these were not shared. The aim of this book is to encourage inexperienced researchers to hone their skills and to explore this environment. Whether you are pursuing an investigation for a research paper for a particular course or subject area; or for a thesis or dissertation for an undergraduate degree, a higher degree, or some other course of study; or simply to satisfy your own curiosity; do it well! That way, when you share your findings with the world, your work would be credible and valuable because you followed rigorous standards for research.

GLOSSARY

Abstract: a synopsis of the research report designed to give the reader a preview of what is conveyed in the report. It should briefly summarise the purpose of the study, the research methodology, major findings and main conclusions. The abstract is written AFTER the research report is completed.

Accessible population: the group of individuals or objects that possess the characteristics in which you are interested, and to which you realistically have access.

Action research: an approach to research that aims at bringing about meaningful, sustainable change by seeking practical solutions to social problems.

Alternate forms (equivalence) reliability: the extent to which two forms of an instrument actually measure the same characteristics.

Anonymity: a state in which the doer of an action is unknown. For example, the identity of the individuals who completed specific questionnaires remains unknown.

Anti-positivism: a philosophical perspective that views knowledge as subjective and relative.

Applied research: research where the aim is to ascertain how theories can best serve the interest of different people.

Attitude scale: a set of items about an object designed to produce a score that is taken as a measure of the respondent's attitude towards the object. There are different kinds of attitude scales.

Basic research: research concerned with the development or refinement of theory.

Bivariate analysis: statistical analysis involving two variables.

Case studies: studies that investigate contemporary phenomena in a specific context. These phenomena or cases include an individual, a group, a policy, an innovation, or any entity that can stand on its own.

Causal-comparative studies: studies that allow the researcher to determine reasons for existing conditions. There is no manipulation of variables and cause effect relationships are tentative at best.

Checklist: a list of events, behaviours or other characteristics on which the occurrence or presence of the characteristics is noted.

Chi square goodness of fit test: a nonparametric test of significance used to determine if observed frequencies (for a single variable) are a good fit for a particular pattern of expected frequencies or whether they differ significantly.

Chi square test of independence: a nonparametric test of significance used to determine whether the observed frequencies in the individual cells (in a cross-tabulation) match an expected pattern. It is used to determine whether there is an association (relationship) between the two variables in the cross-tabulation.

Closed (also **select**) **items**: data collecting items that require the respondents to choose their answers from a number of options that are provided.

Cluster sampling: a sampling technique for which existing groups (clusters) rather than individuals are randomly selected to the sample.

Coding (narrative): a system of attaching symbols to portions of text to identify common issues and themes.

Concurrent validity: the degree to which an instrument matches up against another instrument that measures the same variable.

Confidentiality: a state in which certain information is not revealed. This includes the names of the sources of the information as well as any facts that the sources do not want revealed.

Consequential validity: the degree to which the instrument creates negative consequences for the respondents.

Construct validity: the degree to which the instrument measures the intended theoretical construct.

Content validity: the degree to which an instrument measures what it is intended to measure.

Contingency table: a cross-tabulation.

Convenience sampling: a non-probability sampling technique that involves selecting participants for a study based on their availability; the researcher chooses whoever or whatever is available and convenient.

Correlation: a measure of association or relationship between variables of interest.

Correlational studies: studies that allow the researcher to investigate the relationship or association between variables. There is not manipulation of variables. These studies do not establish cause and effect relationships.

Criterion validity: this form of validity can take two forms, concurrent validity and predictive validity.

Cronbach coefficient: a measure of how well each item correlates with the other items on an instrument.

Cross-tabulation: a two-dimensional grid used to display the distribution across two variables simultaneously; one variable is presented on each dimension.

Data dictionary (codebook): a record of code applied to various items (variables) on a data collection tool.

Decision rule: (for making a decision about the null hypothesis) – If $p_{observed}$ is less than or equal to p_{select}, then the null hypothesis is rejected; if $p_{oserved}$ is larger than p_{select}, then the null hypothesis is retained.

Declarative hypothesis: a hypothesis that suggests the expectation of a relationship or difference between two variables.

Deductive hypothesis: a hypothesis derived from theory.

Deductive reasoning: reasoning that begins with major premises or generalisation, and through deduction, arrives at a specific conclusion.

Degrees of freedom: the number of scores that are free to vary in a set used to calculate a specific statistic (e.g. the mean or a t-value).

Delimitation: the deliberate act of controlling research, making it focused and clear.

Dependent variable: the variable that is affected by the independent variable.

Descriptive statistics: statistics used to describe or summarise a data set.

Developmental research: also called research and development (R & D), this is research conducted to develop effective products for use.

Direct relationship: the interpretation of a positive correlation co-efficient. It indicates that a high (low) score on one variable is matched by a high (low) score on the other variable.

Directional hypothesis: a hypothesis that not only states the expectation of a relationship or difference between two variables, but also states what that relationship might be.

Discourse analysis: the study of how humans use language to communicate (sometimes implicitly) with special attention to how the senders (speakers, writers) construct messages for the receivers (hearers, readers) and how the receivers interpret the received messages.

Discriminant validity: this verified that the instrument is not measuring any construct other than what it is designed to measure.

Equal allocation: a stratified sampling approach in which equal numbers are selected from each stratum in the population.

Ethical principles: a set of rules and conventions that guide professional behaviour. They ensure good professional practice.

Evaluation research: research carried out to make decisions about the worth of alternative entities.

Experimental studies: studies that involve manipulating and controlling variables, and observing the effect on other variables. These approaches are used to establish cause and effect relationships.

External validity (of research): the extent to which the results of a piece of research can be generalised to other populations and conditions.

Face validity: the extent to which the instrument looks like those commonly used for the particular purpose for which you are using it.

Frequency distribution: a summary of a data set that involves showing how often a score appears in the data set, either as counts or as percentages.

Historical studies: studies that investigate events that occurred in the past, in an attempt to understand their influence on current and future events.

Hypothesis: a statement of expected (or suspected) relationship or difference between variables.

Independent variable: those conditions or characteristics that have an effect on some other variables. In experimental research, independent variables are manipulated. Sometimes, there is no manipulation. Also called treatment variable, experimental variable or grouping variables.

Index: a collection of sources of information related to a particular topic.

Inductive hypothesis: a hypothesis formulated based on evidence of several cases.

Inductive reasoning: reasoning that begins with a number of cases of specific observations and arrives at a generalisation.

Inferential statistics: statistical procedures used to make inferences about a population based on data collected from a sample.

Internal consistency: the extent to which items on an instrument 'hang' well together, that is, whether they are assessing the same characteristic.

Internal validity (of research): the extent to which the results of a piece of research can be interpreted accurately and with confidence.

Interquartile range: a measure of dispersion, this is the difference between the median of the lower half of a data set (Q1) and the median of the upper half (Q3).

Inter-rater reliability: the extent to which a rating instrument consistently produces similar results when used by different raters to rate the same entity.

Interval scale: numbers on this scale indicate the quantity of the characteristic that is being measured. The intervals between consecutive values are equal, but there is no absolute zero point. This means that a score of zero does not indicate an absolute absence of the characteristic being measured. Arithmetic computations with numbers on this scale are meaningful. E.g. Scores on tests.

Interview schedule: a list of key questions to be asked during an interview designed to address issues relevant to the area being investigated.

Interviewing: a data collection technique for which the researcher asks questions and the participants supply answers.

Intra-rater reliability: the extent to which a rating instrument consistently produces similar results when used at different times by the same rater to rate the same entity.

Inverse relationship: the interpretation of a negative correlation co-efficient. It indicates that a high (low) score on one variable is matched by a low (high) score on the other variable.

Kruskal-Wallis test: the nonparametric equivalent of the one-way ANOVA.

Levels of measurement: Four numerical scales on which variables can be measured.

Levene test: a statistical procedure that tests parametric assumption of equality of variances among sets of scores.

Likert-type scale: a scale consisting of a number of statements, each accompanied by a range of responses that reflect different degrees of agreement, the most common being Strongly agree, Agree, Neutral, Disagree, Strongly disagree.

Limitation: a condition that weakens the outcomes of a study. The researcher often has little control over such conditions.

Literature review: a critical analysis/discussion of literature related to the problem you are investigating.

Mann Whitney U test: the nonparametric equivalent of the t-test for independent samples.

Mean: a measure of central tendency that uses the value obtained when all the scores in a data set are added and the result divided by the number of scores in the set.

Measures of central tendency: approaches to summarising a data set by finding a single value to represent the set. There are three measures of central tendency: mode, median and the mean.

Measures of dispersion: a measure of how clustered or spread out a data set is, or how homogeneous the scores are. Some common measures of dispersion are the range, the interquartile range, the standard deviation and the variance. (Also called measures of spread or measures of variability.)

Median: a measure of central tendency that uses the score in the middle position of a set of scores after the scores have been organised in numerical order.

Mode: a measure of central tendency that uses the score or category in a data set that has the highest frequency.

Multi-stage sampling: a sampling technique that involves selecting a sample of a sample. For example, voting constituencies can be randomly selected and then voters can be randomly selected from each constituency.

Multivariate analysis: statistical analysis that involves more than two variables.

Narrative data: data collected in the form of extensive text. This includes transcripts from interviews and responses to open-ended items on questionnaires.

Nominal scale: numbers on this scale are used like names or labels, and are used to identify categories. E.g. 1 = female; 2 = male for the variable SEX. Arithmetic computations with numbers on this scale would be meaningless.

Non-directional hypothesis: a hypothesis stated in a way to indicate that a relationship or difference is expected, without stating what the relationship or difference might be.

Nonparametric tests: tests of significance that make few assumptions about the data. These tests are applicable when the assumptions of parametric tests are violated.

Non-participant observation: an approach to observation in which the observer takes no part in the activities being observed.

Non-probability sampling: sampling techniques that do not involve random selection.

Normal distribution: a symmetrical distribution of scores with 68% falling within 1 standard deviation of the mean, 95% within 2 standard deviations and 99.8% within 3 standard deviations. This distribution produces a bell-shaped curve.

Null hypothesis: a hypothesis that indicates that no relationship or difference between the variables is expected.

Numerical data: data collected and/or compiled in the form of numbers.

Observation: a data collection technique that requires the researcher to go into the research setting to look at and listen to events as they occur.

One-way analysis of variance (ANOVA): a parametric test of significance used to determine whether differences in means obtained by three or more groups are statistically significant.

Open-ended (also **supply**) **items**: data collecting items that require the respondents to write their own answers in their own words.

Ordinal scale: numbers on this scale are used like names or labels, and are used to identify categories that can be ordered or ranked. E.g. 1 = Under 20 years old; 2 = 20–29 years; 3 = 30–39 years; 4 = 40 years and over for the variable AGE GROUP. Arithmetic computations with numbers on this scale would be meaningless.

Panic: an overwhelming feeling of fright, terror or dread that you are to avoid feeling when you engage in research, even if everything is not working out as you intended.

Parameter: a measure of a characteristic within a population.

Parametric tests: tests of significance that make certain assumptions about the distribution and variance of the data involved. These tests are applicable for variables measured on the interval or ratio scales.

Participant observation: an approach to observation in which the observer becomes a member of the group or setting that is being observed.

Pearson r: a correlation co-efficient that ranges from 0 to 1, and may be positive or negative. It is applicable when the variables of interest are measured on the interval or ratio scales. (Also Pearson Product Moment)

Piloting: using an instrument with a group similar to the research participants to check the instrument's validity and reliability.

P$_{observed}$: the probability of obtaining observed results by chance. It is compared with p$_{select}$ when deciding whether to reject or retain the null hypothesis.

Population: the entire group of individuals or objects that possess the characteristics in which you are interested.

Positivism: a philosophical perspective that views knowledge as objective, absolute and unchanging. Adherents to this view tend to favour quantitative research methods.

Predictive validity: the degree to which the instrument can predict performance on some other instrument.

Primary sources: sources that present first hand information about events being reported. These are usually participants in or eyewitness of the events.

Probability level: the probability of an event occurring that the researcher assumes is too small to suggest that the occurrence is by mere chance. The researcher uses this value to decide whether to reject or retain the null hypothesis when running a test of significance.

Probability sampling: sampling techniques that involve random selection and/or assignment of participants.

Problem statement: a clear and concise grammatically correct sentence that identifies the intent of a study.

Proportional allocation: a stratified sampling approach in which each stratum is represented in the sample in the same proportion in which it exists in the population.

P$_{select}$: the probability or significance level that the researcher selects at which to carry out the test of significance. Commonly selected probability levels are 0.05, 0.01 and 0.001. It represents the probability of committing a Type 1 error.

Purposive sampling: a non-probability sampling technique that involves selecting participants for a study because they possess characteristics that make them rich sources of information.

Qualitative designs: a range of research designs for which narrative or textual data are collected. Their general purpose is to shed light on or foster understanding (verstehen) of phenomena. They are predicated on the notion that knowledge or 'truth' is subjective, influenced by factors such as culture, past experiences, and context.

Qualitative research: research that involves collecting narrative data that are analysed by coding the text for patterns and themes. It usually relies on inductive reasoning.

Quantitative research: research that involves collecting numerical data that are analysed statistically. It usually involves hypothesis testing.

Questionnaire: an instrument containing a collection of items designed to collect data about a phenomenon from a group of respondents.

Quota sampling: a non-probability sampling technique for which the researcher sets about making contact with individuals that fit particular profiles until the quota for each profile is met.

Random sampling error: a phenomenon that is associated with randomly selecting one sample from several possibilities from within a population. This error can be estimated or measured.

Range: a measure of dispersion, this is the difference between the highest and lowest scores in a distribution (data set).

Rating scale: an instrument that permits the rater to score (rate) some characteristics of an entity on a continuum.

Ratio scale: measurement of this scale is similar to that on the interval scale, except there IS an absolute zero point. This means that a score of zero indicates an absolute absence of the characteristic being measured. Arithmetic computations with numbers on this scale are meaningful. E.g. No. of children in a household.

Reliability (of an instrument): the extent to which the instrument consistently measures what it is intended to measure.

Reliability (of research): the extent to which the results are consistent (internal reliability) and replicable (external reliability). Reliability of the research is a necessary condition for validity.

Research design: a plan outlining the approach to be used to investigate a research problem.

Sample: a sub-group selected from the population, often selected to be representative of the population.

Sampling bias: sampling error that is the result of a flawed sampling procedure. This error cannot be estimated or measured.

Sampling fraction: the ratio of the sample to the population (n/N).

Scatter plot: a two-dimensional graph with the score from one variable plotted on the horizontal axis and the scores from the other variable plotted on the vertical axis. It is used to explore the existence of a linear relationship between two variables.

Secondary sources: sources of information that report events for which they were not present. These are usually sources reporting events about which they heard from others.

Semantic differential scale: a set of bipolar adjectives (e.g. Good – Bad; Weak – Strong; Fast – Slow) about an object. The adjectives are arranged at the extreme ends of a continuum and respondents indicate how they feel about the object by situating themselves along the continuum.

Semi-structured interview: an approach to interviewing that is not as restrictive as a structured interview, and not as open as an unstructured interview. The interviewer has some flexibility when asking the questions.

Simple random sampling: a sampling technique for which each member of the population has an equal chance of being selected to the sample.

Snowball sampling: a non-probability sampling technique in which the researcher locates participants by making contact through other participants.

Spearman rho: a correlation coefficient that ranges from 0 to 1, and may be positive or negative. It is applicable when the variables of interest can be ranked (on at least the ordinal scale).

Split half reliability: an approach to establishing internal consistency by dividing the items on the instrument into two smaller ones and running a correlation procedure.

Stability (test – re-test) reliability: the extent to which the instrument produces similar results over time.

Standard deviation: a measure of dispersion, this is a measure of the variation of each score from the mean of the set. The smaller the standard deviation, the closer the scores cluster around the mean.

Standard error: a measure of the extent to which the mean of the sample deviates from the population mean. A small standard error suggests that the sample mean is a close approximation of the population mean. (Also called standard error of the mean.)

Standard normal distribution: a normally shaped distribution with a mean of 0 and a standard deviation of 1.

Standardised scores: scores converted from different measurement scales to a common scale.

Statistic: a measure of a characteristic within a sample.

Statistically significant: an indication that an observed difference or relationship is not a chance occurrence.

Stratified sampling: a sampling technique that involves dividing the population into component groups (strata) and randomly selecting a sample from each stratum.

Structured interview: an approach to interviewing that requires the interviewer to read the questions to each participant and record the responses in a uniform way. It is like administering a questionnaire orally.

Survey studies: studies that involve the collection of data from a sample of population to learn something about the views, feelings and practices. These kinds of studies are often used to describe the status of phenomena at a particular time.

Surveying: a data collection technique that involves selecting a sample and administering an instrument.

Systematic observation: an observation approach that requires the observer to systematically record the occurrence of events at fixed intervals.

Systematic sampling: a sampling technique for which the research selects every nth member of the population to the sample. The starting point is selected at random.

Test of significance: statistical procedures used to test the null hypothesis that there is no significant difference or relationship between or among two or more variables.

Test: a set of items designed to measure specific characteristics such as personality, aptitude and achievement.

Tests of significance: statistical procedure that provides a basis on which the null hypothesis is rejected or retained.

Theory: an idea that has not yet been established as fact. It is open to being tested in different contexts.

Threats to validity: conditions other than the variables of interest that can have an impact on the outcome of a study.

T-test for independent samples: a parametric test of significance used to determine whether the observed difference between means for two groups is statistically significant.

T-test for paired samples: a parametric test of significance used to determine whether the difference between the means of scores collected from a sample on two different occasions is statistically significant.

Type 1 error: this occurs when a null hypothesis that is true is rejected. It is not a 'mistake' made by the researcher, but a statistical error that is associated with applying probability theory.

Type 2 error: this occurs when a null hypothesis that is false in retained (not rejected).

Univariate analysis: statistical analysis involving one variable.

Unstructured interview: an approach to interviewing that requires the interviewer to raise a general topic of interest and allow the respondent to provide extensive answers.

Validity (of an instrument): the extent to which the instrument measures what it is expected to measure.

Validity (of research): the extent to which the research findings and conclusions are based on evidence collected.

Variables: conditions or characteristics that the researcher manipulates, controls or merely observes. Variables can take on different values.

Variance: a measure of dispersion, this is, the square of the standard deviation.

Wilcoxon signed-ranks test: the nonparametric equivalent of the t-test for paired samples.

REFERENCES AND OTHER USEFUL SOURCES

American Psychological Association. 2001. *Publication Manual of the American Psychological Association*. 5th edn. Washington, DC.

Bell, J. 2005. Doing your research project: A guide for first-time researchers in education, health and social sciences. 4th edn. Milton Keynes, UK: Open University Press.

Berg, B.L. 2006. *Qualitative Research Methods for the Social Sciences*. 6th edn. Needham Heights, MA: Allyn & Bacon.

Best, J.W. and J.V. Khan. 1998. *Research in Education*. 8th edn. Needham Heights, MA: Allyn & Bacon.

Bogdan, R. and S.K. Biklen. 2006. *Qualitative Research for Education: An Introduction to Theories and Methods*. 5th edn. Needham Heights, MA: Allyn & Bacon.

Burns, R.B. 2000. *Introduction to Research Methods*. London: SAGE.

Cable News Network 2005, October 7. Miller: Went to jail for public's right to know. [Online at http://www.cnn.com/2005/US/10/05/miller.dobbs/index.html].

Campbell, D.T. and J.C. Stanley. 1963. Experimental and quasi-experimental designs for research in teaching. In N. Gage, Ed., *Handbook of Research on Teaching*, 171–245. New York, NY: Rand McNally.

Cohen, L., L. Manion, and K. Morrison. 2000. *Research Methods in Education*. 5th edn. London: RoutledgeFalmer.

Field, A. 2005. *Discovering Statistics using SPSS*. 2nd edn. London: SAGE.

Flander, N.A. 1970. *Analysing Teacher Behaviour*. Reading, MA: Addison Wesley.

Fraenkel, J. R. and N.E. Wallen. 2003. *How to Design and Evaluate Research in Education*. 5th edn. NY: McGraw-Hill.

Gall, M.D., W.R. Borg and J.P. Gall. 1996. *Educational Research: An Introduction*. 6th edn. White Plains, NY: Longman.

Gay, L.R. and P.W. Airasian 2003. *Educational Research: Competencies for Analysis and Application*. 7th edn. Englewood Cliffs, NJ: Prentice-Hall.

Gay, L.R., G.E. Mills and P.W. Airasian. 2005. *Educational Research: Competencies for Analysis and Application*. 8th edn. Englewood Cliffs, NJ: Prentice-Hall.

Girden, E. 2001. *Evaluating Research Articles from Start to Finish*. 2nd edn. Thousand Oaks, CA: SAGE.

Glaser, B.G. and A.L. Strauss. 1967. *The Discovery of Grounded Theory: Strategies for Qualitative Research*. Hawthorne, NY: Aldine de Gruyler.

Hinton, P.R. 1995. *Statistics Explained: A Guide for Social Science Students*. London: Routledge.

Johnstone, B. 2002. *Discourse Analysis*. Oxford: Blackwell.

Kvale, S. 1996. *Interviews: An Introduction to Qualitative Research Interviewing*. Thousand Oaks, CA: SAGE.

Layder, D. 1998. *Sociological Practice: Linking Theory and Social Research*. London: SAGE.

Leedy, P.D. 1997. *Practical Research: Planning and Design*. 6th edn. Upper Saddle River, NJ: Prentice-Hall.

Lewin, K. 1959. Group decision and social change'. In E. E. Maccoby, T. M. Newcomb and E. L. Hartley. Eds. *Readings in Social Psychology.* 3rd edn., 197–211. London: Methuen & Co.

Likert, R. 1932. A technique for the measurement of attitudes. *Archives of Psychology*, No. 140.

Merriam, S.B. 1988. *Case Study Research in Education: A Qualitative Approach.* San Francisco, CA: Jossey-Bass.

Miles, M.B. and A.M. Huberman. 1994. *Qualitative Data Analysis: An Expanded Sourcebook.* 2nd edn. Thousand Oaks, CA: SAGE.

Oppenheim, A.N. 1992. *Questionnaire Design, Interviewing and Attitude Measurement.* New ed. London: Continuum.

Oxford Concise Dictionary, 10th edition. Edited by Judy Pearsall. 1999. Oxford University Press.

Pallant, J. 2007. *SPSS Survival Manual: A Step-by-Step Guide to Data Analysis using SPSS.* 3rd edn. Milton Keynes, UK: Open University Press.

Patton, M.Q. 2002. *Qualitative Research and Evaluation Methods.* 3rd edn. Thousand Oaks, CA: SAGE.

Preacher, K. J. 2001, April. Calculation for the chi-square test: An interactive calculation tool for chi-square tests of goodness of fit and independence [Computer software]. Available from http://www.quantpsy.org.

Punch, K. 2005. *Introduction to Social Research: Quantitative and Qualitative Approaches.* 2nd edn. London: SAGE.

Pyrczak, F. and R.R. Bruce. 2000. *Writing Empirical Research Reports: A Basic Guide for Students of the Social and Behavioral Sciences.* 3rd edn. Los Angeles, CA: Pyrczak Publishing.

Robson, C. 1993. *Real World Research: A Resource for Social Scientists and Practitioner-Researchers.* Oxford: Blackwell.

Rowntree, D. 2004. *Statistics Without Tears: A Primer for Non-Mathematicians.* Boston, MA: Allyn & Bacon.

Sammons, P. 1989. Ethical issues and statistical work. In R.G. Burgess, Ed., *The Ethics of Educational Research* 31–59. East Sussex: Falmer Press.

Sarantakos, S. 2005. *Social Research.* 3rd edn. Hampshire: Palgrave.

Siegel, S. and N.J. Castellan. 1988. Nonparametric statistics for the behavioral sciences. 2nd edn. New York: McGraw-Hill.

Spence, E. 2005, September 13. 'The reporter's right not to tell supports the public's right to know.' The *Sydney Morning Herald.* [Online at http://www.smh.com.au/news/ opinion/the-reporters-right-not-to-tell-supports-the-publics-right-tokn ow/2005/09/12/1126377253683. html].

Warrican, S.J. 2006. Action Research: A Viable Option for Effecting Change. *Journal of Curriculum Studies*, 38(1), 1–14.

Wiersma, W. 1995. *Research Methods in Education: An Introduction.* 6th edn. Needham Heights, MA: Simon & Schuster.

Yin, R.K. 1994. *Case Study Research: Designs and Methods.* 2nd edn. Thousand Oaks, CA: SAGE.

Yin, R.K. 1998. The abridged version of case study research. In L. Bickman and D.D. Rog Eds., *Handbook of Applied Social Research Methods*, 229–59. Thousand Oaks, CA: SAGE.

INDEX

www.ingramcontent.com/pod-product-compliance
Lightning Source LLC
Chambersburg PA
CBHW081148270326
41930CB00014B/3078